HISTORY'S WORST BATTLES

HISTORY'S WORST BATTLES

AND THE PEOPLE WHO FOUGHT THEM

JOEL LEVY

METRO BOOKS

NEW YORK

METRO BOOKS
New York

An Imprint of Sterling Publishing
387 Park Avenue South
New York, NY 10016

Conceived, designed, and produced by
Quid Publishing
Level 4 Sheridan House
114 Western Road
Hove BN3 1DD
England

www.quidpublishing.com

ISBN: 978-1-4351-5114-7

For information about custom editions, special sales, and premium and corporate purchases,
please contact Sterling Special Sales at 800-805-5489 or specialsales@sterlingpublishing.com.

Manufactured in Singapore

1 3 5 7 9 10 8 6 4 2

www.sterlingpublishing.com

For my father

CONTENTS

INTRODUCTION

William Tecumseh Sherman, Union general of the Civil War, is supposed to have originated the famous line "War is hell" when addressing the graduating class of the Michigan Military Academy in 1879, warning the cadets that their naïve enthusiasm for war would not survive the awful reality. Whether or not he came up with this exact phrase, it certainly reflected his sentiments. In a famous letter of 1864 to the burghers of Atlanta, explaining why he would not change his mind about burning their city to the ground, he expounded the theme: "War is cruelty, and you cannot refine it . . . You might as well appeal against the thunderstorm as against these terrible hardships of war . . ."

This book can be taken as a lengthy illustration of Sherman's contention, reflecting at least 2,500 years of the horror of war through the exploration of 50 of the worst battles in history. "Worst" is a vague description, which could cover anything from the terrible to the ridiculous. I drew up a list of five broad headings by which to categorize the "bad" battles included in this book.

The first category is the most obvious: the worst battles are surely those with the highest death toll, the most casualties, the greatest amount of bloodshed and carnage. Until the national mobilizations of the late 18th-century French revolutionary era (the *levée en masse*) and the subsequent Napoleonic Wars, truly colossal armies were rare outside China, despite the astonishing claims of ancient authors, which probably reflect the general unreliability of historians until the modern era. Most clashes were relatively small-scale by our modern lights, informed by the world wars of the 20th century, and hence the butcher's bill would typically have been relatively short.

This is why some ancient and medieval battles particularly stand out, owing to the epic scale of the butchery. The locus classicus of this category is the Battle of Cannae in 216 BCE, at which the Carthaginians under Hannibal surrounded a Roman army of over 80,000 men and systematically butchered almost all of them, in the course of a single day. Subsequent bloody engagements were often compared to Cannae, so that there have been innumerable "second Cannaes." This category also covers "heroic last stands," since by definition they tend to result in almost 100 percent casualties, and several instances of this type of bloodbath are represented in the book.

The second category might be termed the "scale of the defeat"; this classification recognizes that one side's greatest battle is the other's worst. This could mean a massive disparity in casualty rates, or the extent of the negative consequences of that defeat. This category also recognizes in particular defeats of large forces by smaller ones.

The third category is Pyrrhic victories, and includes the battle that defined this term—Asculum in 279 BCE. At this battle the Greek king Pyrrhus defeated a Roman army but lost so many troops in the process that he famously remarked, "One more victory like this and we shall be utterly ruined." A battle where the victory is Pyrrhic is "worst" in the sense of strategic utility.

The fourth category is "tactical blunders." Most calamitous defeats owe something to tactical mistakes, but some are particularly marked by the ineptitude displayed. Also included are cases where commanders have made inexplicable, unnecessary, and suicidal decisions.

The fifth category recognizes that "worst" has a specific meaning for combatants—a soldier's worst battle, apart from one where he is wounded or killed, is one where the conditions are particularly grim. Sherman's "War is hell" argument contended that any battle is intolerably awful. But many of the examples in this book suggest that some battles really are worse than others: for instance, in the "green hell" of Hürtgen Forest, in 1944–45, American soldiers had to contend with freezing mist and mud, exploding trees, and deadly snipers.

With the guidance of these five categories I have tried to select a range of battles from around the world and throughout history. There are some notable omissions, usually linked to paucity of sources—for instance, reliable English-language sources on ancient Chinese battles are scarce. Also absent are naval and air battles; I decided to focus exclusively on land conflicts. Any exercise such as this must inevitably be both highly subjective and extremely selective, but every one of the 50 battles featured here is worthy of inclusion on at least one of the five criteria I set out to begin with, usually several at once.

The obvious question is: which of the 50 is the worst of the worst? The combats of ancient and medieval times could undoubtedly be horrific, with the added dimension of proximity between combatants; the visceral violence of hand-to-hand combat. There is no way to imagine the actual terror experienced by a Roman at Cannae as he waited for the Carthaginians to butcher the men crowded in front of him so that he could meet his death in turn; or the brutal horror of the soldiers at Towton, hacking at each other in a crazed melee in the midst of a snowstorm, as the bloody slush melted into the mud and stained the furrows and ditches of the surrounding fields to a distance of nearly 3 miles (5 kilometers).

Yet the scale, duration, and all-consuming nature of modern warfare ultimately outdoes these older conflicts. The worst of all battles must surely be the hell of Stalingrad, 1942–43, where human existence was reduced to its most nightmarish for 199 days of total war, when "the earth breathed fire" and around 2 million people lost their lives.

BATTLE

High casualty rate

Catastrophic defeat

Pyrrhic victory

Tactical blunder

Appalling conditions

GO TELL THE SPARTANS: THERMOPYLAE

480 BCE

Antagonists: Contingents from the Greek states, especially King Leonidas of Sparta and his 300 Hippeis, vs. the armies of Xerxes, king of Persia

Casualties: Greeks (victors): at least 300; Persians: unknown

One of the Trachinian Greeks remarked, "The barbarians are so numerous that when they shoot forth their arrows, the sun will be darkened by their multitude," to which Dieneces the Spartan replied, "So much the better; we will have our fight in the shade."

Herodotus, *The Histories*, 7: 226

The first Battle of Thermopylae remains one of the most celebrated in history, the locus classicus of the heroic last stand, in which King Leonidas and the 300 held off the combined might of the Persian empire for three days and made the great King Xerxes shiver in fear, before succumbing to treachery and meeting a glorious death. Thanks to the success of the 2007 movie *300*, together with other books and movies based on the story, this epic battle has become legendary.

Thermopylae was an episode in the Graeco-Persian Wars of 490–479 BCE. The vast Achaemenid Persian Empire created by Cyrus the Great in the 6th century BCE encompassed territories in Asia Minor (modern-day Turkey), including Greek kingdoms such as Lydia. Under Darius the Persian Empire was extended into Europe with the conquest of Thrace and dominion over Macedon, but later in his reign the Greek Ionian states rebelled, with the help of Athens and Eretria, mainland Greek states. Determined to punish them for their meddling, Darius launched an invasion of mainland Greece but his army was defeated by the Greeks at Marathon in 490 BCE.

THE GRAECO-PERSIAN WARS

In 486 BCE, Darius's son Xerxes succeeded to the Persian throne. In 480 BCE he launched another attempt to conquer Greece, assembling perhaps the largest army yet gathered. The exact size of the Persian force is the subject of considerable scholarly debate, because ancient sources were much given to exaggeration and particularly surpassed themselves in this instance. The primary source for the Graeco-Persian Wars, and the battle of Thermopylae in particular, is Herodotus, known as both the Father of History and the Father of Lies for his sometimes creative approach to verisimilitude. Herodotus was a native of Halicarnassus, a Greek territory in Asia Minor that was part of the Persian Empire. His avowed aim in writing his *Histories* was to preserve the memory of the conflict between the Greeks and the barbarians, but there is a strong element of propaganda in his work; he probably exaggerated the odds facing the plucky Greeks in order to boost the scale of their military achievements by comparison.

According to Herodotus, the Persian army numbered 2.5 million soldiers and a similar number of camp followers; this number is universally regarded as fantastic. The consensus opinion is that his estimate is multiplied by at least a factor of 10, and that 100,000–200,000 troops is more credible. In addition, Xerxes had over 1,000 warships. The invasion

© Public domain

LEONIDAS AT THERMOPYLAE
Napoleonic-era view of King Leonidas at Thermopylae, by Jacques-Louis David.

of Greece was carefully planned, with storage depots set up along the invasion route and colossal feats of engineering, including the construction of a 0.8-mile (1.3-kilometer) boat-bridge across the Hellespont (the straits between Asia and Europe) and excavation of a canal across the headland of Mt. Athos in northern Greece, so that Xerxes' invasion fleet could circumvent the difficult passage around Mt. Athos where a previous Persian fleet had come to grief in 492 BCE. According to Herodotus, 1.4 miles (2.2 kilometers) of rock were cut out of the mountain to make a passage wide enough for two warships to pass abreast, and modern archaeology suggests that in this instance his claims may not be exaggerations.

Canal notwithstanding, earlier naval disasters encouraged the Persians to stick to a land invasion strategy, which meant following the route down the western coast of Greece, through the pass of Thermopylae.

THE HOT GATES

Located about 90 miles (150 kilometers) north of Athens, Thermopylae ("Hot Gates") was named for the volcanically heated sulfurous springs that still characterize the area, and for the narrow pass between the mountains and the Gulf of Malia, through which passed the main route from Thessaly through Lokris and into Boeotia. Today, silt deposition and land subsidence mean that the sea is much farther from the mountainside than in ancient times, with the coastline having advanced 3–5 miles (4.8–8 kilometers) over the last 2,500 years. In ancient times, the pass may have been as narrow as the 50 feet (15 meters) claimed by Herodotus for the narrowest point. In the middle of the pass a wall, known as the Phocian Wall, had been constructed, although it had fallen into disrepair. It was here that the Greeks would make their stand. The date of the battle can be pinpointed to around August, because Herodotus tells us that the Olympic Games were underway and the festival of Carneia in Sparta was nearly over (events also held to account for the sparse numbers of Greek troops).

The Greek force was composed of soldiers from several states, for the habitually quarrelling nations of Greece had come together in the face of the Persian threat. The total number differs depending on the source, but the main contingents seem to have been the Arcadians, Locrians, and Phocians with 1,000 men each, 700 Thespians, and 400 from Thebes. From Sparta came one of the two Spartan kings, Leonidas, with a force of 300 elite soldiers known as Hippeis—essentially the royal bodyguard. Leonidas famously picked only men who had fathered sons, thus ensuring the continuation of the family line; this is generally interpreted as indicating that he did not expect his men to return. In addition to the Hippeis, the Spartan force probably also included an unspecified number of helots— Spartan slaves. Leonidas took overall command of the combined force, which numbered around 7,000, according to Herodotus.

Leonidas set his men to rebuild the Phocian Wall, and here they waited for the onslaught from the massive Persian army. Yet it did not come, for Xerxes camped his forces outside the Hot Gates and waited for five days. Ancient and modern scholars offer a variety of explanations for the pause: Xerxes was uncertain of the size of the Greek force, which was hidden from view inside the pass, behind the wall; he was hoping that his fleet, which had failed to keep pace with the army, would catch up and effect a landing behind the gates, allowing him to outflank the Greeks; or he simply assumed that the Greeks, given time to mull on the hopelessness of their situation, would surrender.

Herodotus relates how scouts sent out by Xerxes to spy on the Greek forces returned bearing strange tidings; the Spartans were doing calisthenics and combing their long hair! Demaratus, a Spartan defector in the service of the king, explained their antics: "It is the custom of the Spartans to pay careful attention to their hair when they are about to risk their lives..."

Xerxes sent Leonidas a message, demanding that he give up his arms. The Spartan king replied in the "laconic" fashion of the Spartans (whose homeland was also known as Laconia): *"Molòn labé"* ("Come and take them"). Herodotus also records another instance of laconic Spartan wit, telling how, when camp gossip spread that the Persian archers were so numerous that their arrows would hide the sun, the Spartan Dieneces joked, "So much the better; we will have our fight in the shade."

On the fifth day Xerxes launched his attack, sending waves of Persian soldiers to storm the Greek position in a frontal assault. This was exactly what Leonidas had counted on; in the narrow pass the superior numbers of the Persians could not be brought to bear, and conditions favored the Greeks. While the Persians were equipped for mobility, with light wicker shields and only quilted cloth for armor, the Greek soldiers were hoplites: heavy infantry named for their hoplons, large wooden shields faced with bronze sheet. Hoplites were also equipped with heavy armor and long spears, enabling them to strike at their enemy before they could come close. Leonidas marshaled his men expertly, rotating units to maintain the stamina of the men in the front line, and utilizing the Spartan tactic of feigned retreat followed by a sudden turn to re-engage. Wave after wave of Persian attacks were cut down, suffering terrible losses. "In this way," comments Herodotus, "it became clear to all, and especially to the king, that though he had plenty of combatants, he had but very few warriors."

On the second day Xerxes threw his elite troops into the battle: the regiment known as the Immortals, so named because any losses were immediately made up so that there were always 10,000 of them. Under their leader Hydarnes they were feared throughout Asia as the finest fighting force in the Persian Empire, but they met with no more success than their fallen comrades and were slaughtered. According to Herodotus Xerxes had set up his throne on a nearby hilltop to watch the battle, and was so appalled by the carnage that three times during the day he leapt to his feet "in terror for his army." The Greeks had lost very few men and it must have seemed that they were on the verge of achieving the impossible and defeating an army that outnumbered them at least 20 to 1.

DINNER IN HADES

Unfortunately, the Greek position was not completely secure; the Hot Gates could be circumvented by paths through the mountains, known only to locals. On the eve of the second day one of these locals, a man named Ephialtes, came to the Persian king to sell this information. (He was richly rewarded but the Greeks later put a price on his head and he was eventually tracked down and killed.) Xerxes immediately dispatched Hydarnes and his Immortals to follow the mountain path, guided by Ephialtes. Leonidas had stationed the Phocians to guard this track but under a hail of Persian arrows they retreated to a more defensible position, leaving the way clear for the Immortals to circle round to the Greek rear.

When news of the outflanking maneuver reached the Greeks they were faced with a grim choice. It was decided to send most of the Greek contingents away to fight another day, but Leonidas and his Spartans chose to stay, together with the Thebans and Thespians, whose homelands were already under Persian occupation. They must have known that they faced certain death and the assumption is that Leonidas planned a rear-guard action to give the others time to retreat. According to the Graeco-Roman historian Plutarch (ca. 45–120 CE), Leonidas told his men: "Breakfast well, for we shall dine in Hades."

© Panos Karas | Shutterstock.com

ANCIENT AND MODERN
Before the modern city of Sparta in Greece lie the ruins of the ancient polis.

Leonidas moved his men clear of the wall to fight on more open ground, and the Persians moved in for the kill. The final battle was of desperate ferocity; according to Herodotus, "they carried slaughter among the barbarians, who fell in heaps," and the Persian soldiers had to be forced into battle under the lashes of their captains. "Many were thrust into the sea, and there perished; a still greater number were trampled to death by their own soldiers; no one heeded the dying. For the Greeks, reckless of their own safety and desperate, since they knew that, as the mountain had been crossed, their destruction was nigh at hand, exerted themselves with the most furious valor against the barbarians."

The Spartan king fell and his men contended fiercely with the Persians for his body, driving them back four times before recovering Leonidas. Retreating to a small hill they made their last stand, their spears by now spent or shattered so that they fought on with just their swords, or even, according to Herodotus, "with their hands and teeth, until the Persians, coming on from the front over the ruins of the wall and closing in from behind, finally overwhelmed them with missiles."

The immediate strategic impact of the battle of Thermopylae was negligible; Xerxes was delayed by just a few days, and although his losses can only be guessed at, the one thing he did not lack for was manpower.

GO TELL THE SPARTANS

The decisive battles in the war came later: the naval battle of Salamis later in 480 BCE, where the Persian invasion fleet was smashed, convincing Xerxes to withdraw from Greece with much of his army, and finally the battle of Plataea in 479 BCE, where the remainder of the Persian army was defeated.

Yet it is Thermopylae that lives on in the Western imagination, and its symbolic impact then and since has been immense. The ancient Greeks were so moved by the heroic last stand of the Greeks and especially the Spartans, that they erected a monument at the site of the battle, inscribed with famous verses: "Go, stranger, and to Sparta tell; That here, obeying her law, we fell."

- - - Persian advance

Mountainous ground

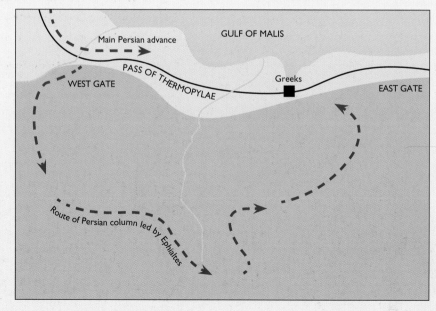

BY SECRET PATHS
The Greeks blocked the main route through the pass between the mountains and the sea, so the Persians circled round behind them, led along secret mountain paths by the traitor Ephialtes.

TO LOSE AN EMPIRE: GAUGAMELA

331 BCE

BATTLE

High casualty rate

Catastrophic defeat

Pyrrhic victory

Tactical blunder

Appalling conditions

Antagonists: Macedonian army under Alexander vs. Persian army under Darius III

Casualties: Macedonian (victors): ca. 300; Persian: ca. 35,000

© Panos Karas | Shutterstock.com

Of Alexander's men about 100 were killed . . . Of the foreigners [Persian army] there were said to have been about 300,000 slain, and far more were taken prisoners than were killed.

Arrian, *Anabasis* of Alexander

If the ancient sources are to be believed, Gaugamela was perhaps the most one-sided victory of all time, with the massively outnumbered Macedonians inflicting total defeat on a vast horde of Persians, achieving a casualty ratio of up to 3,000 Persians killed for every one Macedonian lost. In fact, ancient writers habitually exaggerated to extremes, but it seems clear that at Gaugamela Alexander achieved one of the greatest victories of all time, winning a vast empire and changing the course of history.

BAD OMENS

Alexander the Great, king of Macedon, had already inflicted two defeats on the Persian King Darius III, before the two met at Gaugamela on October 1st, 331 BCE. But on these previous occasions the ground could be said to have favored Alexander, notably at the Battle of Issus in 333 BCE. There, mountainous terrain had prevented Darius from bringing to bear the crushing weight of numbers he was able to marshal, nor had he been able to use effectively his most potent weapon, the scythed chariot, which required a clear run over level ground to operate.

ALEXANDER MOSAIC
Mosaic from Pompeii, dating to the 1st century CE, showing Alexander pursuing a fleeing Darius.

In 331, however, Alexander had allowed Darius to choose the battleground and order everything to his liking, and on the face of it Darius should have been highly confident. He had amassed a colossal army drawn from every corner of his vast dominions, with Bactrians from the foothills of the Himalayas, Greek mercenaries, Scythians from the Black Sea, Cappadocians from Asia Minor, and many more. Ancient estimates of the size of this army vary from 250,000 to over a million. For instance, in his *Anabasis*, the classic account of Alexander's Asian adventures, the Graeco-Roman historian Arrian claims: "The whole army of Darius was said to contain 40,000 cavalry, 1,000,000 infantry, and 200 scythe-bearing chariots." Logistical constraints make it unlikely that the ancients could have fielded armies larger than around 50,000, however.

Darius's army was ranged against the battle-hardened veterans of Alexander's army, made up of 40,000 infantry and 7,000 cavalry, with the elite force led by Alexander himself, the Companions. When the Macedonians arrived on September 30th on the plain of Gaugamela, near Irbil in modern Iraq, they found the Persian host drawn up in a line extending over miles. With a vast, flat plain on which to operate, including lanes cleared specifically for chariot operations, victory should have been assured for Darius. Yet the build-up to the battle had been marked by a series of increasingly ominous portents, cataloged in the only contemporary record of events, the ancient *Babylonian Astronomical Diaries*.

The diaries, preserved in the British Library as a collection of cuneiform tablets, list the bad omens preceding the battle, including, on September 20th, "a lunar eclipse . . . During totality the west wind blew, during clearing the east wind. During the eclipse, deaths and plague occurred." This was followed by flaming meteors, while on the 25th, "A 'fall of fire' occurred in the district . . . entered . . . the Nabû temple and a dog was burned."

According to the Roman historian Quintus Curtius Rufus, Darius put a brave face on this catalog of disastrous portents, declaring to his troops that Alexander was doomed: "Like a wild animal, he sees nothing but the prey he is after as he storms into the trap set for that very same prey."

NOTHING BUT THE PREY

But Darius was to find that Alexander's single-minded focus on the prize—the Persian king of kings himself—would win the day. Alexander had already refused a vast bribe amounting to half the Persian empire to call off his advance; when his general Parmenio commented that he would take it, if he were Alexander, the Macedonian king replied, "I would take it indeed, were I Parmenio." Parmenio was further rebuffed when he advised Alexander to launch a night attack on the Persians, with the Macedonian monarch insisting that he would not steal his victory like a thief in the night. The Macedonians thus enjoyed a good night's sleep, while Darius, fearing a surprise assault, kept his men awake all night.

In fact, Alexander used the time to scout the field, and devised a strategy to counter Darius's plans for the use of scythed chariots. On the next day, October 1st, he drew up his forces slightly to the left of the Persian center, and as he advanced he did so on the oblique, moving farther to the left. This unexpected approach threw the Persian battle plan into disarray: Darius had to launch his chariots too early, depriving them of the cavalry cover they needed to operate successfully. The chaotic battlefront favored Alexander, as the Persians made a fatal mistake, according to Arrian:

". . . when the Persians had made a break in the front line of their army, in consequence of the cavalry sallying forth to assist those who were surrounding the right wing, Alexander wheeled round toward the gap, and forming a wedge as it were of the Companion cavalry and of the part of the phalanx which was posted here, he led them with a quick charge and loud battle-cry straight toward Darius himself. For a short time there ensued a hand-to-hand fight; but when the Macedonian cavalry, commanded by Alexander himself, pressed on vigorously . . . all things together appeared full of terror to Darius, who had already long been in a state of fear, so that he was the first to turn and flee."

Ancient Sicilian historian Diodorus Siculus gives a different version, in which Darius fights bravely, "raining javelins on his enemies," but "as the two kings closed . . . a javelin hurled by Alexander missed Darius but impaled the chariot driver standing behind him. . . the Persians around Darius, and those farther away, thought their king had been brought down." The *Astronomical Diaries* seem to support this version, noting that "Darius's troops deserted him and to their cities [they went]." One theory is that the Persians were in a state of superstitious terror thanks to the series of awful omens leading up to the battle, and that Alexander needed only to show up to carry the day.

NOTHING WANTING

Whatever the chain of events, the consequences were the same—the Persian line broke and in the ensuing rout tens, possibly even hundreds of thousands were killed. Plutarch, in his life of Alexander, comments: "Nothing was wanting to complete this victory, in which he overthrew above a hundred and ten thousand of his enemies, but the taking the person of Darius, who escaped very narrowly by flight."

Darius fled to eastern Persia and would have raised another army, but was murdered by one of his generals. Alexander had won an empire stretching from the Sahara to the Himalayas, while the Persian king had suffered one of the worst defeats in history.

THE ORIGINAL PYRRHIC VICTORY: ASCULUM

279 BCE

BATTLE

High casualty rate

Catastrophic defeat

Pyrrhic victory

Tactical blunder

Appalling conditions

Antagonists: Pyrrhus, King of Epirus, and the Southern Italian Greeks against the Romans under Publius Decius Mus

Casualties: Romans (victors): 6,000–15,000; Greeks: 3,500–15,000

We are told that Pyrrhus said to one who was congratulating him on his victory, "One more victory like this and we shall be utterly ruined."

Plutarch, *Parallel Lives*, Book IX, 21: 9

The Battle of Asculum is the origin of the phrase "Pyrrhic victory," meaning a victory so costly it is no victory at all. Fought between the Romans and the greatest general of his age, Pyrrhus of Epirus, Asculum was confused, bloody, and ultimately indecisive, with rampaging elephants, flaming war wagons, desperate combat across marsh and field, and terrible loss of life.

THE PYRRHIC WARS

Asculum was part of the conflict known as the Pyrrhic Wars (280–275 BCE), which in many ways foreshadowed the Second Punic War (see next chapter). There are many similarities between the strategies, successes, and ultimate failures of Pyrrhus and Hannibal, although Asculum was less bloody and one-sided than Cannae.

In the early 3rd century BCE, the rising power of Rome increasingly threatened the balance of power in Italy and the Mediterranean. Previously the Greek colonies of southern Italy, a region known as Magna Graecia, had controlled the lucrative trade between Sicily, Italy, and Greece, but Rome steadily extended its power in Italy through conquest and alliance. In 282 conflict arose between Rome and the Greek city state of Tarentum, leading to a Roman declaration of war. Tarentum turned for military aid to Pyrrhus, who had a carefully cultivated reputation as a great general.

Pyrrhus was king of Epirus, in northwest Greece. Distantly related to Alexander the Great, he fancied himself a second Alexander and had conquered much of northern Greece. When the Tarentines appealed to him he possessed one of the best-trained and best-equipped armies in the Mediterranean, and probably saw a successful campaign in Italy as a prelude to his real target, the rich agricultural lands of Sicily. Enlisting support from other Greek rulers, Pyrrhus assembled a huge army, and although some of it was lost on the crossing to Italy he was still able to field 25,000 Greek infantry, 3,000 horse, and 20 elephants, in addition to support from his local allies.

Like Hannibal after him, Pyrrhus's strategy was based on the hope that military success against the Romans would incite the various tribes and states of Italy to join his cause. Like Hannibal he was to be disappointed. In 280 BCE he engaged a Roman army of up to 50,000 men at Heraclea (modern Policoro), a battle that marked the first encounter between a Roman army and an Alexandrian one. In particular, it was the first time that Roman troops had encountered war elephants, and the animals had a great impact on their normally doughty infantry, sowing panic and confusion, although typically this affected both sides as rogue elephants ran amok. The Romans lost as many as 15,000 men but Pyrrhus suffered similar casualties. The pattern was to repeat at Asculum.

Die Schlacht bei Asculum. Zeichnung von C. Deutemann.

As Hannibal would later discover, the most remarkable characteristic of Republican Rome was its indomitability; each setback merely hardened Roman resolve. Pyrrhus marched north into Latium, hoping that Roman client city states would flock to his banner, but the Romans had knit a tight network of alliances and he failed to trigger the general uprising for which he had hoped. Meanwhile, the Romans sent a new army to meet him and battle was joined near Asculum (aka Ausculum, modern Ascoli Satriano) in Apulia. With his local allies Pyrrhus had some 45,000 men, and the Roman force was similar; it was one of the largest battles.

Seeking to deny Pyrrhus open space to use his cavalry and war elephants, the Romans engaged him in woody, boggy territory, leading to a day of inconclusive fighting. Determined to choose his own ground, Pyrrhus moved quickly on the second day, seizing the previous day's territory before the Romans had left camp, so that they were forced to meet him in the open. Seeking to engage the Greeks before Pyrrhus could mobilize his elephants, the Roman infantry rushed forward and intense fighting ensued, but eventually the war elephants turned the tide.

Their previous encounter with the terrible beasts had prompted the Romans to develop anti-elephant technology: 300 ox-drawn war-wagons, hung about with spikes and flaming brands to scare off the elephants. According to the ancient sources, however, the wagons were at best only temporarily effective, as Pyrrhus's light infantry disabled them, and the war elephants broke the Roman lines. Graeco-Roman historian Plutarch describes the beasts' impact: "The greatest havoc was wrought by the furious strength of the elephants, since the valor of the Romans was of no avail in fighting them, but they felt that they must yield before them as before an onrushing billow or a crashing earthquake. . ."

ELEPHANTS ATTACK!
In his invasion of Italy, Pyrrhus used war elephants to good effect, terrifying the Romans.

YIELD BEFORE THE BILLOWS

The Romans were chased back to camp, having lost between 6,000 and 15,000 men, according to the varying ancient sources, but as at Heraclea Pyrrhus suffered similar losses, including many of his best Epirote troops and generals and closest comrades. Plutarch relates his famous comment: "One more victory like this and we shall be utterly ruined."

COURAGE IN DEFEAT

Like Hannibal after him, Pyrrhus faced the problem affecting any invasion force far from home with long supply lines: he could not make up his losses, and in addition his Italian allies were losing faith. Meanwhile, as Plutarch puts it, "The army of the Romans, as if from a fountain gushing forth indoors, was easily and speedily filled up again, and they did not lose courage in defeat. . ."

With the war in Italy failing to reach a satisfactory conclusion, Pyrrhus departed to campaign in Sicily. His efforts there also petered out, and in 275 BCE he was recalled by his Italian Greek allies to face renewed Roman threats. This time, however, Pyrrhus had only local troops to call upon: he was defeated at Maleventum (subsequently renamed Beneventum by the victorious Romans) and returned home shorn of conquests and of his army. Roman power in Italy was now unchallenged.

BATTLE

High casualty rate

Catastrophic defeat

Pyrrhic victory

Tactical blunder

Appalling conditions

HANNIBAL HUMBLES ROME: CANNAE

216 BCE

Antagonists: Carthaginian army under Hannibal Barca vs. the legions of Rome under consuls Lucuis Aemilius Paullus and Gaius Terentius Varro

Casualties: Carthage (victors): ca. 8,000 dead; Rome: 10,000 captured, ca. 70,000 dead

When morning broke, the Carthaginians turned to gathering spoils and inspecting the carnage, which even they found horrifying. Thousands of Roman soldiers lay there ... united in a death which the blind chances of battle or flight had brought upon them.

Livy, *History of Rome*, Book 22, Chapter 51

© Getty Images

The battle of Cannae was the worst military disaster in Roman history, and remains the worst single day of slaughter on European soil. For military historians it ranks as one of the great examples of tactical planning and execution, earning the victorious commander, Hannibal Barca, a place among the most revered commanders of all time. To the ancient Romans Hannibal was a terrifying bogeyman, and his bloody victory at Cannae still had the power to strike fear into Roman hearts even after Rome had acquired a vast empire. Yet for all the superlatives, the long-term strategic consequences of the Roman defeat and slaughter were limited.

SWORN TO HATRED

Cannae was a battle in the Second Punic War (218–201 BCE) between Rome and Carthage. Carthage was a city state near present-day Tunis in North Africa, founded by colonists from Phoenicia (hence "Punic") in modern-day Lebanon. It became the focus of a trading and military empire in the western Mediterranean, competing for power first with the Greek colonies in Sicily and later with the rising power of Rome in Italy. In the First Punic War Carthage lost control of Sicily and other Mediterranean territories, but the Carthaginian general Hamilcar Barca extended Punic power in the Iberian Peninsula. This became the power base of his family, including his sons Hannibal and Hasdrubal. According to Roman legend, Hamilcar made his sons swear eternal enmity to Rome. When Hannibal was elected by the troops to lead Carthaginian forces in Spain he soon made good on his oath, launching in 219 BCE an attack on Saguntum, a territory under Roman hegemony. The Romans protested that Hannibal had broken the treaty that defined the borders between Roman and Carthaginian influence, and in 218 BCE they declared war—the Second Punic War had begun.

The Romans expected Hannibal to attempt the recapture of Sicily, but in a daring gambit Hannibal led his army overland across the Pyrenees, the Rhône, and the Alps to invade Italy and strike at the Roman heartland. His strategic master plan was to rouse the subject peoples of Italy, some of whom were actively hostile to Rome or had only recently been subjugated, introducing a new dispensation to

MOUNTAIN MADNESS
Hannibal's daring but perilous march across the Alps cost him many men and a few elephants.

the Italian peninsula and destroying the carefully constructed network of alliances and tribute engineered by his enemy. Rome depended on its allies and subjects for manpower, materiel, and money—the normal practice in raising armies, for instance, was for half the manpower to be Roman citizen soldiers and the other half from allies. Hannibal knew that he did not have the resources to conquer Rome single-handedly, but he hoped to be the spark that would light the fuse of rebellion, bringing Rome to its knees and forcing it to reverse the humiliations inflicted on Carthage in the First Punic War.

After many tribulations and skirmishes, including a disastrous encounter with an avalanche, Hannibal and his army arrived in northern Italy where they won support from some Gaulish tribes. Despite victories against the Romans at the rivers Ticinus and Trebia in 218 BCE, and again at Lake Trasimene in 217 BCE, where the Romans lost 15,000 men, the rest of Italy refused to throw off the Roman yoke. The Romans doggedly raised more armies, resorting under the leadership of Quintus Fabius Maximus to a strategy of shadowing Hannibal so as to impede the foraging of his armies, while refusing to engage him in direct battle. Meanwhile, Roman forces in Iberia cut Hannibal's lines of possible reinforcement.

In 216 BCE, the Roman Senate decided that the so-called Fabian strategy was unmanly, and resolved to crush Hannibal with a massive force. Normally Rome would field just four legions a year, and often this force would be split between different theaters of conflict. Now they mobilized an unprecedented 16 legions, increasing the size of each one from four to five thousand foot and from two to three hundred horse. Even four centuries later, when at the height of its power, the total size of the Roman Empire's military was 25 legions, spread from Britannia to the deserts of Mesopotamia. The force dispatched to take on Hannibal thus amounted to some 80,000 infantry and 6,000 cavalry. In charge of this colossal army were two consuls (normally each consul would take sole charge of an army of his own), Aemilius Paullus and Terentius Varro. According to the Graeco-Roman historian Polybius, who knew Aemilius personally, the consuls were instructed "to fight a decisive battle with a courage worthy of Rome."

A COURAGE WORTHY OF ROME

Ranged against the Romans was the army of Hannibal, consisting of around 40,000 infantry and 10,000 cavalry. The core elements of his army were the much-feared heavy cavalry and the battle-hardened Libyan infantry units equipped with Roman armor acquired from previous victories, while the rest were of mixed ethnicity including Gauls from the Alps and Celtiberians and Lusitanians from Spain. Crucially, Hannibal had the advantage in cavalry, in both quality and quantity, and the Romans' fear of the Carthaginian horse was to prove both justified and their undoing.

BY THE RIVER AUFIDUS

Seeking to provoke Rome to engage with him directly, Hannibal had moved to capture Roman storehouses at Cannae (modern-day Canne della Battaglia), breaking the Roman army's supply lines. The two armies engaged in a few days of indecisive skirmishing along the banks of the Aufidus (the modern-day River Ofanto), before Hannibal planted his army directly in front of the main Roman encampment on the left bank. On August 2nd, realizing that Hannibal wanted to draw them into a pitched battle on this more open side of the river, where his cavalry would have full room to maneuver, the Romans forded the river and took up position between the Aufidus and a small hill about half a mile away. According to the two Roman sources, Polybius and the later Roman historian Livy, the crossing was on the initiative of the plebeian consul Varro. Command of the army alternated daily between the two consuls, and on this fateful day it was Varro's turn. Polybius and Livy go to some lengths to heap blame for the ensuing disaster on Varro, who is portrayed as boastful, conceited, and foolhardy, in contrast to the noble and wise Paullus. But Paullus himself had supposedly been given explicit advice by Fabius Maximus to avoid confronting Hannibal in terrain favorable to cavalry, in which context the choice of battleground might have seemed logical.

© Public domain

ROMAN ROUT
John Trumbull's 18th-century version of the death of Aemilius Paullus, one of the two consuls leading the Romans at Cannae.

In fact, it was a huge tactical blunder. The Romans' main advantage was their massive numerical superiority in infantry, and even though this freshly raised army was inexperienced, Roman infantry had proven themselves one of the most formidable fighting forces in the ancient Mediterranean world.

In frontal combat their tactics and equipment made them tough in defense and irresistible in attack. A line of Roman infantry would usually outmatch an equal number of opposing troops, and Hannibal had learned from his previous encounters that meeting them head-on was inadvisable. But the Romans' choice of a constricted battlefield, with limited space between the hill and the river, meant that the numerical superiority of their army could not properly be brought to bear. Instead of achieving a broad front that could envelop the Carthaginians, the Romans would now be arrayed narrow and deep, with the bulk of the army impotently massed behind the front line, unable to affect the action. Seeking to obstruct Hannibal's cavalry in their choice of ground, the Roman generals had succeeded mainly in nullifying their own numerical superiority. Furthermore, events were shortly to prove that the Carthaginian cavalry was far from nullified.

When the armies were drawn up the Romans were ordered in customary fashion, with their infantry in the center and cavalry on either side. Paullus led the cavalry on the Roman right, Varro the cavalry on the left, while the center was under Gnaeus Geminus Servilius. Opposite them, facing west, Hannibal had drawn up his forces in unexpected fashion. Rather than placing his best infantry in the center where the main thrust of the Roman attack would evidently fall, he ranged his Gallic and Spanish soldiers there. The Libyan foot divisions were drawn up on their flanks. By the river on Hannibal's left, opposite Paullus, was the Spanish and Gallic heavy cavalry under his brother Hasdrubal; on the far right was the Numidian heavy cavalry under its leader Maharbal; Hannibal himself commanded the center, which was to play the crucial and most difficult role in his tactical master plan.

As the battle began Hannibal bowed out his center line toward the Romans, but the power of the Roman infantry soon drove the Gauls and Spaniards back. Meanwhile, the heavy cavalry on the left smashed the Roman horse under Paullus; seeing they were routed, Hannibal moved quickly to join up with the infantry and threw himself into the fray in the center. Here, Hannibal marshaled his troops in the most perilous phase of the battle; his plan teetered on a knife's edge as the Gallic and Spanish infantry slowly gave ground before the advancing Roman legions. The key moment in ancient warfare tended to be the rout—when the morale and discipline of one side crumbled and defenders started to worry not simply that the battle

ENVELOPMENT

was lost, but that the men on either side of them would turn tail and flee. In such a situation those who broke and ran first would be the ones most likely to survive, but at the same time getting caught up in a rout was the worst fate that could befall soldiers—unable to present a collective defense with shields and weapons, troops suddenly became easy prey. A stalwart defense could turn into a massacre in seconds, and the rout was when most casualties occurred. Normally it was troops such as the Gauls and Spaniards who would be thought at most risk, with their mix of ethnicities and perceived lack of discipline in combat. The true measure of Hannibal's quality as a leader was that he instilled sufficient discipline and trust in this heterogeneous collection of troops that they could maintain an ordered retreat. As the main mass of Roman infantry advanced, the Carthaginian center slowly gave ground, bowing back in a U-shape.

Having dispersed his opposition by the river on the left, Hasdrubal led his heavy cavalry across the back of the advancing Roman center and joined with Maharbal's horse in attacking Varro's cavalry. The Roman horse was now completely neutralized, and Hasdrubal was able to leave Maharbal to chase off Varro while he turned to strike the Roman infantry from behind. By the time he fell on the Roman rear, Hannibal had sprung his trap. As his center gave way and the Romans bulged forward, the Libyans had maintained their positions on the flanks; now they closed in to take the Roman infantry from either side. With Hasdrubal's cavalry crashing in from the rear, the Romans found themselves caught in a box and completely enveloped. Though they turned to face outward on all sides, forming a desperate defensive square, their numbers counted for little with so many men packed into the center unable to engage the enemy.

The battle descended into grim carnage. The doomed Romans fought on with obstinate courage while Hannibal's army systematically butchered them. Fleeing men were hamstrung (crippled by cutting the tendons on the back of the leg) and left to be finished off later. According to the Roman sources, Hannibal circled the fray, inciting his soldiers to complete the slaughter, driven on by his implacable hatred of Rome. Livy reported that over 45,000 infantry and 2,700 cavalry were killed, and a further 10,000 soldiers were taken captive. Other estimates put the Roman casualties as high as 70,000. Hannibal lost around 8,000 men. Paullus and Servilius were among the dead, but Varro had fled in ignominy.

Livy paints a vivid picture of the battlefield on the following day:

"When morning broke, the Carthaginians turned to gathering spoils and inspecting the carnage, which even they found horrifying. Thousands of Roman soldiers lay there, infantry and cavalry scattered everywhere, united in a death which the blind chances of battle or flight had brought upon them. A few, whose wounds had been staunched by the morning frosts, even rose from among the heaps of dead all covered in blood—only to be slaughtered there and then by their enemies. Others were discovered, still alive, but lying there with their knees or hamstrings sliced apart, baring their necks or throats and begging their enemies to drain the rest of their blood. Some were even found with their heads buried in the ground, having dug small pits for themselves and buried their faces in the earth, and then simply smothered themselves to death."

This overwhelming victory had turned on two key elements. The first was the Carthaginians' superiority in terms of cavalry, and Polybius records that the Romans drew a hard-learned lesson from Cannae: better to be outmatched in infantry and stronger in cavalry than vice versa. If Hannibal's heavy horse had not gained the upper hand, Roman cavalry charges would have turned the day against him. The second key to Hannibal's success was the remarkable courage and discipline displayed by his Gallic and Spanish infantry, who, despite taking the bulk of Carthaginian casualties, had held their lines without collapsing into rout.

THE FATAL BLOW

According to the ancient accounts, Hannibal's commanders urged him to take advantage of his stunning victory by marching on Rome without delay. "The worth of this battle will be revealed when you are feasting on the Capitol in five days' time," Maharbal supposedly advised. But Hannibal demurred, raising objections, which prompted the exasperated Maharbal to declare: "The gods do not give all their gifts to any one man. You can win a battle, Hannibal. But you have no idea how to exploit it." In Livy's version Hannibal's delay proves fatal: Rome is given respite from terror and despair and manages to pull together its defenses, steeling itself to continue the war.

In practice Hannibal was almost certainly right to dismiss the notion of advancing on Rome. His exhausted army was too small and lacked the equipment and ability successfully to lay siege to Rome, which lay 250 miles (400 kilometers) distant and still possessed formidable defenses, the massacre at Cannae notwithstanding. Hannibal maintained faith in his original strategy, hoping that his crushing victory would set off a general rebellion against the Roman yoke and rally the Italian provinces to his banner. But the Romans had built their local empire too strong, and while some groups did join Hannibal's cause he was never able to bring Rome to terms. Roman resolve was simply hardened by the disaster at Cannae; fresh legions were raised and Fabian strategy employed once more, with Hannibal eventually held at bay in Campania. He would spend a further 14 years in Italy without achieving another great victory, while the Romans successfully took the war first to Iberia and later to Carthage itself.

In 202 Hannibal was finally recalled to Carthage to take charge of the defense of the homeland, only to be defeated at the Battle of Zama in 201 BCE. Rome had won the Second Punic War and Carthage was stripped of her Iberian dominions. Hannibal would later be forced into exile, find employment as an anti-Roman general for hire, and eventually commit suicide in the face of relentless Roman pursuit.

LOST LEGIONS OF ROME: TEUTOBURG FOREST

9 CE

BATTLE

High casualty rate

Catastrophic defeat

Pyrrhic victory

Tactical blunder

Appalling conditions

Antagonists: Three Roman legions under the Publius Quinctilius Varus vs. the Cherusci and other Germanic tribes led by Arminius

Casualties: Romans: 15,000 legionaries, uncertain number of camp followers; Germanic tribes (victors): unknown

Never was there slaughter more cruel than took place there in the marshes and woods, never were more intolerable insults inflicted by barbarians.

Florus, Epitome, *The Roman History*, XXX

© Getty Images

A military disaster that scarred the Roman psyche and changed history, the battle of the Teutoberg Forest saw three entire legions wiped out in horrific circumstances. Mired in mud and tangled in forest thickets, lashed by storms and ambushed on all sides, Roman soldiers and their families prayed for death in battle in preference to capture followed by gruesome torture and sacrifice.

The military successes of Julius Caesar had pushed the limits of the Roman Empire to the shores of the Atlantic, but with the Rhine forming the eastern boundary of Roman territory, hostile regions of Germanic "barbarians" lurked not far from Italy itself. In the early years of the 1st century CE, the first Roman emperor, Augustus, devoted much attention to securing the German frontier. His adopted son and heir, Tiberius, had successfully pacified the region, projecting Roman control across the Rhine as far as the Elbe. Now began the slow work of Romanizing the region, in which high-ranking Germans served in the Roman military and even won citizenship, while Roman colonies introduced urban living to the Germanic peoples. Most contentiously, new provinces were expected to start paying tax.

Under Tiberius the Romanization process seemed to be going slowly but smoothly, but in 7 CE Augustus recalled him, sending in his place Publius Quinctilius Varus, a well-connected nobleman related to the imperial family by marriage. Varus was unaware that a rebellion was being plotted in secret, and that the ringleader was one of his closest native aides, a German prince named Arminius (the Latinized version of Hermann).

INTO THE FOREST

Arminius laid his plans carefully, but word nonetheless leaked out and Varus was warned by other Germans. Apparently completely taken in by Arminius, the Roman governor dismissed the allegations and blundered into the German's trap. According to the Roman historian Paterculus: "Fate now dominated the plans of Varus and had blindfolded the eyes of his mind." In 9 CE Arminius arranged for Varus to receive pleas for assistance from communities scattered around the region, so that the Romans would disperse part of their force in peace-keeping detachments. In late summer he manufactured reports of unrest from far-flung regions, prompting Varus to march deep into a region that is now Lower Saxony with three of his legions: the XVIIth, XVIIIth, and XIXth; Arminius went with him. Evidently not expecting trouble, Varus decided to deal with the unrest en route to his winter quarters, so as well as soldiers the Roman column included supply wagons and camp followers—many of them the wives and children of the legionaries.

Arminius's scouts led the straggling Roman column, strung out through the forest in widely separated groups, toward a carefully prepared ambush. At this crucial juncture, according to the ancient Roman historian Cassius Dio, Arminius and his co-conspirators among the German auxiliaries "begged to be excused from further attendance, in order, as they claimed, to assemble their allied forces, after which they would quietly come to his aid." In fact, Arminius was leaving to set the rebellion in motion, ordering the massacre of Roman peace-keeping detachments that had been sent to the various tribes in the region, before gathering his men to set upon Varus and his legions in the depths of the forest.

HERMANN'S HEIGHTS
The Hermann Monument in Germany's Teutoburg Forest celebrates the exploits of Arminius.

As the Romans struggled painfully through thickly wooded country cut with deep ravines, the Germans harassed them with a continuous stream of guerrilla attacks on the fringes of the column. At the same time the heavens opened and heavy rain and storms lashed the forest, turning the difficult paths into quagmires. The main ambush came as the Romans arrived at a narrow strip of land between hills and a swamp; here, at a hill known as the Kalkriese, north of modern Osnabrück, the Germans had erected a palisade of wooden screens from behind which they launched their main ambush. By now the Roman column was broken into small groups which fought as best they could, but over four days of bloody fighting they were slaughtered to a man. The Germans reserved particularly grisly deaths for captured officers, so Varus and others took their own lives. His three legions, numbering around 15,000 men, were completely destroyed, along with an unknown number of camp followers.

LAST STAND AT THE KALKRIESE

The utter destruction of the main Roman army in Europe meant that Germania and even Italy itself was now in imminent peril. However, quick action by commanders on the Rhine, coupled with the failure of the Germans to press their advantage and cross the river, stabilized the situation. Yet the damage had been done. When the 72-year-old emperor

Augustus heard the news he was distraught, bewailing the loss of the legions for the rest of his life. According to Suetonius, "He was so greatly affected that for several months in succession he cut neither his beard nor his hair, and sometimes he could dash his head against a door, crying 'Quinctilius Varus, give me back my legions!'"

Tiberius was despatched to bring the rebellious tribes to heel, and later his brother Germanicus reached the site of the disaster to recover and bury the bones. As recorded by the ancient Roman historian Tacitus, a dreadful sight greeted him: "In the field, the bones of the soldiers lay scattered about, each where he had fallen either standing his ground or trying to flee. There were bits of weapons, and the bones of horses among them, and human heads had been nailed to the trunks of the surrounding trees."

Arminius was murdered by other Germans 12 years later, but his ambush in the Teutoburg Forest had shaped the course of history. The ancient Roman historian Florus wrote that "The result of this disaster was that the empire, which had not stopped on the shores of the Ocean, was checked on the banks of the Rhine." The Rhine would form the eastern European boundary of the Empire in perpetuity, with the result that Germany was never Romanized and Germanic culture endured. Germanic tribes would later bring down the Roman Empire, conquer much of Europe, and spread Anglo-Saxon culture around the globe.

BATTLE OF BRITONS: WATLING STREET

61 CE

BATTLE

High casualty rate

Catastrophic defeat

Pyrrhic victory

Tactical blunder

Appalling conditions

Antagonists: Boudicca, Queen of the Iceni, and the ancient British tribes vs. Roman XIVth Legion under Gaius Suetonius Paulinus

Casualties: Romans (victors): 400; Britons: 80,000

Our soldiers spared not to slay even the women, while the very beasts of burden, transfixed by the missiles, swelled the piles of bodies.

Tacitus, *Annals*, Book XIV, Chapter 37

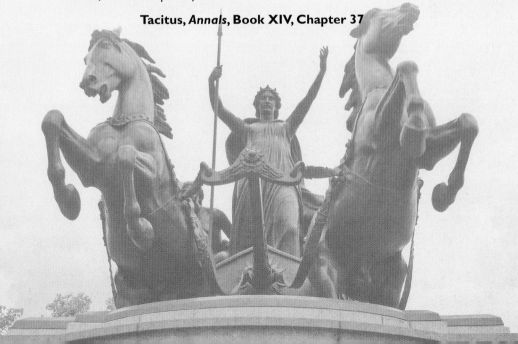

© Claudio Divizia | Shutterstock.com

The Battle of Watling Street is hedged about with uncertainties: it may not have happened anywhere near Watling Street, the number of combatants and casualties varies by source, and the primary antagonist may never have existed. Yet it has become a defining battle in British history and made Boudicca, the Warrior Queen, a legendary figure. The name "Watling Street" derives from the Anglo-Saxon term *Waetlinga* for the people of Verulamium (modern St. Albans), an important settlement on the road, with the name later being applied to the whole length of the route. The only Roman-era reference to the road refers to the stretch between Dover and London as "Iter III" (Route III) and the stretch from London northwest toward Wales as part of the long "Iter II" from Hadrian's Wall.

THE BRITONS ARE REVOLTING

In 60 CE Prasutagus, king of the Iceni, died. This was bad news for the Iceni, a tribe in modern-day East Anglia; Prasutagus had been a client king of the Romans, allowed to keep his throne on the understanding that he would name the Roman emperor as his heir. In addition he had run up huge debts, so when he died the Iceni suddenly found that they and their kingdom had become Roman property. Severe taxes were imposed and Prasutagus's widow, Boudicca, was whipped and her daughters were raped. The Iceni rose up in revolt, along with the neighboring tribe, the Trinovantes. Other tribes would join their cause as the rebellion progressed.

Leading the angry Britons was the formidable Boudicca, described by the ancient source Cassius Dio as "very tall, in appearance most terrifying, in the glance of her eye most fierce, and her voice was harsh; a great mass of the tawniest hair fell to her hips; around her neck was a great golden torc. . ." She led a vast force of warriors to sack the nearest Roman colony, Camulodunum (modern Colchester), massacring most of the inhabitants. Then they defeated an understrength legion that had rashly marched against them, before moving on, in 61 CE, to Londinium (modern London), only recently established but already one of the major towns in Britain.

Meanwhile, the Roman governor Suetonius Paulinus was away in North Wales campaigning against the Druids on Anglesey. When he heard of the revolt he promptly marched his legion—the XIVth—toward London, expecting to join up with reinforcements. To his dismay one legion refused to budge from Exeter and the other had already been destroyed by Boudicca; Suetonius decided on a strategic retreat, pulling his forces back from London. Those who couldn't travel were left to their fate as the marauding Britons razed first Londinium and then Verulamium, slaughtering everyone they found. Tacitus, the primary source for the story of Boudicca, which he based on the account of a first-hand witness, estimates that over 70,000 people were murdered.

Boudicca rallied her troops for one last battle, determined to crush Suetonius and end the Roman occupation of Britain. It is assumed, although there is no hard evidence, that the XIVth Legion retreated up Watling Street and that Boudicca chased them, forcing them to come to battle. The only clues to the location of the battlefield come from Tacitus, who records that Suetonius carefully chose ground that would prevent the vast horde of Britons from encircling his much smaller force: "He chose a position approached by a narrow defile, closed in at the rear by a forest, having first ascertained that there was not a soldier of the enemy except in his front, where an open plain extended without any danger from ambushes."

Tacitus estimates that the Britons numbered 100,000 and Cassius Dio claims a quarter of a million; Suetonius had one legion and a smattering of other forces numbering 10,000. Yet by the time battle began the Britons had already doomed themselves: so confident of victory were the warriors that they had brought their families to watch the spectacle, arranging a great circle of wagons at the back of the battlefield. This would impede their retreat and trap them when the tactics and discipline of the Roman legionaries turned the fight into a rout. The lay of the land funneled the British forces into a relatively narrow front, and their wild charge was checked by the initial volley of pila (javelins) hurled by the Romans, before the close-quarter fighting tactics of the legionaries broke them entirely. The butchery that followed extended to the gathered families, and Tacitus claims that 80,000 Britons were slaughtered for the loss of just 400 Romans. If this is true, the Battle of Watling Street is the worst single-day loss of life in the history of European warfare.

Tacitus says that Boudicca committed suicide with poison, while Cassius Dio says she sickened and died after the battle. Her resting place, and the location of the battlefield, remain great historical mysteries. Since the only record of Boudicca comes from these two Roman sources (with Dio's likely based in large part on Tacitus's), some historians question whether there ever was such a historical personage. If the Battle of Watling Street did take place, it secured Roman control of Britain for centuries to come.

UP THE STREET

BATTLE

High casualty rate

Catastrophic defeat

Pyrrhic victory

Tactical blunder

Appalling conditions

AN EMPEROR IN CHAINS: EDESSA

260 CE

Antagonists: Roman army under Emperor Valerian vs. Persians under the Emperor Shapur I

Casualties: Romans: 70,000, including the emperor: Persians (victors): unknown

The vigorous attempt of the Romans to cut their way through the Persian host was repulsed with great slaughter; and Sapor, who encompassed the camp with superior numbers, patiently waited til the increasing rage of famine and pestilence had ensured his victory.

Edward Gibbon, *Decline and Fall of the Roman Empire*

For the first two centuries CE, the greatest enemy of Rome was the Parthian Empire in the east, but in the 220s the Parthians were overwhelmed by a Persian rebellion that instituted the Sassanid Persian Empire. The Sassanids were to prove an even greater threat to the Roman Empire and to Roman emperors in particular.

In 240 the second Sassanid shah, Shapur I, came to the throne. He waged a series of campaigns against the Romans in the east. In 242 he destroyed the army of Emperor Gordian, who perished in the battle, becoming the first emperor to die in this way. In 252–56 Shapur campaigned in Mesopotamia and Syria, sacking Antioch, the chief and richest city in the region.

Meanwhile, in Europe, the Western Roman Empire was racked by repeated Germanic invasions and infighting between rival claimants to the imperial purple. Valerian (Publius Licinius Valerianus) was a Roman nobleman and able soldier who had been a high-ranking general under the emperor Gallus. The usurper Aemilian rose against Gallus and, as Valerian marched to assist his master, Gallus was murdered by his own soldiers who went over to Aemilian. When Valerian drew near, however, the soldiers promptly defected to him and in 253 Aemilian met the same fate as Gallus. Valerian was acclaimed emperor and split the empire with his son, Gallienus, taking the eastern half for his remit.

In 260 Shapur again invaded Roman territories in Mesopotamia and Valerian marched to meet him. The ancient accounts of what happened next differ depending on perspective. The deeds of Shapur are recorded in a remarkable set of inscriptions on the walls of the Ka'ba-ye Zardost (the Cube of Zoroaster), an ancient building near Persepolis. According to these, Shapur met Valerian in battle near Edessa in 260:

TWO SIDES TO EVERY STORY

"And in the third campaign, we set upon Carrhae and Edessa, and as we were besieging Carrhae and Edessa, Valerian Caesar came against us, and with him was a force [of 70,000]. . . And to the west of Carrhae and Edessa a great battle took place for us with Valerianus Caesar. And we with our own hands took Valerian Caesar prisoner and the rest who were the commanders of this army, the Praetorian Prefect, and the senators, and the officers, all of these we took prisoners and we led them away into Persia."

Roman and Byzantine accounts of the Battle of Edessa tell a rather different story, perhaps in order to save face and lessen the extraordinary

PERSIAN PRIDE
Rock relief at Naqsh-e
Rustam, showing the triumph
of the Persian emperor
Shapur I over Valerian.

blow to morale involved in the loss of the emperor himself. According to these accounts, Valerian was successful in some minor skirmishes before his forces were laid low by an enemy greater than any army: plague. Having lost some. 70,000 men, Valerian retreated behind the walls of Edessa but was forced by either his desperate plight or the imminent threat of mutiny by his dispirited soldiers to sue for peace, agreeing to ride out to parley with a delegation from Shapur. In the "Western" version of events Valerian is only taken captive through the perfidy of the Persians. Edward Gibbon, for instance, drawing on ancient Roman sources, tells the story like this: "Valerian was reduced to the necessity of entrusting his life and dignity to the faith of an enemy. The interview ended as it was natural to expect. The emperor was made a prisoner, and his astonished troops laid down their arms." Whichever account is true, the Battle of Edessa led to vast loss of Roman life and the first time that a Roman emperor was captured by his enemies.

THE GREAT HUMILIATION

In the Western version of the story, Shapur subjects Valerian to terrible indignities and reserves a gruesome fate for his body. According to Gibbon: "Valerian, in chains, but invested with the Imperial purple, was exposed to the multitude, a constant spectacle of fallen greatness; and that whenever the Persian monarch mounted on horseback, he placed his foot on the neck of a Roman emperor." Worse still, when Valerian eventually "sunk under the weight of shame and grief, his skin, stuffed with straw, and formed into the likeness of a human figure, was preserved for ages in the most celebrated temple of Persia. . ." In some accounts the emperor's skin is first painted bright red.

This story may well be fanciful, anti-Persian propaganda. A series of famous Persian reliefs show Shapur and the captured emperor, and it is notable that in all of them Valerian is depicted in imperial regalia and without chains, contradicting the Roman version of his ill-treatment.

THE END OF THE WORLD: ADRIANOPLE

378 CE

BATTLE

High casualty rate

Catastrophic defeat

Pyrrhic victory

Tactical blunder

Appalling conditions

Antagonists: 60,000 Romans under Emperor Valens vs. 60,000 Goths under Fritigern

Casualties: Romans: 40,000, including Valens; Goths (victors): unknown

The ground, covered with streams of blood, made their feet slip...At last one black pool of blood disfigured everything, and wherever the eye turned, it could see nothing but piled up heaps of dead, and lifeless corpses trampled on without mercy.

Ammianus Marcellinus, *The Roman History*, Book XXXI

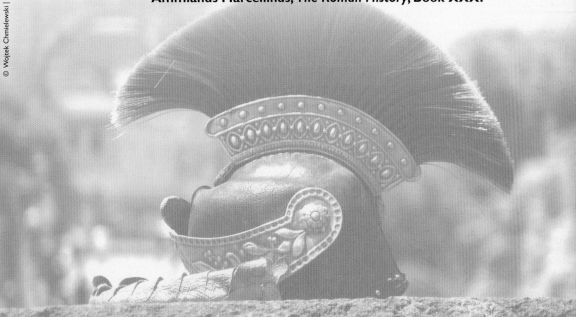

The Battle of Adrianople is widely regarded as the defining battle of Late Antiquity and the death knell for the Western Roman Empire. It was a bloody slaughter on a dry and dusty plain, in which Roman legionaries suffered first from appalling conditions and then at the hands of heavy cavalry in a manner strikingly reminiscent of the disaster at Cannae (see pages 25–32).

ALIEN NATION

By the late 4th century the Roman Empire had long been loosely divided into eastern and western halves, each half ruled by an Augustus ("senior" emperor) and his Caesar (junior partner and anointed successor) in a system known as the Tetrarchy. This arrangement had been devised to help the empire face the multiplying threats on its borders, primarily from the Persians in the east and the Germanic barbarians along the Rhine/ Danube frontiers. All across Eurasia tribes and nations were on the move, and in eastern Europe the arrival of the Huns had displaced the Goths (Visigoths and Ostrogoths), perennial flies in the Roman ointment. Now the Visigoths sought permission to move across the Danube, into the empire, and in 376 CE the eastern emperor Valens reluctantly agreed.

Right from the start, however, relations between the Romans and their new "subjects" went sour and the Visigoths, joined by the Ostrogoths, started marauding across the provinces in great hordes. Valens was in Mesopotamia preparing for a long-planned campaign against the Sassanids when he received news that the Goths were running amok in Thrace (modern-day Bulgaria), and he was forced to return to Europe with a force of 40,000 infantry and 20,000 mainly light cavalry. The plan was for him to join forces with the western emperor Gratian, but politics or revolts, or a combination of both, delayed the arrival of these reinforcements.

According to the main source for the history of the battle, the former soldier turned historian Ammianus Marcellinus, Valens was swayed by counsel that he should strike without waiting and thus claim all the glory. More importantly, he also seems to have made a series of devastating errors and miscalculations. Facing Valens were the Visigoth leader Fritigern and his Ostrogoth counterparts Alatheus and Saphrax, who commanded the heavy cavalry. Fritigern drew the Roman army to meet him near the strategically important city of Adrianople (modern Edirne, in Turkey), wisely avoiding a direct assault on the fortified city which his "barbarian" horde was not equipped to besiege. Instead, Fritigern prompted Valens to make a catastrophic mistake: marching for hours across the dry and dusty plains without food or water.

Valens sent ahead his scouts and spies, who reported back that the Ostrogoth cavalry was nowhere to be seen. The Romans assumed they were off raiding elsewhere in the Balkans, leaving a relatively small force of Visigoth infantry—possibly as few as 10,000—drawn up in a defensive wagon circle known in modern parlance as a laager. On the basis of this intelligence Valens dismissed the final pleas of the western emperor, Gratian, to delay, and advanced. In fact, the Ostrogoth cavalry was not far away, and Fritigern played for time. He had the surrounding fields torched, denying the Romans access to foraging and ensuring that clouds of acrid smoke would choke the thirsty, weary, and sun-baked legionaries.

Perhaps realizing that his army was ill-prepared for battle, Valens seemed willing to discuss a truce, but ill-discipline in the ranks betrayed him. A unit of auxiliaries attacked the Goths, triggering an all-out battle. At first the Roman infantry, flanked by light cavalry, pressed the Visigoth infantry back and had the upper hand, but then the huge force of heavy Ostrogoth cavalry suddenly appeared to turn the tide.

The light Roman cavalry was quickly scattered and the Roman infantry, weakened by hunger and thirst, found themselves encircled as at Cannae. Their situation hopeless, the Romans fought to the death; according to Ammianus: "with such vehemence did they resist their enemies who pressed on them, that some were even killed by their own weapons." But it was to no avail. Among the 40,000 Roman dead were almost all the high-ranking officers and generals, and even the emperor himself. "Nor, except the Battle of Cannae, is so destructive a slaughter recorded in our annals," wrote Ammianus just a decade or so later.

This stunning defeat shattered Roman morale and emboldened the Germanic invaders. It was now clear that the Roman army, largely invincible for over 500 years, was vulnerable, and over the next century the Western Roman Empire would collapse in the face of the "barbarian" invasions. Little wonder that the 4th-century CE Archbishop of Milan, St. Ambrose, called the Battle of Adrianople, "the end of all humanity, the end of the world."

LAAGER LOUTS

BATTLE

High casualty rate

Catastrophic defeat

Pyrrhic victory

Tactical blunder

Appalling conditions

THE SWORD OF GOD: YARMOUK

636 CE

Antagonists: Byzantine army under Vahan the Armenian vs. Arab Muslim army of Khalid ibn al-Walid

Casualties: Muslims (victors): unknown; Byzantines: 25,000–70,000

The Greeks [Byzantines] and their followers in this battle tied themselves to each other by chains, so that no one might set his hope on flight. By Allah's help, some 70,000 of them were put to death, and their remnants took to flight.

Ahmad ibn Jabir al-Baladhuri, *Kitab Futuh al-Buldha*

(Golan Heights) © Ella Hanochi | Shutterstock.com

The Battle of Yarmouk, or Yarmuk, was a key battle in the early stages of the Islamic expansion, where the forces of the Eastern Romans or Byzantines (who became known as Greeks rather than Romans, because their language and culture was mainly Hellenic) had a chance to defeat decisively the main Muslim army in the Near East and to check and even reverse the advance of Islam.

DESERT RAIDERS

Byzantium was well used to incursions by desert raiders into its Near Eastern holdings such as Syria and the Levant. The Eastern Romans had set up buffer kingdoms around the region such as the non-Muslim Ghassanids of the Levant; they also maintained garrisons around the region and could put armies into the field to deal with unrest. They also made frequent use of the time-honored trick of buying their way out of trouble. None of these methods would avail against the new challenge rising out of the east—the Arab tribes united under the banner of Islam. Under the control of their wily general Khalid ibn al-Walid, aka the Sword of God, small but highly effective units of Arab cavalry had struck blows across the region, culminating in the capture of Damascus in September 635.

The loss of such an important city roused the Byzantine emperor Heraclius to attempt decisive action. He gathered a great army composed of units from across the ethnically diverse empire and sent it south under the leadership of his top general, Vahan the Armenian. The exact size of this force is uncertain. According to the 9th-century Islamic historian Ahmad ibn Jabir al-Baladhuri, "Heraclius gathered large bodies of Greeks, Syrians, Mesopotamians, and Armenians numbering about 200,000," but such a vast number probably owes more to propaganda than reality. Based on the levels of manpower known to have been available to the Byzantines at this time, an estimate of 50,000 is probably closer to reality.

Initially, the Muslim Arabs gave way in the face of this large force, giving up Damascus and other gains. Eventually, the Muslim commander Khalid decided that he needed to force a decisive battle, gathering together all of the smaller armies and raiding parties into a single force. Even so, he could muster only 25,000 or so: highly mobile Arabic cavalry, together with spear and bow wielding infantry.

The Byzantine army had established a base at Yaqusah, at the edge of the Golan Heights on the strategically important road from Damascus to Egypt. Khalid pitched his camp to the south, near the Yarmouk River north of Jerusalem. This was broken country with deep valleys, gorges, and cliffs. Khalid would use the terrain to great effect. The Muslim army was accompanied by camp followers, including many of the warriors' wives; they too would play an important role in the battle.

When the two armies lined up opposite one another on August 15th, 636, the Muslims were outnumbered at least two to one. Mindful that attacking expended more energy and manpower than defending, Khalid let the Byzantines come to him, even if this meant they appeared to be dictating the battle. Vahan lined up his forces in four groups, each with supporting cavalry, as well as a large contingent of heavy cavalry, or cataphracts, in reserve. Khalid matched the four infantry groups, supporting his flanks with cavalry and keeping a highly mobile cavalry force in reserve.

The battle is said to have taken six energy-sapping days. The first day opened with the customary contests between the elite "champions" of each army, but the Muslim champions vanquished all comers and Vahan felt the morale of his army slipping. Morale was to prove a crucial factor, with the religious zeal of the Muslims helping to counteract the imbalance of forces. Cutting short the contests between champions, Vahan ended the first day with inconclusive probing of the enemy front.

THE DAY OF LOST EYES

Over the next three days Vahan attempted to crush the Muslims' right flank, creating enough disruption to attempt a breakthrough here or elsewhere along their front for his cavalry to smash through, allowing him to outflank and rout the smaller army. The hard-pressed Muslim infantry were repeatedly pressed right back into their camp, which was just behind the battlefield. Again and again Khalid deployed his cavalry reserve to support the right flank and break up the Byzantine attack. According to Islamic sources, when fighting was at its most desperate and the soldiers on the Muslim right threatened to break and run, their wives forced them back into the fray by hurling stones and epithets at them. Eventually some of the women even threw themselves into battle; according to al-Baladhuri, they "fought violently." On the fourth day Vahan launched his entire army at the Muslims, but his right flank was beaten back by a cavalry charge and only saved itself by deploying a massive volley of arrows and javelins. This rain of projectiles led to this stage of the battle being known as the Day of Lost Eyes.

After four days of exhausting combat both sides had lost many men but the attacking Byzantines had suffered most in terms of casualties and damage to their morale. Although there was no fighting on the fifth day, with Vahan pursuing fruitless negotiations with Khalid, the Sword of God knew that the attritional warfare had set up conditions for a Muslim victory. He despatched a unit of cavalry behind the Byzantine army to capture the bridge across the Yarmouk — the Byzantines' only line of retreat was now cut off.

THE SIXTH DAY

On the sixth day Khalid went on the offensive, launching an all-out assault on the Byzantines' exhausted and depleted left flank, which eventually disintegrated under the pressure. Throughout the battle the Byzantines' heavy cavalry had failed to enter the fray, for reasons that are not clear, and now they were harried off the battlefield by the more mobile Islamic cavalry. The center and right of Vahan's army was now exposed and when they attempted to retreat they found the bridge was held against them. Driven back into an angle between the river and a gorge, the Byzantines were trapped and slaughtered. Some escaped across the river but nearly half are said to have been butchered. According to Al-Qa'qa' bin Amr, a commander in Khalid's army, "We killed those who stood against us; With flashing swords, and we have their spoils; We killed the Romans until they were reduced; Upon the Yarmuk, to withered leaves."

The consequences of this emphatic victory for the Muslims were immense: if the Byzantines had crushed Khalid at Yarmouk, it is possible that the Muslims would have been pushed out of the Near East and Mesopotamia, and might never have expanded their territory farther than Arabia. Instead, Islamic control of Syria was consolidated, opening the way to the conquest of Egypt and North Africa. Within less than a hundred years Islamic armies controlled all of Spain and were raiding into France, while in the east the Caliphate stretched to Central Asia and the borders of China.

BATTLE

High casualty rate

Catastrophic defeat

Pyrrhic victory

Tactical blunder

Appalling conditions

DEATH IN THE DESERT: HORNS OF HATTIN

1187

Antagonists: Saladin, Sultan of Syria and Egypt, and 30,000 Muslim troops vs. Crusader army of ca. 20,000 under Guy, King of Jerusalem, Raymond of Tripoli, and Reynald de Châtillon, Master of the Templars

Casualties: Muslims (victors): unknown; Crusaders: ca. 20,000 killed or captured

And so, in sorrow and anguish, they camped on a dry site where, during the night, there flowed more blood than water ...Throughout the night the hungry and thirsty men were harassed further by arrows and by the fire's heat and flames ...That night God indeed gave them the bread of tears to eat and the wine of remorse to drink.

Anon., *Libellus de Expugnatione Terrae Sanctae per Saladinum* ("The Book of the Capture of the Holy Land by Saladin")

© Amitai | Dreamstime.com

The Horns of Hattin is an extinct volcano near the Sea of Galilee in what is now Israel. On its slopes and in the valley leading toward it, one of the largest armies assembled in the history of the Crusader kingdoms met with disaster, undone by hubris, folly, discord, and hellish heat. It was a battle that fatally undermined the Christian presence in the Holy Land and made its victor, Saladin, the most famous ruler in the world.

By the 1180s the Crusader kingdoms of Outremer ("beyond the sea," as they were known in Europe) were in an increasingly precarious situation. Europe was deaf to entreaties for Crusader reinforcements and the Byzantines were consumed by intrigues and murder; meanwhile, their Muslim opponents were gathering under a single banner—that of Saladin, sultan of Egypt and Syria. By 1183 he had crushed Muslim rebels at Edessa and Aleppo, but with both sides reeling from the effects of a drought, he had brokered a peace treaty with the leper king of Jerusalem, Baldwin IV. The uneasy peace was shattered, however, by the actions of Reynald of Châtillon, an adventurer from the Second Crusade who persistently raided unarmed caravans of Islamic pilgrims and sponsored a pirate fleet that pillaged the Red Sea. Saladin mobilized his army, intent on punishing the criminal Reynald, but his progress was checked by Frankish fortresses and another prolonged famine. In 1185 Baldwin, the one man who might have maintained the truce with the Muslims, died, leaving his sickly infant nephew to inherit the crown as Baldwin V.

In 1186 the infant king died and the throne was seized by his mother Sibyl and her new husband, Guy of Lusignan. A newcomer to the Holy Land, Guy's accession to the throne of Jerusalem caused resentment among the nobles of Outremer, particularly Raymond of Tripoli. Raymond went as

THE HORNS
A view of the Horns of Hattin from the Arbel Valley to the north.

THE LEPER KING

far as agreeing a truce with Saladin to allow the Saracens (as the Muslims were generically known to the Crusaders) free passage across his lands so that they could raid the Kingdom of Jerusalem.

Yet Saladin had achieved limited success against the Crusaders. Their heavily fortified strongholds and cities were almost impossible to take, especially while they were able to put armies in the field. An attempted siege would expose Saladin's forces to attack by an army of heavily armored knights on horseback and their infantry support, and the Crusaders had a good record against the Muslim forces.

A CARAVAN TOO FAR

In 1186 a truce still held between Saladin and the Kingdom of Jerusalem, but once again the actions of Reynald of Châtillon shattered it. He seized a caravan in contravention of the truce and refused to make restitution to Saladin, who declared all-out war on the Franks (as the Crusaders were known to the Muslims). He gathered an army of 30,000 men, forcing the squabbling Crusaders to make common cause. Even Raymond of Tripoli reluctantly agreed to join the army that Guy was raising.

Guy was determined to meet Saladin with full force and raided every garrison in the Holy Land for soldiers. According to one of the main Frankish sources for the battle, the *Libellus de Expugnatione Terrae Sanctae per Saladinum* ("The Book of the Capture of the Holy Land by Saladin"):

"Not a man fit for war remained in the cities, towns, or castles without being urged to leave by the King's order. Nor was this host sufficient. Indeed, the King of England's treasure [money donated by Henry II for the defense of the Holy Land and kept in the treasury of one of the holy orders] was opened up and they gave a fee to everyone who could bear a lance or bow into battle."

The forces of the military religious orders, the Knights Templar and Hospitaller, were also called up. The combined forces, led by Guy, Raymond, and Balian of Ibelin, numbered over 20,000. According to the *Libellus*, "The army was quite large: 1,200 knights, innumerable Turcopoles [light cavalry], and 18,000 or more infantry." They even brought with them parts of the Holy Cross, one of the most venerated relics in Christendom, so that it might be paraded in the midst of the host.

Though formidable, this army was hamstrung by mistrust, mutual loathing, and vanity. According to the *Stratagems of al-Harawis*, a Muslim military manual from ca. 1192, "[the Franks] have little religious sentiment and are capable of treachery and disloyalty; they desire the things of this world and are indifferent to the things of the next; [they are] irresponsible, thoughtless, petty, and covetous . . . being concerned with rank and status . . ." The exception to this was deemed to be the orders of the warrior monks: "beware of the [Hospitallers and Templars] . . . for they have great fervor in religion, paying no attention to the [things of this] world; [they cannot be] prevented from interfering in political affairs . . ."

In July 1187, Saladin moved his army across Jordan to the shores of Lake Tiberias (modern Sea of Galilee) and sought to provoke the Franks into battle. His armies roamed across the land setting fires and allegedly even desecrating the holy site atop Mount Tabor. Saladin himself rode to the Springs of Saforie (Saffuriyah) where the Franks were camped, but they refused to be lured away from their ample water source. On July 2nd Saladin had siege equipment brought up and laid siege to the town of Tiberias. Although the town soon fell, the wife of Raymond of Tripoli held out in the citadel. She sent pleas for help via messengers to Saforie, just as Saladin must have hoped. His aim was to draw the Franks out and make them march across open country, exposing them to tactics that favored his army's fighting style, with its emphasis on mobility and archers.

Raymond counseled wisely that they should steer clear of Saladin's trap, but the king ignored his advice. Guy was keenly aware that his reputation had still not recovered from his inaction in similar circumstances back in 1183, when he had refused to meet the Saracens in open battle. He also needed to justify having raided the King of England's battle fund. Perhaps he was egged on by Reynald and the zealous Templars and Hospitallers. On July 3rd Guy ordered his army to march toward Tiberias.

A DAY OF SORROW AND TRIBULATION

Guy's march to Lake Tiberias ranks among the greatest tactical blunders of all time. It was more than 16 miles (26 kilometers) to the lake, across an arid plateau with just a few scanty springs available en route, and the Franks must have known that these were held by the Saracens. Predictably, the heavily armored Franks quickly began to suffer from heat and thirst, and Saladin's forces harried them on all sides. The army made it as far as the springs of Tur'an, about a third of the way to Lake Tiberias, but these were insufficient to support such a large force, and so they struggled on.

They advanced only 1 or 2 miles (3–4 kilometers) farther. Saladin's forces had surrounded them, and Saladin himself led the main attack which fell on the Frankish rear, guarded by the Templars. Raymond was in the vanguard, and managed to advance to the edge of the plateau, achingly close to the descent to the lake. He sent word urging the king to push on, but the weight of Saracen attacks caused Guy to order that camp be pitched.

During the night the Muslims tightened their encirclement, setting fire to the surrounding heath and bombarding the thirst-crazed Franks with arrows. After a terrible night, the author of the *Libellus* records, "light dawned on a day of sorrow and tribulation, of grief and destruction." The Muslim army waited until the heat of the day had mounted, and then both sides drew up their forces for a climactic confrontation, but the lack of water immediately caused the collapse of Frankish discipline. The Frankish army was composed of knights, whose charge could beat off any frontal assault, and infantry, whose job it was to screen the vulnerable knights from enemy archers. But the infantry, crazed by thirst, immediately charged up to the summit of the Horns of Hattin and refused to come back down. According to the *Libellus*: "The King, the Bishop, and others sent word, begging them to return to defend the Lord's cross . . . the Lord's army, and themselves. They replied: 'We are not coming because we are dying of thirst and we will not fight.'"

TO THE VICTOR
Saladin receives the captured Crusader knights and princes after the battle.

Raymond and Balian managed to break free of the encircling forces and flee, but the king and the knightly orders made a last stand. With arrows raining down, the Frankish knights launched a series of desperate charges, aiming directly at Saladin himself. His son gave an account of the climax of the battle:

"I was at my father Saladin's side during the battle, the first that I saw with my own eye. The Frankish king had retreated to the hill with his band and from there he led a furious charge against the Muslims facing him, forcing them back upon my father. I saw that my father was alarmed and distraught, and tugged at his beard as he went forward, crying: 'Give the Devil the lie!' The Muslims turned to the counterattack and drove the Franks back up the hill . . . But they returned to the charge with undiminished ardor and drove our army back toward my father. His response was the same as before, and the Franks retired back to the hill . . ."

Finally, Guy surrendered. Saladin had captured the King of Jerusalem, together with many leading nobles, including the hated Reynald. He treated his captives graciously, filling a cup for the king with his own hands. The king then passed the cup to Reynald. What happened next is related in the *Account of the Battle of Hattin*, written around 1197 by a local Frank named Ernoul:

"Prince Reynald would not drink. When Saladin saw that . . . he was irritated and told him: 'Drink, for you will never drink again!' The prince replied that if it pleased God, he would never drink or eat anything of his (Saladin's). Saladin asked him: 'Prince Raynald, if you held me in your prison as I now hold you in mine, what, by your law, would you do to me?' 'So help me God,' he replied, 'I would cut off your head.' Saladin was greatly enraged at this most insolent reply, and said: 'Pig! You are my prisoner, yet you answer me so arrogantly?' He took a sword in his hand and thrust it right through his body. The mamluks who were standing by rushed at him and cut off his head. Saladin took some of the blood and sprinkled it on his head in recognition that he had taken vengeance on him."

THE FALL OF JERUSALEM

Guy and the other nobles were ransomed, but over 200 Templars and Hospitallers were executed and the common soldiers enslaved. Frankish morale was crushed and defensive manpower across the Crusader kingdoms was drained. A string of cities soon fell to Saladin; he took Acre in July and Jerusalem in October. Tyre, Antioch, Tripoli, and a few castles were all that remained of the Crusader kingdoms.

The fall of Jerusalem triggered the Third Crusade, but despite limited successes against Saladin the Crusade was a failure and Jerusalem was never recovered. By 1192 the Franks were confined to a narrow coastal strip. Saladin's crushing victory at Hattin and his subsequent defeat of the Third Crusade had made him renowned from England to India.

High casualty rate

Catastrophic defeat

Pyrrhic victory

Tactical blunder

Appalling conditions

MONGOL MASTER PLAN: LIEGNITZ
1241

Antagonists: Mongol horsemen under Kadan and Baidar vs. mixed force of European knights and infantry under Duke Henry II of Silesia

Casualties: Europeans: ca. 25,000 men, including Henry and many nobles; Mongols (victors): unknown

As the Prince [Henry of Silesia] is raising his arm to bring his sword down on an enemy, a Tartar [Mongol] thrusts his lance into the Prince's armpit and the Prince slides from his horse. The Tartars pounce on the Prince and, dragging him clear, cut off his head with a sword, tear off all his badges, and leave his corpse naked.

Jan Długosz, *Annals*, ca. 1480

The year 1241 was a dark one for eastern Europe, with a string of defeats to invading Mongol armies. Two of these, the battles of Liegnitz (modern Legnica) in Poland and Mohi in Hungary, which took place within a few days of one another, were particularly catastrophic bloodbaths.

The carnage at Liegnitz was merely a minor element in a grand master plan for destruction and despoliation on a continental scale. The plan had its genesis in the world-conquering ambitions of Genghis Khan, who welded the diverse nations of the Mongolian steppe into an all-conquering army. After his death, overlordship of the Mongols passed to his son, Ogodei, but actual command was devolved to a series of khans who ruled khanates, also known as hordes. In the west, Genghis's grandson Batu established the Kipchak Khanate, aka the Golden Horde, with the help of the veteran general Subedei. Together they planned in meticulous detail the conquest of Russia and the subjugation of the Pontic and Caspian steppes, followed by an incursion deep into Europe. In 1237, Batu's hordes crossed frozen rivers into Russia, conquering all the Russian principalities save Novgorod, and by 1241 they were ready to execute the next phase of their plan.

Batu and Subedei had gathered a force of 70,000 men—all on horseback, most of them light cavalry with some heavy cavalry. All of them wielded composite bows, cunningly fashioned weapons capable of hurling arrows over great distances despite their small size. A geographer, Richard Hakluyt, described what were known in Europe as the Tartars in his 1589–1600 work, *The Principal Navigations, Voyages, Traffiques, and Discoveries of the English Nation*:

"They used to fight constantly and valiantly with javelins, maces, battle-axes, and swords. But specially they are excellent archers, and cunning warriors with their bows."

Tartar warriors could shoot on the gallop and even fire backward without breaking stride. Hakluyt also recorded that they wore little armor on their backs, to discourage them from turning tail and fleeing, but in fact the false rout was one of their primary tactics. The light Mongol cavalry would appear to be withdrawing in disarray, luring their enemies into headlong pursuit onto ground more favorable to the Mongols, whereupon they would spring an ambush on all sides while the "fleeing" horsemen would turn and fight.

FROM RUSSIA WITH HATE

These tactics, along with their unrivaled savagery to conquered populations, had earned them a fearsome reputation. According to Hakluyt, "Vanquished, they ask no favor, and vanquishing, they show no compassion . . . suddenly diffusing themselves over an whole province, and surprising all the people thereof unarmed . . . they make such horrible slaughters, that the king or prince of the land invaded, cannot find people sufficient to wage battle against them, and to withstand them."

HOW CAN YOU FLEE FROM MY GRASP?

The Mongol expansion had dislodged a tribe known as the Cumans, nomadic steppe people like themselves, and they had crossed the Carpathian mountains and taken refuge in Hungary, appealing to King Béla IV for protection. Despite disquiet among his nobles, to whom the Cumans were little different from the Tartars themselves, this was granted. Batu seized upon this as a pretext for launching an invasion of Hungary. In December 1240 he dictated an ominous letter to Béla:

"I have learned that you keep the Cumans, my slaves, under your protection. Whence I charge . . . that you do not make me your enemy on their account. For it is easier for them to escape than for you . . . But you, living in houses and possessing fortresses and cities, how can you flee from my grasp?"

BATU KHAN
Medieval Chinese depiction of Batu Khan, leader of the Golden Horde.

© Mary Evans | INTERFOTO | Bildarchiv Hansmann

In December 1240, the Mongols seized Kiev, the most important Russian city, and in February of the following year they crossed the frozen rivers into eastern Europe. Batu and Subedei had divided their force in two; 50,000 men under their command would cross the Carpathians directly into Hungary, while a northern force of 20,000 under Baidar and Kadan circled north into Poland to draw off any sources of support that might come to Béla from the north.

This northern force skirted the Carpathians in early March and blazed a trail of destruction across Poland, defeating Polish armies at Krakow and Chmielnik. Bypassing fortified Wrocław, the Mongol commanders sought out the army of the most powerful noble in Poland, Henry II of Silesia. Their scouts had discovered that Henry was planning to rendezvous with his brother-in-law, King Wenceslas I of Bohemia, and his army of 50,000; they were determined to meet Henry's force of 30,000 before this could happen.

Henry was waiting for Wenceslas at Liegnitz, where he had gathered a force of Polish knights, Templars from France, Teutonic Knights from Prussia, and foot soldiers from Poland and Germany, including German gold miners from Goldberg. What Henry lacked was reliable intelligence; he did not know where Wenceslas was or when he might arrive. Fearing to allow the Mongols free reign to terrorize his lands, he led his army out to meet them on a nearby plain, on ground of the Mongols' choosing. According to The *Annals* of Jan Długosz, a major source for the battle, Henry's exit from Liegnitz was accompanied by an ill omen: "On April 9, Prince Henry, in splendid armor, rides out from Legnica to do battle with the Tartars. As he rides past the Church of the Blessed Virgin, a stone falls from the roof narrowly missing his head."

The Mongols knew that their lighter horsemen would suffer in hand-to-hand combat with the heavily armed European knights. They preferred to use their greater mobility and circle the knights, staying out of range of their swords and lances and peppering them with arrows. For this to work, however, the knights had to be separated from their infantry support. Here, the indiscipline of the European forces served the Mongols well. While the Tartars followed commands issued by signal without seeking personal glory, their opponents lined up in small groups according to personal allegiance, and thought as much about individual glory as battle tactics.

RUSES AND STRATAGEMS

The first to attack was a Polish division under Duke Boleslav, who rushed forward but soon found themselves surrounded by Mongol horsemen showering them with arrows, and withdrew. Next, a charge by Teutonic Knights and Polish knights under Meshko of Opole seemed to force the Mongols to retreat, but perhaps wisely Meshko declined to pursue them. Unfortunately, Henry himself, leading Polish knights and French Templars, did fall for the classic Mongol stratagem of the false rout, especially when they saw a particularly garish Mongol standard, with a yak's tail atop crossed sheep shoulder blades, join the retreat.

Outpacing its infantry support and in a ragged charge, Henry's division was in trouble. The Mongol cavalry wheeled round and rode past them, while a standard deployed a secret weapon, as Długosz reports:

"As the Tatars withdraw . . . the bearer of a huge [standard] with a giant X painted on it . . . topped with an ugly black head with a chin covered with hair . . . begins violently shaking [it], and there suddenly bursts out a cloud [of smoke] with a foul smell that envelops the Poles and makes them all but faint, so that they are incapable of fighting."

Shrouded in smoke, cut off from support, and surrounded on all sides, Henry and his knights had their horses shot out from under them and were then cut down with lances and sabers. Henry himself was killed, and the Mongols cut off his head and paraded it on a lance. The Europeans were now routed and some 25,000 of them were slaughtered. Długosz records that "The Tartars, wishing to know the exact number of the dead, cut one ear off each corpse, filling nine huge sacks to the brim."

MASSACRE AT MOHI

With victory at Liegnitz, the northern Mongol force had achieved its strategic goals. Béla received no assistance from the north, and his own lands were in turmoil. Distrust of the Cumans triggered a race riot in which their leader was murdered, to which the angry nomads responded by hacking and burning their way south. Nonetheless, Béla managed to gather a force of 70,000 (or 100,000, according to some sources). Leaving Pest on the same day as the disaster at Liegnitz, the Hungarian army advanced on the Mongols, who gave ground until they reached the plains of Mohi by the River Sajó. Here, with a forest to guard their back and screen their movements, Batu and Subedei planned their enemy's destruction.

In the early hours of April 11th, Batu led a large portion of his force across the river while other elements circled round to surround the Hungarian camp. Assaulting the Europeans with arrows, catapults, burning petroleum weapons, and even primitive gunpowder devices, the Mongols harried and terrified their enemy. In the confusion the Mongols seemed to have left an exit corridor, down which thousands of European soldiers fled, but this was another ruse—the fleeing men, vulnerable in their rout, were ridden down and slaughtered. Between 45,000 and 60,000 Europeans were lost and Béla barely escaped with his life. As a Bavarian chronicler for 1241 succinctly summarized: "This year the kingdom of Hungary, which has existed for the past 350 years, was destroyed by the Tartars."

Shortly after this the Mongol forces, apparently poised to invade Austria and perhaps rampage all the way to the Atlantic, abruptly disappeared.

Kadan and Baidar had withdrawn from Poland immediately after Liegnitz, leading later German writers to claim that the heroic sacrifice of the Teutonic Knights and their companions had saved Germany from the Mongol hordes. In fact, the northern Mongol force had never intended to penetrate farther. What Batu could have achieved had he continued west is one of the great "what-ifs?" of history, but at this moment fate intervened and the Great Khan Ogedei died. As was customary, all the lesser khans were called back to Karakorum in Mongolia for a meeting to elect a new Great Khan. The invasion of Europe was called off and a Mongol army never again threatened Europe directly. The sacrifices of Liegnitz and Mohi were both atrocious and pointless.

THE TARTAR TRAP
The leading European division under Boleslav is drawn forward before being attacked from the flanks by Mongol units. Prince Henry charges forward to relieve them but Mongol ruses scatter the European knights leaving Henry to attempt an unsuccessful breakout to the south.

PHASE I

PHASE 2

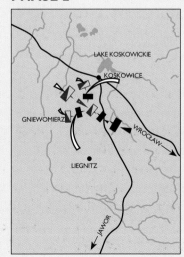

PHASE 3

⊢ Duke Henry's units

▮ Mongol units

BATTLE
High casualty rate
Catastrophic defeat
Pyrrhic victory
Tactical blunder
Appalling conditions

UPON SAINT CRISPIN'S DAY: AGINCOURT

1415

Antagonists: English army under Henry V vs. the flower of French nobility under the Constable of France, Marshal Boucicaut, and various royal princes

Casualties: English (victors): fewer than 1,000; French: 5,000–10,000, including numerous dukes and other nobles

The [French knights] had their horses so severely handled by the archers, that, smarting from pain, they galloped on the van division and threw it into the utmost confusion, breaking the line in many places. The horses were become unmanageable, so that horses and riders were tumbling on the ground, and the whole army was thrown into disorder.

Enguerrand de Monstrelet, *Chronicles*

Agincourt has become one of the legendary battles of English history, a stirring story of triumph against the odds, rousing speeches, and plucky yeoman archers getting one over on arrogant French aristocrats. What is obscured by the legend is the awful reality of the battle, with horrific scenes of carnage played out in terrible conditions, along with atrocities and the murder of prisoners.

In 1413 England had a new, young king, eager to gain the laurels of military glory and win back territory in France that had once belonged to his dynasty. Henry V wasted little time in provoking a new chapter in the long-running conflict with France, the Hundred Years' War, starting off by pressing his claim to the French throne and then making unacceptable demands of the increasingly alarmed French. The souring of relationships between the French and English courts was fictionalized by Shakespeare (*Henry V*, Act 1, Scene 2) with an incident in which Henry promises to return as cannon shot a barrel of tennis balls sent by the Dauphin (the heir to the French throne and son of King Charles VI).

BALLS TO BUCKSHOT

Henry had no desire for negotiations to succeed; he was preparing for war, and wished to achieve more than the raids of his ancestor Edward III—he wanted to conquer and hold territory. In the winter of 1414–15 the king had ships commandeered to ferry to France the army of 12,000 men he was assembling at Southampton. In early 1415 a diplomatic mission to France predictably failed, but Henry did not launch his invasion until relatively late in the season, in August. His plan was to capture Harfleur, a port in Normandy, thus establishing a secure bridgehead via which he could conquer swathes of Normandy and northern France.

Unfortunately, the siege turned out to be costly in both time and men, mainly thanks to the dysentery that afflicted his army. When the port finally fell on September 22nd there was little of the campaigning season left, in addition to which the disunited French looked like finally coming together in the face of the English threat. Large armies were being marshaled against him, with even the traditionally pro-English Burgundians sending men to the French side. The sensible move would be to sail home from Harfleur, but Henry had not achieved the glory he sought.

To the dismay of his counselors, the young English king decided it would be better to sail home from Calais, but rather than sail there he would march 100 miles (160 kilometers) across hostile territory. His force had been greatly reduced by disease and he had to leave a garrison at Harfleur, so Henry would be traveling with just 8,000 men, across at least two major rivers. Perhaps Henry intended merely to demonstrate his bravado, and hoped to avoid a pitched battle. But French armies were hunting him.

ENOUGH TO KILL

On October 8th the English marched out of Harfleur, expecting to meet the Governor of Calais, Sir William Bardolph, at the Somme crossing. When Henry reached the estuary of the Somme, however, he found the crossing held against him by the French and was forced to take a different route. By October 24th the English reached Frévent, just 30 miles (48 kilometers) from Calais, but here they were brought to bay by the gathering French forces. Scouts reported that a huge army blocked the road ahead. According to legend, when Henry quizzed a Welshman, David Gambe, about the size of the enemy forces, he replied: "There are enough to kill, enough to capture, and enough to run away." The king ordered his men to prepare for battle, sharpening stakes that could be set in the ground to protect his bowmen and disrupt cavalry charges.

Archers formed a sizable contingent of Henry's army; they would prove to be the decisive factor in the battle. With a longbow measuring roughly the height of a man, a skilled archer could hit a target 590 feet away. The English had been stockpiling armor-piercing arrows in the Tower of London for months, in preparation for the campaign. Together, longbow and armor-piercing arrows were the medieval equivalent of an antitank missile, able to penetrate the plate of the heavily armored French knights.

Beyond the village of Maisoncelles, near Agincourt, the English could see the French force blocking the valley ahead. Although medieval sources do not give the precise number, it is thought that there were at least 20,000 French soldiers, including the flower of French nobility. Present were the Constable of France, Charles d'Albret; Marshal Boucicaut; and the dukes of Orléans, Bourbon, and Alençon, but it is not clear who, if anyone, had overall command. Henry ordered his men to make camp and they sat in gloomy silence, soaked by rain, brooding on the likely outcome of the next day's battle. The French camp was filled with carousing and laughter.

The next day was the feast of St. Crispin, a holiday in England, which features in Shakespeare's famous version of the rousing speech Henry is said to have given that morning. In fact, the most contemporary sources do not mention any speech, and slightly later ones put pious words in the king's mouth. Henry drew up his forces in three divisions of knights and men-at-arms, with all his men dismounted to fight on foot. Either between the divisions, or at the flanks, were the bowmen, protected by screens of sharpened stakes. Surveying the battlefield, Henry saw that it was flanked by woods on either side that drew in to narrow the field, and between them lay freshly ploughed ground soaked with rain. Beyond this were the French forces, drawn up in three lines of dismounted men, flanked by

cavalry. Constable d'Albret was in command of the front line, in which the leading nobles jostled for space, each wanting to take pride of place. According to the French chronicler, Pierre Cochon, "In their arrogance the French had proclaimed that only those who were noble should go into battle, so all the men of lower ranks . . . were pushed to the rear."

The English waited but the French did not move. According to the earliest chronicle of the battle

composed in England, the *Gesta Henrici Quinti* (Deeds of Henry V) of ca. 1417, this was because they well realized the disadvantages of the ground before them: "The king [Henry V] realized the astuteness of the French in standing firm in one place so that they might not be exhausted by advancing on foot through the muddy field . . . it was necessary for the English, if they wished to come to grips with the enemy, to traverse the middle ground on foot, burdened with their arms."

What seemed like French wisdom would turn out to be a tactical blunder that gave Henry the advantage. The king ordered his men to pull up the sharpened stakes, advance, and reset the defensive screen farther down the field in the narrows between the woods. At the same time he sent contingents of archers down each side, hidden by the trees. Unaccountably, the French, possibly due to their lack of a clear command structure, did not attack at this moment when the English were most vulnerable.

ENOUGH TO KILL
Victorian engraving showing the English army butchering the French knights.

© Georgios Kollidas | Shutterstock.com

Having allowed the English to set up within bowshot, the front ranks of the French now paid the price. Trumpets blared and volley after volley of arrows poured into the French lines. Attempts to sweep away the bowmen with a cavalry charge were hindered by the screen of stakes, while of the force of 800 men-at-arms under the Duke of Brabant detailed to take out the archers, 660 were cut down before getting anywhere near them.

When the French attempted to close with the English they got bogged down in the terrible mud. According to Pierre Cochon, "As the night had seen much rain, the ground was soft so that the men-at-arms sank into it by at least a foot." Worst affected were the French knights in their heavy armor. Adding to the confusion, the French cavalry were thrown back in disarray, their horses crashing into the foot soldiers. According to the 15th-century account of Enguerrand de Monstrelet, "Horses and riders were tumbling on the ground, and the whole army was thrown into disorder."

The English seized their advantage, pressing forward for close-quarter butchery. According to Enguerrand, "Throwing down their bows, [the bowmen] fought lustily with swords, hatchets, mallets, and bill-hooks, slaying all before them." The narrow front prevented the French from engaging with their superior numbers, negating their advantage. According to some accounts, the mass of Frenchmen pressing forward caused hundreds to die from suffocation and trampling under the growing heap of dead and dying. This may be an embellishment, but with men slipping about in mud and gore, the combat must have been intense and horrific.

AN INSTANTANEOUS AND GENERAL MASSACRE

After two hours it was clear that the English had won the day and surviving Frenchmen fled the field. The last line of French forces hovered behind the melee, unsure of what to do; around noon Henry ordered them off the battlefield and they left with their tails between their legs. But there was to be a final and tragic act in the narrative. The original French plan of battle had called for a small force, led by local knights making use of their knowledge of the terrain, to circle round via the woods and come on the English camp and baggage train from the rear. This was the only part of the plan that succeeded, and as Henry and his men were mopping up on the main battlefield and turning their thoughts to the mass of prisoners they had taken, they were alarmed to see renewed fighting breaking out to their rear. Enguerrand relates what happened next:

"This distressed the king very much, for he saw that though the French army had been routed they were collecting on different parts of the plain in large bodies, and he was afraid they would renew the battle. He therefore caused instant proclamation to be made by sound of trumpet, that every one should put his prisoners to death, to prevent them from aiding the enemy, should the combat be renewed. This caused an instantaneous and general massacre of the French prisoners . . ."

BATTLE SITE
Monument marking the site of the battle at Agincourt.

This seems like a war crime to modern eyes but contemporary authors blamed the French knights involved, who were later imprisoned despite giving away the treasure they had managed to loot from Henry's own baggage. It is not clear to what extent the king's command was obeyed, anyway, since the ransom of prisoners was the main source of remuneration for the victorious soldiers.

Against English losses of fewer than 1,000, French casualties numbered somewhere between 5,000 and 10,000, including the Constable and many leading nobles, the royal princes the Dukes d'Orléans and de Brabant among them. Henry paused to ransack the French baggage train (at which point, according to legend, he threw a feast for his generals, with captured French nobles acting as servants) before marching unopposed to Calais and sailing back to England to celebrate his great victory. It was said that the mentally unstable French king, Charles, was taken by a fit of madness on hearing the news from Agincourt. French chronicler Sieur Louis de Conte, just a boy at the time, later recalled: "[In 1415] the prodigious disaster of Agincourt fell upon France; and although the English King went home to enjoy his glory, he left the country prostrate . . ."

BATTLE

High casualty rate

Catastrophic defeat

Pyrrhic victory

Tactical blunder

Appalling conditions

BLOODY SUNDAY: TOWTON
1461

Antagonists: Yorkist army under Edward IV vs. Lancastrian army under Henry Beaufort, Duke of Somerset

Casualties: 20,000–35,000 Yorkists (victors) and Lancastrians died, mainly the latter

. . . [T]he wounds they died of being made by battle axes, arrows, and swords, caused an immense effusion of blood, which lay caked with the snow, which at that time covered the ground, and afterwards dissolving with it, ran down, in the most horrible manner, the furrows and ditches of the fields for two or three miles.

Thomas Langdale, *A Topographical Dictionary of Yorkshire*

© Jane Rix | Shutterstock.com

Towton may have been the biggest, longest, and bloodiest battle ever fought on British soil (with the possible exception of the battle of Watling Street — see pages 37–9), yet it is virtually unknown and rarely features in history books. Towton involved huge armies comprising a sizable proportion of the population, engaged in hours of exhausting combat in the midst of a snowstorm, and culminating in a gory massacre without mercy.

The dynastic struggle known as the Wars of the Roses pitched the House of York against the House of Lancaster for control of the throne of England. The heraldic emblem of York was a white rose and of Lancaster a red rose, hence the name. Both houses belonged to the Plantagenet dynasty, and could trace their ancestry back to Edward III. The Lancastrians had ruled since Henry IV deposed his cousin, Richard II. He was succeeded by Henry V, but when he died his son, crowned Henry VI, was just an infant. His long rule was marked by increasing infirmity, both politically and personally. According to the medieval abbey chronicle, *The Second Continuation of the History of Croyland Abbey*, "In consequence of a malady that had been for many years increasing upon him, [Henry VI] had fallen into a weak state of mind, and had for a length of time remained in a state of imbecility and held the government of the realm in name only."

Henry VI's reign saw the disastrous conclusion (from an English point of view) of the Hundred Years' War with France, and his right to the throne was challenged by his cousin, Richard of York. In 1455 open warfare broke out between the two, launching the Wars of the Roses, which evolved into a long-running and increasingly bitter series of battles up and down the countries. Most of the nobles in the realm were drawn in, and the wars would eventually claim over 100,000 lives (at a time when the population of England and Wales was probably less than 3 million).

In January 1461 Richard of York was killed in battle and his 18-year-old son Edward, previously Earl of March, became duke. Edward was a giant, standing at 6 feet 4 inches (1 meter 90 centimeters) and according to the admittedly biased *Croyland Abbey Chronicle*: "He was now in the flower of his age, tall of stature, elegant in person, of unblemished character, valiant in arms, and a lineal descendant of the illustrious line of king Edward the Third." Although young and inexperienced, he would prove to be a capable and ruthless military leader. Edward now became head of the Yorkist faction, whose main strength lay in the

THE WARS OF THE ROSES

south of the country, and although he was acclaimed king in London he refused a coronation, knowing that he would have to prove his claim to the throne through force of arms. Gathering an army, he marched north to confront the Lancastrians.

BEFORE THE GATES OF YORK

Somewhat ironically, the main Lancastrian stronghold in the north was York, and this was Edward's target. He wanted not just to defeat the Lancastrians but to utterly destroy them, securing his position permanently. To this end he had raised a huge army; opinions differ markedly as to how huge, with contemporary sources inflating the numbers involved to absurd levels of 100,000 or more, and modern writers downplaying the size of the forces—leading scholar of the era Professor Charles Ross suggests a force of 20,000, while the general consensus puts the Yorkists at 40,000. However, a sizable detachment of Edward's overall strength was marching separately under the Duke of Norfolk, and it was not clear when they would arrive.

YORKIST KING
Formerly Earl of March and Duke of York, Edward became the fourth king of this name in 1461.

Opposing the Yorkists, the Lancastrians seemed to hold most of the cards. Their force was larger—generally thought to have been around one-third bigger, giving them 30,000–60,000 men. (Given that in this era an army of 5,000 men was considered large, the forces gathering for the battle were truly titanic. Ross, whose figures are at the lower end of the scale, estimates that, out of all Englishmen and Welshmen eligible to fight—those aged between 16 and 60—one-tenth were present at the Battle of Towton.) Their men were better trained and supplied, and with the Yorkists advancing on them they had the advantage of choosing the battleground and meeting an army tired from a long march with fresh, rested troops.

EDWARDVS · IIII

In the event, the speed of Edward's march north surprised the Lancastrians and they were not able to secure the River Aire against the Yorkists. They had, however, chosen a second line of defense, between the villages of Towton and Saxton, and here the two armies would meet on March 29th, Palm Sunday (normally a holiday). Here, on a small plateau, the Lancastrians chose the higher ground, with a clear field of view ahead and their rear secured by woods, while the left and right flanks were protected by steep drop-offs to marshy ground and a small river, the Cock Beck, respectively. The Yorkists would have to attack uphill.

Alongside Edward at the head of his army were his commanders, Richard Neville, Earl of Warwick (aka the Kingmaker), and William Neville, Baron Fauconberg,

© Public domain

BLOODY BECK
Yorkist troops massacre retreating Lancastrians in the midst of the raging torrent of Cock Beck.

a veteran of French wars and uncle to both men. As they marshaled their forces and surveyed the unfavorable situation, the weather took a decisive turn when a snowstorm hit the battlefield. Strong winds from the south blew snow and sleet into the eyes of the Lancastrian archers, unsighting them at a crucial moment and adding range to the shots of the Yorkists. Wily Fauconberg took advantage immediately, ordering his archers to take a ranging shot and then take up positions accordingly, from where they poured a devastating hail of arrows into the enemy ranks. Lancastrian arrows fell harmlessly short and were picked up and used by the Yorkists.

Suffering under the withering barrage, the Lancastrians were forced to forsake the advantage of the high ground and rush forward to engage the enemy directly. So began many hours of ferocious hand-to-hand combat. The superior numbers of the Lancastrians put the Yorkists under great pressure, but they were encouraged by the presence in their midst of Edward, highly visible thanks to his great stature, and even more so because the standard that accompanied him was borne by the Welsh giant David ap Matthew, 2 inches (5 centimeters) taller even than the king himself. Battle raged as snow and mud were churned into bloody slush. According to the *Croyland Abbey Chronicle*: "They engaged in a most severe conflict, and fighting hand to hand with sword and spear, there was no small slaughter on either side . . ." The battle was fought with other weapons too: archaeological excavations of the battlefield have revealed the presence of the first handguns and the first bullet ever to be recorded on a European battlefield.

© northallertonman | Shutterstock.com

DACRE'S CROSS
Stone cross set up on the
site of the Battle of Towton,
in remembrance "of the men
slain at Palme Sunday Field."

The Yorkists hung on until early afternoon, when the Duke of Norfolk arrived with around 5,000 men, who launched themselves at the Lancastrian left flank. The fighting front wheeled around so that behind the Lancastrians was the valley of the Cock, which was in full spate. Their line held until late afternoon when the Yorkists broke through. There is speculation that an important Lancastrian commander was lost at this point—for instance, it is known that Lord Dacre was shot by a sniper hiding in a tree, while the Earl of Northumberland was severely wounded.

With the line broken the rout began, and the tactical advantages of the battlefield from a Lancastrian point of view suddenly became traps. To the left lay boggy marshes, and toward Towton an uphill retreat to open land where they could easily be chased down. Most of the Lancastrians attempted to flee across what is now known as Bloody Meadow to the Cock Beck, but when they reached it they found it in full spate. So many men died crossing it that their bodies formed a bridge, earning this location the name "The Bridge of Bodies." In the pursuit of the fleeing men, the unrivaled savagery of the age and the brutality of Edward of York were revealed. Before the battle Edward had given a proclamation: "No prisoner should be taken, nor one enemy saved." Now his men enacted it. According to the Croyland chronicle: "The [Lancastrians'] ranks being now broken and scattered in flight, the king's army eagerly pursued them, cutting down the fugitives with their swords, just like so many sheep for the slaughter, made immense havoc among them for a distance of ten miles [16 kilometers], as far as the city of York."

On Edward's orders, 42 captured Lancastrian nobles, who might normally have expected to be ransomed, were executed, and archaeological digs at the site have uncovered a mass of bodies. Examination showed that their arms had probably been tied and that they had died from multiple head wounds, and also that their ears had probably been cut off as trophies. In all, around half the Lancastrian forces are thought to have died, along with many Yorkists, suggesting a death toll of anywhere between 20,000 and 30,000 men, meaning that over 1 percent of England's population may have died that bloody Sunday.

FALL OF THE AZTECS: TENOCHTITLAN

1520–21

BATTLE

High casualty rate

Catastrophic defeat

Pyrrhic victory

Tactical blunder

Appalling conditions

Antagonists: Cuautemoc's Aztecs vs. Hernán Cortés's Spaniards and their Indian allies

Casualties: Unknown, but high on the Aztec (losing) side

Broken spears lie in the roads;
We have torn our hair in our grief
The houses are roofless now, and their walls
Are red with blood.

Aztec lament on the fall of Tenochtitlán

Tenochtitlán was the capital and heart of the Aztec empire, and more specifically the state they called Mexico. When Hernán Cortés and his conquistadors first saw it they were astounded by its size, beauty, and unearthly qualities, but a year later they would utterly destroy it, erasing the city from the Earth after a brutal siege that bears comparison with Stalingrad (see pages 217–22).

AN ENCHANTED VISION

On November 8th, 1519, Cortés and his band of Spanish adventurers marched along a causeway and entered the city of Tenochtitlán for the first time. To Bernal Díaz del Castillo, one of Cortés's soldiers who later penned an account of the conquest of Mexico, it "seemed like an enchanted vision . . . Indeed some of our soldiers asked whether it was not all a dream . . . It was all so wonderful that I do not know how to describe this first glimpse of things never heard of, seen, or dreamed of before."

At this time Tenochtitlán was possibly the biggest and arguably the greatest city on Earth. Founded two hundred years earlier by the Aztecs (who called themselves the Mexica), it was a city of around 200,000 people, with nearly a million people in the surrounding valley. According to the Spanish account, crowds of up to 60,000 attended one of the city's great markets — more people than lived in the biggest city in Spain.

MEXICAN CONQUEROR
The Spanish conquistador Hernán Cortés (1485–1547), who engineered the fall of the Aztec empire.

The Aztecs had migrated to the Valley of Mexico, probably from the north, and when they got there they found a great lake surrounded by swamps, rivers, and smaller lakes, already inhabited by many warlike tribes. Relegated to a marshy island in the middle of a brackish lake, they worked hard to drain and reclaim farmland and build causeways both literal and political, through networks of allegiances. After a flood had destroyed much of the original city, the Aztecs rebuilt on a grid pattern of streets and canals, dividing the city into four quarters with a fifth district set aside for a huge sacred precinct. Aqueducts and sophisticated sewage systems kept the city clean and fresh, and the whitewashed walls, clean streets, huge, gaudily painted pyramids, and colorful inhabitants of this city that seemed to float on the lake made a powerful impression on the Spanish conquistadors as they processed toward the palace of Moctezuma, the Aztec emperor.

To the Aztecs the Spanish were aliens of fearful provenance, attended by disquieting prophecies and omens. Word had already reached Tenochtitlán of a massacre perpetrated by the Spanish some time earlier, and there was an air of millenarian doom about the city. According to an Aztec account of the period, it was, "as if everyone had eaten stupefying mushrooms . . . as if they had seen something astonishing. Terror dominated everyone, as if all the world were being disemboweled . . . People fell into a fearful slumber . . ."

They were right to be frightened; the Spaniards' lust for gold overwhelmed their wonder at the city and fear of its massed inhabitants. In June 1520, one of Cortés's lieutenants ordered a massacre during a spring festival. An Aztec account relates: "The dancers and singers were completely unarmed . . . but without warning they were all put to death. The Spaniards attacked the musicians first, slashing at their hands and faces until they had killed all of them. The singers—and even the spectators—were also killed. This slaughter in the Sacred Patio went on for three hours." The people of Tenochtitlán turned on the Spanish and Cortés found himself under siege in Moctezuma's palace. On June 30th he forced the Aztec emperor to appear before his people to try to calm the situation but when he was met with a hail of stones it was apparent that he had lost authority and therefore any utility. He was almost certainly murdered by the Spanish.

That night the Spanish tried to escape along the causeways but over 600 were lost, many weighed down with stolen gold, along with thousands of Cortés's Indian allies, the Tlaxcalans. It became known as the Noche Triste, or Night of Tears. Cortés and what remained of his force fled across the mountains to Tlaxcala.

The Aztecs believed the Spaniards had gone for good and attempted to restore the city. According to the *Codex Florentino*, a compendium of native accounts compiled by Bernardino de Sahagún: "They repaired and decorated the temple of their god, sweeping it clean and throwing out all the dirt and wreckage." But the invaders had unwittingly unleashed their deadliest weapon of all—smallpox. The *Codex Florentino* recounts:

"A great plague broke out in Tenochtitlán. It lasted for seventy days, striking everywhere in the city, and killed vast numbers of people. Sores erupted on our faces, our breasts, our bellies; we were covered with agonizing sores

THE GREAT PLAGUE

from head to foot . . . The sick were so utterly helpless that they could only lie on their beds like corpses . . . many others died of hunger. They could not get up to search for food, and everyone else was too sick to care for them, so they starved to death in their beds."

With the city stricken by disease, the Spanish returned. Cortés had rallied his troops and native allies and constructed a fleet of small ships to enable naval operations on Lake Texcoco. Despite the terrible pestilence ravaging their population, the Aztecs put up desperate resistance and the Spanish and their allies could only advance street by street, house by house, leveling city blocks as they went.

WEEPING WARRIORS

The south of the city—the original "old town" of Tenochtitlán—fell to the besiegers when the Aztecs abandoned it to make a last stand in the northern Tlactelolco quarter. According to the Aztec accounts in the *Codex Florentino*: "The Aztec . . . deserted the Tenochtitlán quarters all in one day, weeping and lamenting like women. Husbands searched for their wives, and fathers carried their small children on their shoulders. Tears of grief and despair streamed down their cheeks."

Some 300,000 defenders crowded into the northern quarter where the Spanish besieged them for 80 days. There was heavy fighting, during which, according to native accounts contained in the *Codex Florentino*, "None of our enemies and none of our warriors escaped harm. Everyone was wounded, and the toll of dead was grievous on both sides." The remnants of the Aztec forces finally surrendered on August 13th, 1521. The last Aztec emperor, Cuautemoc, approached Cortés and, according to Fernando de Alva Ixtillxochitl, a descendant of one of the allied kings who fought for Cortés, "Cuautemoc then asked Cortés to kill him: 'For you have already destroyed my city and killed my people.'" In fact, he was tortured by having his feet roasted over a fire, as the Spanish interrogated him about the whereabouts of Aztec treasure. When the Spanish entered the devastated northern quarter they found that

CITY SACKERS
The conquistadors enter the ravaged city, in William de Leftwich Dodge's 1899 painting, *The Last Days of Tenochtitlan*.

© Public domain

smallpox had continued its ravages; 50,000 of the defenders are thought to have perished from the disease. Bernal Díaz recorded, "We could not walk without treading on the bodies and heads of dead Indians. The dry land was piled with corpses."

Cortés had Tenochtitlán leveled, founding Mexico City in its place. Díaz later wrote: "Of all the wonders I beheld that day, nothing now remains. All is overthrown and lost."

BATTLE

High casualty rate

Catastrophic defeat

Pyrrhic victory

Tactical blunder

Appalling conditions

TO CATCH A KING: PAVIA
1525

Antagonists: French under King Francis I vs. Imperial army under Charles de Lannoy, Charles, Duke of Bourbon, and others

Casualties: French: 10,000; Imperial army (victors): 1,500

And many were slain by the edge of the sword; and they were like dung upon the face of the field, and like the corn after the reaper, which none gathered.

"The Battle of Pavia," from the *Chronicle of Rabbi Joseph ben Joshua ben Meir*

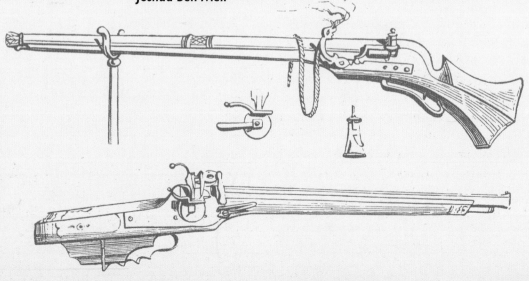

(Arquebuses) © Roger Viollet | Getty Images

Though not the bloodiest battle, Pavia must rank as one of the worst in terms of tactical aptitude, clarity of command, and use of victory. A melee of extreme confusion, fought in scattered skirmishes across a mist- and smoke-shrouded battlefield, saw the French King Francis I repeatedly snatching defeat from the jaws of victory, resulting in his humiliating loss to, and capture by, a smaller force.

The Battle of Pavia was a showdown between the two superpowers of Renaissance Europe: France and the Hapsburg Empire. Their struggle became entwined with the Italian Wars, a conflict that had been going on for decades. Dating back to 1494, it had initially concerned French claims to the Kingdom of Naples but latterly had come to focus on the richest principality in Europe, the Duchy of Milan. When the young Francis I came to the French throne in 1515, the conquest of Milan was his ambition. But soon the odds began to stack against him, as his greatest rival, the Hapsburg Charles V, grew in power and territory. Between 1516 and 1519 Charles united the Spanish and Austrian thrones, succeeded in getting himself elected ahead of Francis as Holy Roman Emperor, and inherited the Duchy of Burgundy. Imperial Hapsburg territory in Spain, the Netherlands, Germany, and Austria now ringed France on three sides, while across the Channel Henry VIII of England was an ally of Charles.

"I WANT NOTHING LESS"

KNIGHT-KING
Francis I was known as the "Roi-Chevalier" because he personally led his forces on the battlefield, with mixed results.

Francis was brave and determined, however, and continued to launch forays into Italy, meeting with fluctuating fortunes. After victory at Marignano in 1515 he was defeated at Bicocca in 1522. By 1523 all his gains in Italy were reversed as Francesco Sforza, another Imperialist ally, became Duke of Milan. At the same time Francis was forced to deal with a rebellion at home, led by Charles, Duke of Bourbon. When this was crushed in 1524, Charles fled to the Imperialist camp, while French armies successfully chased off Imperial forces threatening Marseille. Francis decided personally to lead a decisive strike against the Imperialists and seize the Italian prizes at the same time, marshaling a huge army with naval support. In October 1524 he crossed the Alps into Italy at the head of an army of 30,000 men, twice the size of the force defending Milan. Writing to

© Public domain

Henry VIII in November, he warned: "I have taken all necessary measures; my supplies are ready and my troops are paid . . . I have not crossed the Alps in person or invaded Italy with 30,000 good infantry and the support of a fleet . . . to stop now. I want nothing less than the entire state of Milan and the kingdom of Naples."

Francis's army was diverse (though not as diverse as the Imperial army—see below), with Swiss, German, and Italian mercenaries, including formidable German Landsknechts, supported by French heavy cavalry (known as gendarmes) and over 50 cannon, along with other firearms. There were several notable features about this force—the importance of cannon and arquebuses (predeccessors of the musket) in the battle has led to it being known as the first modern battle in Europe. A large proportion of the French army were mercenaries, and although they were experienced and effective they bore little loyalty to their commander-in-chief. "The French infantry numbers 24,000 to 26,000 men, but not 10,000 of them are as staunch as ours," wrote the Abbé of Najera, the Imperial war treasurer, to Charles V. The strongest force in the French army was the gendarmes, heavy cavalry equivalent to medieval knights. They were both the military and social elite of the army and their ranks were mostly made up of aristocrats, comprising the flower of French nobility. This would have devastating consequences when they were so badly mauled in the battle.

"WE WERE DEFEATED, SOON WE WILL BE VICTORIOUS"

The strength of this French force, swollen to around 33,000 by reinforcements, convinced the Imperialist commander Charles de Lannoy to abandon poorly fortified and disease-ridden Milan and withdraw to Lodi. Another Imperialist garrison remained at nearby Pavia. At this stage Francis's most experienced commanders urged him to strike a decisive blow at Lodi, but Francis was prone to heeding bad advice. A man of old-fashioned ideals about chivalry and knightly virtues, he placed more value on the personal loyalties and fine sentiments of his inner circle than on more pragmatic voices. His childhood friend Guillame Gouffier, Seigneur de Bonnivet and Admiral of France, fatefully advised Francis to besiege Pavia, an ill-starred decision that would result in the capture of the king and his own death. Imperial forces breathed a sigh of relief, and Fernando Francesco d'Ávalos d'Aquino, Marquis of Pescara, commander of the garrison at Lodi, is said to have remarked, "We were defeated, soon we will be victorious."

Accordingly the French army descended on Pavia, a heavily fortified city protected to the south by the River Ticino and guarded by a garrison of 6,000 German and Spanish Imperial troops under the capable command of Antonio de Leyva. An initial attack on November 21st was repulsed and a long siege began.

Imperialist forces regrouped under Lannoy and Charles of Bourbon, but time seemed to be against them. The people of Pavia suffered terrible famine, as Rabbi Joseph ben Joshua ben Meir recorded: "And they ate in her every unclean thing, by reason of famine . . ." Meanwhile, the Imperialist troops were threatening to mutiny over unpaid wages. Lannoy decided to force the issue, and marched his army to Pavia. He had around 20,000 mainly German and Spanish troops, including Landsknechts of his own, 5,000 horse, and 17 guns. But the strength of the French positions and their numerous artillery made a frontal assault impossible.

ARMS AND HEADS

Lannoy cooked up a cunning plan, combining a strong sortie by the garrison of Pavia with a night raid on the walled park to the north of the city where a sizable portion of the French army was encamped. During the night of February 23rd Imperialist sappers quietly breached the walls of the park, and in the early hours of the 24th the troops moved in. At this time of year heavy morning fog was a feature of the landscape, and throughout the battle the field would be shrouded in mist and gun smoke, leading to confusion and poor tactical intelligence, particularly on the French side. As Rabbi Joseph puts it: "Much people fell of the French, for fear came upon them as desolation, suddenly, and the soldiers could not find their own hands."

The first objective of the Imperialists was to seize the fortified hunting lodge, north of the park, the Castello Mirabello, and a force of arquebusiers under D'Ávalos d'Aquino managed to seize it. At this point, however, the fog cleared enough for the French to see their targets and volleys of cannon-fire ripped into the Imperialist ranks. Martin Du Bellay, a contemporary chronicler, recorded the effect of the French artillery on the advancing Imperial troops: "Shot after shot made great gaps in their battalions, so that all you could see was arms and heads flying through the air."

Meanwhile, farther to the south and east a strong force of Imperial German Landsknechts painfully but successfully pushed back the Swiss pikemen of the French army. Behind them Imperial troops still poured into the park through the breach in the wall, their entrance covered by a force of light cavalry under Lannoy. This was the pivotal moment in the battle: the French artillery could have continued to pound the Imperial ranks, but Francis intervened. Seeing the Imperial cavalry there for the taking, he allowed his sentimental ideals about proper knightly combat to overwhelm a more hard-headed, modern sensibility regarding battle. To Francis, shooting at the enemy from a distance was unchivalrous. As the 19th-century German historian Max Jähns put it, "The king was much put out by the idea that the artillery would have all the honor of the battle, and he did not want to miss the chance of breaking a lance; he could no longer restrain his ardor for the fight." Marshaling his gendarmes, he charged the Imperial horse, making the cardinal error of advancing across the front of his own guns, which were forced to cease firing. The French cavalry charge seemed successful, easily scattering the lighter Imperial horse, and Francis famously turned to the Maréchal de Foix, who was beside him, and declared, "Monsieur de Lescun, now I really am the Duke of Milan."

CHAOTIC SCENES
A 16th-century Brussels tapestry depicts the confused state of the battlefield at Pavia.

© Public domain

In fact, Francis had completely failed to grasp the tactical reality, having mistaken the melee into which he had rushed for a mere skirmish. Lannoy had immediately appraised the situation and maneuvered his troops to encircle the king and his gendarmes, who found themselves mired in boggy ground. With bristling hedges of pikes hemming them in, the gendarmes were cut down by arquebusiers firing from a distance. The social composition of the gendarmes meant that the carnage took a fearful toll on the nobility of France. For instance, out of 100 nobles from the Dauphiné region who fought at Pavia, just one survived. Historian of the battle of Pavia, Angus Konstam, compares the decimation of the French aristocracy at Pavia to the devastation of Scottish nobility at the battle of Flodden in 1514. The king himself was surrounded and captured; many of his favorites and old friends were killed.

Meanwhile, the Imperial Landsknechts fought bitterly with their counterparts in the French army, and a sortie by the defenders of Pavia drove off remaining Swiss formations. By 9 a.m. the battle was over and the last French force, the 5,000 men under Charles de Valois, stationed to the west of Pavia, retreated to Milan without joining the fight.

The battle was a disaster for Francis, who in order to secure his release was forced to sign the Treaty of Madrid, conceding all his Italian territories and Burgundy to Charles V. Yet in the long run the Imperialist faction completely failed to make their victory count; Francis immediately repudiated the Treaty and the Italian Wars continued.

FRANCIS INTO ITALY
The French drove the Imperial forces out of Milan and pushed them back to Lodi. But then, rather than advance on Lodi, King Francis surrounded Pavia, allowing the Imperial armies time to regroup.

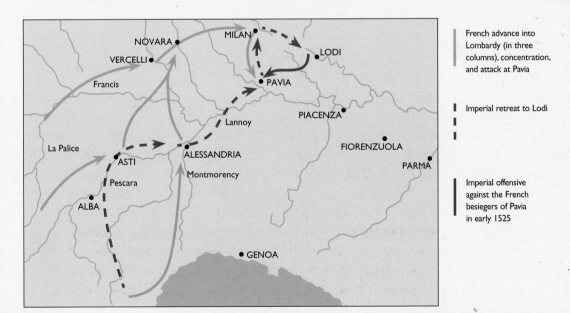

French advance into Lombardy (in three columns), concentration, and attack at Pavia

Imperial retreat to Lodi

Imperial offensive against the French besiegers of Pavia in early 1525

BATTLE

High casualty rate

Catastrophic defeat

Pyrrhic victory

Tactical blunder

Appalling conditions

MASSACRE OF THE INCA: CAJAMARCA

1532

Antagonists: Conquistadors under Francisco Pizarro vs. Inca under Atahualpa

Casualties: Spanish (victors): none; Inca: 2,000–7,000

The Spaniards fell upon the Indians and began to cut them to pieces. The Indians were so filled with fear that they climbed on top of one another, formed mounds, and suffocated each other. Since they were unarmed, they were attacked without danger to any Christian.

Spanish soldier's eyewitness account of the massacre at Cajamarca, 1532

The encounter between a small force of conquistadors led by Francisco Pizarro and the Inca emperor Atahualpa is regarded as one of the great turning points in history, memorably described by historian of civilization Jared Diamond as the "collision at Cajamarca." Diamond views the incident as a collision between two histories of human development—a crunch point where the exigencies of history doomed one civilization to destruction at the hands of the other. In other words, there was a lot riding on this one battle, for it spelled utter catastrophe for the loser. But the traditional account of Cajamarca raises many questions. Can the relative numbers of antagonists be trusted? Was it really a battle in the normal sense of the word, or simply a massacre?

The Spanish conquest of Peru is generally regarded as an even more incredible feat than Cortés's dismantling of the Aztec empire to the north a decade earlier. Certainly, many of Pizarro's contemporaries viewed it in this fashion, his secretary Francisco Xerez memorably declaring, in his *Report on the Discovery of Peru*:

WHOSE DEEDS CAN BE COMPARED WITH THOSE OF SPAIN?

"When has it ever happened, either in ancient or modern times, that such amazing exploits have been achieved? Over so many climes, across so many seas, over such distances by land, to subdue the unseen and unknown? Whose deeds can be compared with those of Spain? Not even the ancient Greeks and Romans."

Yet the "amazing exploits" owed much to deception, betrayal, and murder, particularly at Cajamarca, a town in the Peruvian highlands. Atahualpa, the Inca ruler (known simply as "the Inca"), had arranged to meet with the Spanish after an unpromising first encounter. According to Atahualpa's nephew, Titu Cusi, at the first meeting between Atahualpa and the Spanish the Inca offered them *chicha*, a maize beer, in gold cups, but they angered him by pouring it on the floor. When the Spanish noted that the Inca's entourage were scared of their horses, the conquistador Hernando de Soto rode his mount right up to Atahualpa's litter, "spurring his horse so close to Atahualpa's face that its breath tousled the crimson tassels on the Inca's royal headband. Atahualpa, however, was unmoved and unblinking."

Most of his subjects, however, were not so sanguine about the strange creatures, the like of which they had never seen. According to Wamán Poma, a mixed-race Spanish-Indian nobleman writing in the early 17th century, some of the sacred virgins sent by Atahualpa as gifts to the Spanish when he heard of their arrival "were also offered to the Spaniards' horses, because, seeing them eating maize, the Peruvians took them for a kind of human being. Until that time, horses were unknown to our people and it seemed advisable to treat them with respect."

A FRIGHTENING SIGHT

Atahualpa was fresh from victory in a battle in the ongoing civil war with his brother Huáscar, over the disputed succession to the throne. The dispute had arisen after their father, Huayna Capac, had succumbed to smallpox, one victim of the epidemic sweeping the Americas, brought by the Spanish invaders. Because of the fighting, Atahualpa was accompanied by a huge army, which was encamped outside Cajamarca. Conquistador accounts explain that: "Governor Pizarro wished to obtain intelligence from some Indians who had come from Cajamarca, so he had them tortured." Learning that the Inca was encamped there, Pizarro led his men to the city. The Inca account claims that Atahualpa invited them there.

On arrival, the Spanish were shocked at the size of the Indian army. "All of us were full of fear," recalled one of the conquistadors:

> " . . . because we were so few in number and we had penetrated so far into a land where we could not hope to receive reinforcements. Few of us slept that night, and we kept watch in the square of Cajamarca, looking at the campfires of the Indian army. It was a frightening sight. Most of the campfires were on a hillside and so close to each other that it looked like the sky brightly studded with stars."

Pizarro and his men were quartered around a central plaza, and on the following day the Spanish leader hid most of his men out of sight around the square. He was accompanied by just 106 foot soldiers and 62 horsemen, a tiny force with which to attempt the subjugation of a mighty empire. One of the conquistadors, Pedro de Candia, was sent with a small force to set up some small cannons in a high place, to be fired as the signal for a general attack. Pizarro himself waited in the center of the plaza, accompanied by just 15 men.

LAST EMPEROR
Atahualpa, last Inca emperor of Peru, captured by Pizarro and put to death.

© Getty Images

ATABALIPA frere de GUASCAR
Inca ou Empereur du PEROU

With great ceremony Atahualpa arrived, borne on a litter and accompanied by thousands of followers (who may have been unarmed, according to the conquistadors' own accounts). When Friar Vicente de Valverde, the priest accompanying the Spanish, passed him a Bible, things went horribly awry. The Inca had no writing system of their own, so unsurprisingly Atahualpa seemed uncertain what to do with the book, which he had been told would reveal great truths. Either frustrated, or angered with the priest's impudence in attempting to show him how to read it, the Inca tossed it aside.

This was the cue for Valverde to call for the Inca's head. "Come out! Come out, Christians! Come at these enemy dogs who reject the things of God," he cried out, "March out against him, for I absolve you!" Pizarro complied, signaling Candia. Pedro de Cieza de León, one of Pizarro's conquistadors who later became a historian, recalled what happened next in his book, *The Discovery and Conquest of Peru*:

"Candia fired the shots, a novelty for them and frightening, but even more so were the horses and the horsemen who loudly shouting 'Santiago, Santiago!' came charging out . . . against the enemies, who were stunned and did not make use of the artifices they had planned. They did not fight; rather, they looked where they could flee . . . Many were killed or wounded."

Pizarro and his squadron of foot soldiers threw themselves into the fray, desperate to capture Atahualpa. They pushed toward the Inca's litter, hacking at the bearers, says de Cieza, with "slashes that would sever the hand or arm of those who held the litter, who then with great courage would hold it with the other, wishing to protect their Inca from death or prison." Panic swept through the Indians, with many dying in the crush. "They wailed loudly," wrote de Cieza. "They were shocked by what they were seeing. They asked each other if it was real or if they were dreaming." Eventually a "furious throng" pushed down one of the walls of the plaza and fled through the gap, but the Spanish continued to slaughter any in their path. According to Spanish accounts, the massacre only abated when the light failed and evening came.

THEY DID NOT FIGHT

© Jose AS Reyes | Shutterstock.com

HORSEMAN OF THE APOCALYPSE
Equestrian statue of Pizarro, ironically regarded as a poor horseman by his fellow conquistadors.

Estimates of the Indian dead range from 2,000 to 7,000, and most of the accounts specify that the massacre lasted just an hour. This would imply that each Spaniard was killing at the rate of 12–41 people per hour (although it is likely that a large proportion of the casualties were sustained in the crush). Possibly the contemporary sources exaggerated the number of Indian dead, but by any assessment the fight at Cajamarca must rank as one of the most unbalanced victories in world history. Given, however, that the Indians seemed to think they were attending a diplomatic conference and were unarmed, it may be more accurate to describe the encounter as a spectacularly cruel massacre, rather than a battle.

THE NEW TROY: OSTEND
1601–04

High casualty rate

Catastrophic defeat

Pyrrhic victory

Tactical blunder

Appalling conditions

Antagonists: Ostend garrison of Dutch, English, and other nationalities under Sir Francis Vere vs. Spanish army under Archduke Albert of Austria

Casualties: Unknown; both the Spanish (victors) and the Dutch incurred high losses

. . . [I]t was a bloody business. Night and day the men were knee-deep in the trenches delving in mud and sand, falling every instant into the graves which they were thus digging for themselves . . .

John Lothrop Motley, *History of The United Netherlands*

© Getty Images

The Siege of Ostend was the epic battle of its age; described as a "long carnival of death," it lasted more than three years and earned the beleaguered town the title of the New Troy. Terrible casualties were inflicted on the besieging armies as they struggled against the elements as well as the defenses, while conditions inside the town were horrific.

THE UNASSAILABLE AND THE INDEFENSIBLE

"Among the many battles, sieges, naval encounters, and all manner of other military engagements of the Eighty Years' War," wrote book historian Anna Simoni, late curator of the Dutch section of the Department of Printed Books at the British Library, "none was, and perhaps is, more famous than the long drawn-out siege of Ostend in which the Spaniards assailed the unassailable and the Dutch defended the indefensible." The siege was supposed to be the last act in the Spanish reconquest of Flanders, one of the territories of the Netherlands. Spanish rule had been imposed on all of the Netherlands in 1519, but after a revolt in 1567 the northern, mainly Protestant, United Provinces of the Netherlands (aka the Dutch Republic) had waged a long and bitter war with the powerful overlords of the southern or Spanish Netherlands. In 1598 Philip II of Spain granted sovereignty of the Netherlands to his daughter Isabella and her husband, Archduke Albert of Austria, who continued to wage war against the Republic. Ostend was a particularly important prize: the last Republican possession in Flanders, it controlled access to the sea. Albert decided to lay siege to it, declaring that it would fall even if it took 18 years.

On July 5th, 1601, an army of 20,000 laid siege to Ostend and its garrison of roughly 8,000 Dutch, Flemings, English, Scots, Germans, and French, all under the command of Englishman Sir Francis Vere. The city was protected to the north by a dyke and to the east by a newly constructed harbor known as the Gullet, but although it was more vulnerable to the west it was nonetheless protected by the latest technology in fortifications, including strong ravelins (V-shaped earthworks protecting bastions from direct attack). Albert had 18 fortresses of his own constructed, from which to fire cannons, installing 50 siege guns.

Early in the siege the Spanish launched an ill-advised attack on the Gullet, hoping to cut off Ostend from resupply by sea so that it could be starved into submission. But the inrushing tide and the unrelenting bombardment from the Republican fortification overlooking the approaches to the Gullet turned the assault into a disaster. In his landmark *History of The United*

Netherlands, the 19th-century American historian John Lothrop Motley described the scene:

" . . . it was a bloody business. Night and day the men were knee-deep in the trenches delving in mud and sand, falling every instant into the graves which they were thus digging for themselves, while ever and anon the sea would rise in its wrath and sweep them with their works away . . . It was a piteous sight, even for the besieged, to see human life so profusely squandered."

With the sea lanes remaining open, the Dutch were able to keep supplies and reinforcements coming to the city, but the inhabitants lived under intolerable stress. Constant bombardment, fires, rowdy mercenaries looting, sorties, and assaults made life hazardous and hard.

On January 7th, 1602, the Spanish launched their largest assault, but the Republicans had been warned in advance by spies and opened a sluice, letting the sea flood into the Spanish trenches, drowning some attackers and sweeping others out to sea. Among the Spanish dead was discovered the body of a woman dressed in man's clothing. According to Henricus Bilderbeke, author of a near-contemporary account of the siege, she had apparently joined in with the battle, "as was obvious from certain of her wounds . . . under her clothes she wore a gold chain studded with gemstones and also some other valuables and money."

THE FINISHER
Genoese-Spanish General Ambrogio Spinola (known as Ambrosio to the Spanish) took over the Siege of Ostend in 1603.

The siege dragged on for so long and was so bloody that Ostend gained a reputation as a training ground for all the arts of warfare, from soldiering to engineering to surgery, earning the nickname "University of War." Between July 1602 and July 1603, 4,000 defenders and 8,000 besiegers died, and two Dutch surgeons working in the city amputated more than 1,700 arms and legs between them.

THE UNIVERSITY OF WAR

In September 1603 a new commander, Ambrogio Spinola, took control of the investing forces, and slowly but surely he pushed back the defenders. By June 1604 the Republicans had retreated to their innermost fortifications, which they declared they would hold for as long as the Trojans had defended

Troy, earning Ostend the name of New or Little Troy. Dead bodies were used to shore up the ramparts when earth ran short. The defenders clung on until September, their long battle tying down the majority of Spanish forces in the Netherlands and making it possible for Prince Maurice of Orange and his allies to win a string of victories for the United Provinces. These included the conquest of Sluis, which meant that Ostend no longer held such vital strategic importance, and the defenders were given leave to surrender.

On September 20th, 1604, the garrison marched out with full honors and the officers were treated to a banquet by Spinola. When Albert and Isabella entered Ostend, it was said that the Duchess wept at the sight of the ruined city. According to legend the fabric color known as Isabelline — the grayish-yellow of soiled linen — derives its name from Isabella's vow not to change her linen until Ostend was taken. Exhausted by the cost of the victory, Albert sued for peace with the United Provinces, signing a 12-year truce and decreeing that Ostend should be rebuilt.

CAVALIER CARNAGE: MARSTON MOOR

1644

BATTLE

High casualty rate

Catastrophic defeat

Pyrrhic victory

Tactical blunder

Appalling conditions

Antagonists: Royalist armies under Prince Rupert of the Rhine vs. Parliamentarian armies under the Earl of Leven, including cavalry under Oliver Cromwell

Casualties: Royalists: 4,000 killed, 1,500 captured; Parliamentarians (victors): ca. 300 killed

Upon the alarum the Prince mounted to horse and galloping up to the right wing, met his own regiment turning their backs to the enemy which was a thing so strange and unusual he said "swounds, do you run, follow me," so they facing about, he led them to a charge, but fruitlessly ...

Sir Hugh Cholmley, Royalist governor of Scarborough

© Popperfoto | Getty Images

The English Civil War pitted Royalist forces loyal to Charles I against the forces of Parliament. Though known as the "English" war, this conflict in fact involved other parts of Britain, and it was the intervention of the Scottish that turned the tide of war decisively in favor of Parliament. Up until 1644 the Royalist commander, the Marquess of Newcastle, had won a string of victories, but when an army of 20,000 Scots known as Covenanters marched south under the Earl of Leven, Newcastle found himself facing a war on two fronts. In April he retreated to York, the major town in the north of England and the seat of Royalist power in the region, where he was besieged by "the Army of Two Kingdoms."

IF YORK BE LOST

In June King Charles wrote urgently to his nephew, the dashing Cavalier general Prince Rupert of the Rhine, who had garnered an aura of invincibility with his cavalry exploits, begging him to relieve the besieged city. "If York be lost I shall esteem my crown little less," wrote Charles, adding fatefully, "But if York be relieved, and you beat the rebels' army of both kingdoms which are before it; then (but otherwise not) I may make a shift . . ." The clear implication of the letter was that Rupert was under royal command not just to relieve the siege, but also to engage the Parliamentarian army. Supposedly Lord Culpeper, learning the contents of the letter after it had been sent, warned dolefully, "Why then, before God you are undone, for upon this peremptory order he will fight, whatever comes on't."

Prince Rupert was already engaged on an epic tour of the west of Britain, known as the York March, having left Shrewsbury in May and followed a zigzag course through Lancashire, picking up reinforcements and besieging Liverpool. On receiving the king's despatch on June 19th he immediately set out for York. Arriving at Knaresborough, 14 miles (23 kilometers) west of York, on June 30th, he sent an advance guard east to fool the allied generals into thinking he was marching directly on York. They repositioned their armies, concentrating their forces on Marston Moor to the west of the city to block his likely route, only for Rupert to outflank them by marching around to the north. On July 1st he raised the siege and linked up with Newcastle's infantry.

Newcastle probably expected Rupert to enjoy his victory or possibly head south to link up with his uncle, the king; certainly this is what the allies thought, because they began moving to block the route south, sending

their infantry toward Tadcaster. But Rupert believed that he had direct orders, and curtly informed Newcastle to march his garrison out of York and join him in offering battle. The allied commanders were startled to receive word that Rupert was drawing up his forces to engage them at Marston, and quickly recalled the foot. On the morning of July 2nd, the Parliamentarian forces drew up on the lower slopes of Marston Hill, between the villages of Long Marston and Tockwith. According to Parliamentarian eyewitness Simeon Ashe, "being on a hill, we had the double advantage of the ground, and the wind." On the left of the main infantry force was cavalry under Lieutenant-General Oliver Cromwell, including his famous Ironsides regiment.

© Public domain

Opposing them were the forces of Rupert, who was frustrated to learn that the peremptory tone of his note to Newcastle had ruffled feathers, so that the 4,000-strong garrison from York, under Lord Eythin, was slow to arrive. Even when they did turn up, Rupert's forces only came to 18,000 men against the allies' 28,000. By this time Rupert had lost any advantage he might have had by pressing his attack while the allies were still in disarray, and he and Eythin fell to arguing. Most of the day had passed and Rupert decided that it was too late to offer battle.

CAVALIER PRINCE
Prince Rupert, Count Palatine, most celebrated and dashing of Royalist commanders.

Even as the Royalist troops started to relax, however, Lord Leven decided to take the initiative. At seven o'clock in the evening, just as a huge thunderstorm burst overhead, the Parliamentarian forces attacked.

AT SWORDS' POINT

Cromwell launched his cavalry at the opposing horse and overcame the first lines, but was briefly forced to retire from the fight with a wound. Prince Rupert himself rallied the Royalist cavalry in a counterattack, as eyewitness Lionel Watson related: "Cromwels own division had a hard pull of it: for they were charged by Ruperts bravest men, both in Front and Flank: they stood at the swords point a pretty while, hacking one another . . ." But Cromwell returned to the fray and, "at last (it so pleased God) he brake through them, scattering them before him like a little dust." Rupert himself was forced to hide in a bean field to avoid capture, while his great hunting dog, Boy, was killed in the battle.

DOOMED MONARCH
Charles I of England, whose clashes with Parliament led to the Civil War and his eventual execution.

In the center the infantry battle was going less well for the allies; several units were routed, sowing general confusion. Several of the allied commanders, believing the battle lost, fled the field, but two Scottish regiments held firm. As darkness fell it was unclear who, if anyone, had won, and soldiers from both sides were leaving in disarray. The allied commander Lord Fairfax found himself behind enemy lines, but made it back to safety by removing his insignia and simply riding through the confusion. Meeting up with Cromwell, they decided to launch a last attack.

The Parliamentarian horse fell on the by-now disorganized, leaderless, and exhausted Royalists, routing them. Only Newcastle's elite troops, the Whitecoats, stood their ground in a ditched enclosure, fighting bravely for an hour. Scotsman Lieutenant-Colonel James Somerville described their doomed last stand:

"Here the parliament horse of that wing received their greatest loss, and a stop for some time to their hoped-for victory, and that only by the stout resistance of this gallant battalion . . . until at length a Scots regiment of dragoons, commanded by Colonel Frizeall [Hugh Fraser], with other two, was brought to open them upon some hand, which at length they did; when all their ammunition was spent, having refused quarters, every man fell in the same order and rank wherein he had fought."

Only 30 of the Whitecoats survived, but their rearguard action bought time for many more Royalist troops to make it back to York.

The battle had taken just two hours, and had swung from a draw to a shattering defeat in an instant. On the field lay 4,000 Royalist dead with a further 1,500 taken prisoner, for the loss of just 300 Parliamentarians. Marston Moor is often touted as "the largest battle ever fought on British soil," although this book features two that may have been larger (see Watling Street, pages 37–9, and Towton, pages 68–72). It was, however, by far the largest battle of the Civil War, with important consequences for the course of the conflict. The aura of invincibility about Prince Rupert was shattered while the reputation of Cromwell was enhanced, leading to his eventual command of Parliamentarian forces.

OTTOMANS AT THE GATES: VIENNA

1683

BATTLE

High casualty rate

Catastrophic defeat

Pyrrhic victory

Tactical blunder

Appalling conditions

Antagonists: Ottoman army under Grand Vizier Kara Mustafa Pasha vs. garrison of Vienna under Count Ernst von Starhemberg and Polish and Imperial relief force under Polish king Jan III Sobieski

Casualties: Ottomans: 10,000; Christians (victors): 2,000

. . . [A] Siege of Sixty days, accompanied with a Thousand Difficulties, Sicknesses, Want of Provisions, and great Effusion of Blood, after a Million of Cannon and Musquet Shot, Bombs, Granadoes, and all sorts of Fire Works, which has changed the Face of the fairest and most flourishing City in the World . . .

Samuel Crouch, *A True and Exact Relation of the Raising of the Siege of Vienna*, 1683

From the 1660s the Ottoman Empire steadily encroached on Christian territories in the Balkans and eastern Europe, under a succession of capable viziers. The Hapsburg Austro-Hungarian emperor, Leopold, more concerned with troubles to the west, pursued a policy of appeasement toward the Turks, readily ceding them conquests in Hungary. Coupled with his failure to suppress revolts by Ottoman-supported insurgents in Hungary, particularly the rebellion of Imre Thököly, Leopold's stance was perceived as weakness by the Ottoman sultan, Mehmed IV, and his ambitious Grand Vizier Kara Mustafa Pasha, who plotted a major campaign into Hapsburg territories.

NOTHING TO EXPECT BUT DEATH

In February 1683 the Ottoman Sultan issued a blood-curdling declaration of war from Edirne, worth quoting at length for the exhaustive range of its threats:

"You have for some time past acted to our prejudice, and violated our Friendship . . . and thereby have exposed your People to fear and danger, having nothing to expect but Death, which you have brought upon your selves. For I declare unto you, I will make myself your Master, pursue you from East to West, and extend my Majesty to the end of the Earth; in all which you shall find my Power to your great prejudice. I assure you that you shall feel the weight of my Power; and for that you have put your hope and expectation in the strength of some Towns and Castles, I have given command to overthrow them, and to trample under feet with my Horses, all that is acceptable and pleasant in your Eyes, leaving nothing hereafter . . . For I have resolved without retarding of time, to ruin both you and your People, to take the German Empire according to my pleasure, and to leave in the Empire a Commemoration of my dreadful Sword . . . I will according to my pleasure put your Sacred Priests to the Plough, and expose the Brests of your Matrons to be Suckt by Dogs and other Beasts."

A huge force set off to conquer cities in Hungary, but at the beginning of July the Grand Vizier decided to strike at Vienna itself, advancing on the Hapsburg capital with an army of 90,000 men (contemporary sources inflate the number to 150–200,000). A large portion of this army was effectively non-combatant, but nonetheless it

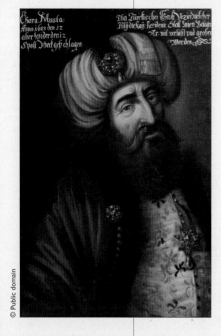

OTTOMANIAC
Kara Mustafa Pasha, Ottoman Grand Vizier. Disastrous handling of the siege of Vienna cost him his head.

included tens of thousands of crack troops such as Janissaries and Tartars. Unfortunately for them, Kara Mustafa Pasha had made a giant strategic error. By attacking Vienna, the bulwark of Christendom in the East, he made a regional conflict with the Hapsburgs into a crusade for Christian Europe, mobilizing the forces of Austria, Germany, and Poland to unite against the Turks, thus negating their major military advantage: strength of numbers.

Vienna had had ample warning of the Turks' intent, and Leopold and his court were long gone before the Ottoman armies arrived to find the city's defenses repaired and strengthened, with strong bastions protected by ravelins. Ottoman engineers, however, were expert at siege warfare, and set about digging a complex network of trenches and mines. Counter-mines were dug by the Austrians, through which they could attack the sappers and defuse the explosives, leading to a "subterranean battlefield" of gnawing tension and sudden shocking violence. *A True and Exact Relation of the Raising of the Siege of Vienna*, a 1683 pamphlet written in English by Samuel Crouch, relates how Vienna, fortified with "so many new Retrenchments, Pallizadoes, Parapets, new Ditches in the Ravelins, Bastions, Courtins," put up "a Vigorous Defense and a Resistance without parallel," but how the Turks, "by endless Workings, Trenchings, and Minings, reduced it almost to its last gasp."

The city held out until September 6th, when a huge Turkish mine breached one of the bastions in the city walls. The defenders, weakened by hunger, exhaustion and dysentery, waited for the final assault to come, but Kara Mustafa made another tactical blunder. Instead of launching an attack, he paraded his army before the city walls, hoping to intimidate the defenders into surrender. Little did he know that the cavalry was coming.

CHARGE OF THE HUSSARS

Back in March the Hapsburg Empire had made an alliance with Jan III Sobieski, king of Poland, and he had brought a force of 20,000 men to join up with a Hapsburg army of 20,000 men and around 35,000 German troops, giving a huge army of 75,000 men and 160 cannons. After a forced march the Austrian and German troops engaged the Turks at dawn on September 12th near Kahlenberg at the edge of the Vienna Woods, on the Danube northwest of the city. Sobieski's army had taken a longer route, planning to outflank the Turks and crash into their left flank after the other Christians had tied them down. Meanwhile, Kara Mustafa had made

© Public domain

KINGS' MEET
Jan Sobieski, flanked by
Polish Hussars, meets up
with the Emperor Leopold
after the relief of Vienna.

yet another error, underestimating the size of the relief force and thus keeping many of his best troops back to continue the siege, and ordering his men to stay awake all night on the 11th, mistakenly believing that the Christian attack would come a day earlier.

At around 1 p.m. the Poles arrived at the edge of the woods, and by 3 p.m. in fierce heat the Polish cavalry broke the Ottoman left wing. Leading the charge were the Polish Hussars, the most advanced fighting force in Europe at the time. These lightly armored cavalry were famous for their exotic appearance and close-knit, knee-to-knee charges, which drove all before them. Charles Ogier, Comte D'Artagnan (the model for the famous musketeer of Dumas), observing Hussars in 1635, had written:

" . . . never have I seen a more peculiar sight than this. Polish nobility all on beautiful chargers, in superb shining armor, with panther, lion, and tiger skins thrown over their shoulders, having long lances held up by cords hanging from the saddle, on the end of which, beneath the point, were silk pennons which fluttered in the air and confused the enemy's eyes. This was all very brilliant, but it was hard not to laugh at the sight of the tall wings fixed to their backs, from which, as they say, enemy horses are frightened and escape from . . . at their side they wear sabers and near the saddle pistols, maces, hammers, axes, and swords."

Crouch relates how the Turkish lines crumbled and the Christian allies sent them fleeing:

"The Christians being ravish'd with the Victory, pursued them with so much heat, that they were not only forced to leave their great Camps, but likewise all their others; flying toward Hungary: And it is certain, had not the Night come on, they had totally defeated and routed the Ottoman Army."

In fact, the bulk of the Ottoman army lived to fight another day, but the allies enjoyed the spoils of battle thanks to the huge amount of loot left behind in the Ottoman encampment. Writing to his wife shortly after the battle, Sobieski described his exotic plunder:

"Ours are treasures unheard of . . . tents, sheep, cattle, and no small number of camels . . . it is victory as nobody ever knew of, the enemy now completely ruined, everything lost for them. They must run for their sheer lives . . . Commander Starhemberg [of the Viennese garrison] hugged and kissed me and called me his savior."

Sobieski caught up with and crushed the Turks later that year at Párkány, and the Ottomans never again threatened the gates of Vienna. They had succeeded only in uniting Christian Europe against them in the form of the Holy League, and would lose Hungary before the end of the 17th century. Kara Mustafa Pasha's reward for failure was to be strangled by a silk rope pulled by several men on each end, and Sultan Mehmed IV was deposed shortly afterward.

BATTLE

~~High casualty rate~~

Catastrophic defeat

~~Pyrrhic victory~~

~~Tactical blunder~~

Appalling conditions

MARLBOROUGH'S WORST BUTCHER'S BILL: MALPLAQUET

1709

Antagonists: British, Dutch, and Imperial allies under the Duke of Marlborough and Prince Eugene of Savoy vs. French army under the Duc de Villars

Casualties: Allies (victors): 25,000; French: 10,000–15,000

They hewed in pieces all they found before them... even the dead when their fury found no more living to devour.

German observer at the Battle of Malplaquet

© Ivy Close Images | Alamy

The War of the Spanish Succession pitted the French against an alliance of Imperial, British, and Dutch forces. Led by John Churchill, Duke of Marlborough, and Prince Eugene of Savoy, the allied forces inflicted a string of defeats on the French. By 1709 the French had been forced back within their own borders and in September Marlborough and Eugene were besieging Mons. The French dredged together a last army under Maréchal Claude, Duc de Villars, and he marched north to relieve the siege with a force of 80,000 men, including French, Bavarian, Swiss, and Irish contingents, taking up a strong position near Malplaquet where woods abutted the road to Mons. Here, Villars set up lines of fortifications, with entrenchments and "entanglements" (obstacles akin to modern barbed wire). Sensing his chance to crush the last army in France, Marlborough advanced with 110,000 Dutch, Prussian, Hanoverian, Irish, Swiss, Danish, Scottish, Hessian, Saxon, and English troops.

Marlborough and Eugene planned to employ their usual tactics of pressing the flanks so that Villars would weaken his center. The allied infantry reserve would then occupy the redoubts in the French center, so that the cavalry could pass safely through and fall on the French infantry from the flanks and rear. However, poorly communicated orders may have meant that the young Prince of Orange, commanding the allies' left wing, believed that, rather than simply containing the French right, his task was to overwhelm it completely. The misunderstanding would exact a heavy toll.

The allied advance was disrupted by woodland, undergrowth, and, near the center, by boggy ground. A contingent of 22 battalions under General Lottum was detailed to attack a projecting salient in the French lines, where the French were entrenched in the Sars woods, but quick thinking by the French artillery commander saw a battery of guns rushed forward to enfilade Lottum's lines from the side, while musket fire poured into them from the woods. Desperate to escape the withering crossfire, Lottum's infantry charged forward and started trying to tear down the French fortifications with their hands, but it took them three hours to make an impact on the French lines.

HORROR IN THE WOODS

GENERAL SUCCESS
John Churchill, 1st Duke of Marlborough, said to have been Britain's greatest general.

© Public domain

© Public domain

PARTNER PRINCE
Prince Eugene of Savoy
forged a successful
military partnership with
Marlborough.

**ORKNEY
GAINS THE
DAY**

Meanwhile, on the left, the Prince of Orange, at the head of his Dutch, Swiss, and Scottish battalions, walked into a deadly setup, with a hidden battery of 20 cannon ripping into them from the side, while 3,000 French muskets volleyed into their front ranks. Two-thirds of the prince's staff was cut down and his horse was shot out from under him. After just half an hour the prince's battalions had suffered 5,000 casualties, a dead general among them. Tragically misconceiving his instructions, the prince re-formed his lines and tried again, but once more the attack was beaten off with heavy casualties and the loss of two more generals. Only the arrival of Marlborough himself prevented a third ruinous assault.

Maréchal Louis François, Duc de Boufflers, was in charge of the French right, facing the prince . If he had seized the initiative and attacked, he might have won the day but, mindful of his orders, he remained on the defensive. Meanwhile, at the salient in the wood of Sars, Lottum's forces finally broke through the French fortifications and poured forward, the battle degenerating into brutal hand-to-hand combat under the trees. By 11.30 the combat there had become animalistic in its savagery. Sir Richard Temple's regiment, badly mauled by the French during their advance, went into a killing frenzy. "They hewed in pieces all they found before them . . . even the dead when their fury found no more living to devour," wrote a German observer. Some 7,000 men fell in the woods.

Observing the battle, Eugene was nicked in the side of the neck by a musket ball. "If we are to die here it is not worth dressing," he is supposed to have said, "If we win, there will be time tonight." By 1 p.m. Marlborough's tactics had worked sufficiently for him to order Lord Orkney to advance on the center. Orkney later wrote: " . . . my 13 battalions got to the entrenchments, which we got very easily for as we advanced they quitted them and inclined to their right. We found nothing to oppose us. Not that I pretend to attribute any glory to myself, yet I verily believe that these 13 battalions gained us the day, and that without firing a shot almost."

At this point the French commander Villars was hit by a musket ball that shattered his knee, and he passed out from loss of blood. As the allied cavalry poured through the breach in the center, Maréchal Boufflers took charge of the French and counter-charged, holding up the allies for long enough for the French forces on either flank to withdraw in good order. Finally, Boufflers disengaged his horse and skillfully maneuvered to cover the retreat, and by 3:30 p.m. the battle was over, with the exhausted and depleted allies in possession of the field. It was a Pyrrhic and inconclusive victory for Marlborough, whose reputation suffered as a result of the carnage, which produced the highest casualties of any of the battles of the War of the Spanish Succession.

THE BATTLE OF MALPLAQUET

Villars was entrenched in a wood and Lottum's infantry was savaged by cannon. The Prince of Orange led several costly advances against Bouffler. Eventually, the British under Orkney broke through in the center, winning the day.

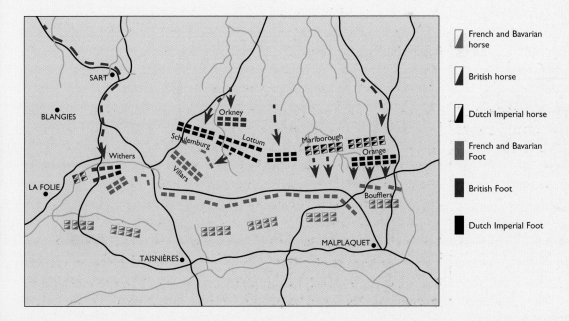

French and Bavarian horse

British horse

Dutch Imperial horse

French and Bavarian Foot

British Foot

Dutch Imperial Foot

BATTLE

High casualty rate

Catastrophic defeat

Pyrrhic victory

Tactical blunder

Appalling conditions

INTO THE FIRE-VOLCANO: TORGAU

1760

Antagonists: Prussian Army under Frederick II of Prussia vs. Austrian and Saxon army under Marshal Daun

Casualties: Prussians (victors): 16,670 men killed and wounded; Austrians: 8,500 men killed and wounded, 7,000 captured, and 49 guns lost

A corporal of the fourth company remarked to a guard: "If we have got to stand here and be shot at, because they won't let us attack, give me a pinch of snuff." The guard took his box from his pouch, and as he was lifting the cover, a cannon-ball shot off his head. In the most cold-blooded way, the corporal turned to his second neighbor and said: "Well, now, you give me a pinch; that one has gone to the devil."

Ferdinand Schrader, *Frederick the Great and the Seven Years' War*, 1905

Frederick the Great of Prussia won a series of famous victories, earning him a reputation as one of history's finest generals. Napoleon was a particular admirer, describing Frederick's famous victory at the Battle of Leuthen as "a masterpiece of movements, maneuvers, and resolution. Alone it is sufficient to immortalize Frederick and place him in the ranks of the greatest generals."

Leuthen was one of a series of ten great victories won by the armies of Prussia during the Seven Years' War (1756–63), eight of which were personally overseen by Frederick, that beat off attacks by a grand alliance encircling the embattled state, comprising Russia, Austria, and France. Napoleon Bonaparte would later claim that "Prussia was not defended for seven years against the three most formidable European powers by the Prussian soldiers but by Frederick the Great," and supposedly told his generals of the Prussian king, "Gentlemen, if this man were still alive I would not be here." Of the ten victories, the one that Frederick savored least was the bloody Battle of Torgau, in which poor intelligence saw him throw his elite regiment into the teeth of an Austrian cannonade, with terrible consequences. The battle finished with the victors losing twice as many men as the vanquished.

LAST ORDERS
Frederick of Prussia writing orders during the Battle of Torgau, in Bernhard Rode's 1793 painting.

In October 1670, poorly defended Berlin fell to an invasion force of Russians and Austrians, but they promptly withdrew from the city when Frederick started to march his army toward them. On November 2nd, Frederick got word that an Austrian army under Daun had come up from the south and set up camp at Torgau on the River Elbe north of Dresden. Actually made up of multiple nationalities including Austrians, Hungarians, Bohemians, Silesians, Croats, Italians, and Moravians, with a force from Saxony, the army comprised 42,000 infantry, 10,000 cavalry, and 275 guns. The Prussians knew Torgau well, having previously occupied it themselves—it provided a highly defensible camp, with a long, flat-topped west–east-running ridge guarded at the east end by a lake. Despite his army being marginally smaller—35,000 infantry, 13,500 cavalry, and 309 guns—with the Russian and Austrian armies from Berlin still lurking nearby, Frederick felt he must strike a decisive blow against Daun.

INTO THE FIRE-VOLCANO

Reasoning that the confines of the Torgau ridge would constrict the Austrian forces and prevent Daun from mobilizing his full strength, Frederick planned a bold outflanking maneuver. In the early hours of November 3rd, while 18,000 men under General Zieten attacked the south of the ridge near the eastern end as a diversion, Frederick would lead the bulk of the force in a wide swing through the woods around the ridge and come at it from the north. Unfortunately for the Prussians, they encountered Austrian skirmishers, and the ensuing gunfight alerted Daun to the maneuver. While he rearranged his forces to meet threats on both sides of the ridge, Frederick was being led astray on the woodland paths by incompetent guides.

Finally in position just after lunchtime, Frederick fell into another error when he mistakenly believed that the sound of cannon fire from the Austrian lines indicated that Zieten's diversion was underway. At 2 p.m. he ordered his elite grenadier battalions, the cream of the Prussian infantry, to assault the ridge. As they emerged from the woods they were met with the most concentrated artillery bombardment that veterans on either side had ever experienced. In his *History of Friedrich II of Prussia*, Thomas Carlyle depicted the scene:

"The Grenadiers have their muskets, and their hearts and their right-hands. With amazing intrepidity, they . . . rush into the throat of this Fire-volcano . . . The Grenadiers plunge forward upon the throat of Daun; but it is into the throat of his iron engines and his tearing billows of cannon-shot that most of them go. Shorn down by the company, by the regiment, in those terrible 800 yards . . ."

Within minutes, two thirds of the grenadiers were dead or wounded.

THE HIDDEN CAUSEWAY

Frederick's forces were unable to take the ridge and by 5 p.m. the Prussian attack on the north of the ridge had failed. Frederick himself was hit by a musket ball, and although it was stopped by his clothing, his chest was heavily bruised and he retired to nearby lodgings, fearing the worst for the battle. But events conspired to swing things in his favor. First, Daun was forced to retire with a wounded foot, leaving the Austrians leaderless, and secondly, a Prussian officer bringing a message to Zieten noticed a causeway up the southwest face of the ridge that was partially hidden and hence had been left unguarded. Zieten had been slow in starting his attack and had not made much headway, but now his Garde brigade stormed the causeway and turned the battle. The Prussian commanders to the north saw the successful attack and joined in, and soon the Prussians held the western end of the ridge. The Austrians withdrew, albeit in good order, and Zieten was able to ride to the king and inform him that the day was theirs. It was a hollow victory; Frederick wrote gloomily to a friend: "We have just defeated the Austrians. They have lost an extraordinary number as well as we. This victory will perhaps allow us a little rest this Winter and that is about all. Next year we must begin anew."

© Public domain

FIELD MARSHAL
Austrian Field Marshal Leopold Joseph von Daun, wounded at Torgau.

BATTLE

High casualty rate

Catastrophic defeat

Pyrrhic victory

Tactical blunder

Appalling conditions

DON'T FIRE 'TIL YOU SEE THE WHITES OF THEIR EYES: BUNKER HILL

1775

Antagonists: British redcoats of the Boston garrison under Major General Howe vs. militiamen of the American Continental Army under General Artemas Ward and General Israel Putnam

Casualties: British (victors): 1,054; Americans: ca. 400

Nothing could be more shocking than the carnage that followed the storming [of] this [fortification]. We tumbled over the dead to get at the living, [with] soldiers stabbing some and dashing out the brains of others.

Royal Marine involved in the Battle of Bunker Hill

The Battle of Bunker Hill has a special place in the mythology of the Revolutionary Wars, despite being both a defeat for the Americans and misnamed (it actually took place on neighboring Breed's Hill). Yet, it was such a costly Pyrrhic victory for the British that it profoundly influenced the course of the War of Independence.

Tensions between the American colonists and the British authorities had boiled over in April 1775 when British troops sent to seize militia stores in Concord, Massachusetts, had been humiliatingly rebuffed by Minutemen militia. The British were forced to hole up in their garrison at Boston, while various militias that would shortly be enrolled in the American Continental Army occupied positions ringing the city. A tense standoff ensued, until the night of June 16th when a force of militiamen were sent to occupy Bunker Hill, a high point on the Charlestown peninsula on the other side of the harbor from the British garrison. In the dark, however, they bypassed Bunker Hill and moved on to Breed's Hill, which lay closer to the British garrison and thus constituted a more provocative position. As morning broke on the 17th the British could see Americans throwing up fortifications on the hill. A British warship in the harbor started bombarding them with cannon; one man had his head knocked off as the militia frantically dug trenches and put up fences. They were, recorded one of the American soldiers, "fatigued by our Labor, having no sleep the night before, very little to eat, no drink but rum . . . The danger we were in made us think there was treachery, and that we were brought there to be all slain."

In the Boston garrison General Thomas Gage, commander of the British forces, decided that the hill would have to be taken before the militia could set up artillery there. He ordered Major General William Howe to lead a party of 2,400 troops across the harbor, but after sorting out transport and waiting for the tide it was 3:30 p.m. before they could land. The Americans put the time to good use by extending their line of fortifications from the hilltop redoubt down to the shore, intending to frustrate any attempt to outflank them.

As the battle neared, the odds seemed stacked against the 1,500 American militia on Breed's Hill; they were ill trained, with little in the way of leadership or command structure. The redcoats disembarking on the shores of Charlestown were among the best-trained soldiers in Europe.

THE WRONG HILL

Meeting sniper fire, the British turned their cannon on the town and set it alight, the blazing buildings adding to the sweltering heat of the day. The redcoats advanced across what looked like open pasture toward the hill; onlookers feared the worst for the defenders.

"A CHOAKY MOUTHFUL"

But the British found that the long grass of the pasture concealed multiple obstacles, and that the militia would prove a tougher nut to crack than expected. "Our three generals," wrote a British officer involved in the attack, "expected rather to punish a mob than fight with troops that would look them in the face." In fact, the militia were disciplined and effective; according to legend, the Americans were told, "Don't fire 'til you see the whites of their eyes." While this line was probably invented decades later, the militiamen did hold their nerve, waiting until the British were in range and then opening fire to devastating effect. "[The British] advanced toward us in order to swallow us up," wrote militiaman Peter Brown, "but they found a Choaky mouthful of us."

© Public domain

FAMOUS DEATH
The death of American revolutionary Joseph Warren in the redoubt on Breed's Hill.

A detachment of redcoats sent to outflank the Americans on the left ran into the hastily prepared shoreline defenses and met with a hail of fire from up the slope. The British fell back in disorder, but quickly re-formed and advanced again. The colonials kept up a withering barrage of musket fire, particularly aiming for the striking uniforms of the officers. Soon, recalled an American officer, "the dead lay as thick as sheep in a fold." A British officer bitterly quoted Shakespeare: "They make us here but food for gunpowder."

Twice rebuffed, the British again regrouped and planned a more considered assault, bringing their artillery more into play, targeting the redoubt on top of the hill, and marching in widely spaced columns. Poor coordination among the various militias comprising the colonial force had caused problems with their supplies, and now the lack of powder began to bite.

As ammunition ran low the firing from the American lines slowed and "went out like an old candle," according to William Prescott, commanding the redoubt. The determined British advance reached the breastwork, cut through the defenses, and stormed into the redoubt, meeting rifle butts with bayonets as the battle reached an intense and gory climax. "We tumbled over the dead to get at the living," wrote a British officer, "soldiers stabbing some and dashing out the brains of others."

TOO DEARLY BOUGHT

The surviving Americans fled and the British were too exhausted to pursue them farther than Bunker Hill. The battle had lasted just two hours, yet Howe had lost 40 percent of his force, with over 1,000 casualties set against around 400 for the Americans. Howe lost every member of his staff and admitted that "the success is too dearly bought." The British would eventually have to quit Boston

© Jorge Salcedo | Shutterstock.com

MISTAKEN MEMORIAL
The plaque on the Bunker Hill Monument, actually sited on Breed's Hill.

thanks to their terrible losses, while the American army took heart from a clear demonstration that it could stand up to the worst Britain had to offer. Despite losing the battle, their efforts would earn them a place in history commemorated by an enormous monument erected at the site. Yet confusion over the proper name of the site—and hence the battle— continues to this day, with the memorial sitting squarely atop Breed's Hill yet labeled the Bunker Hill Monument. US historian Nathaniel Philbrick, author of *Bunker Hill*, argues that "the whole thing's a screwup . . . The Americans fortify the wrong hill, this forces a fight no one planned, the battle itself is an ugly and confused mess. And it ends with a British victory that's also a defeat."

BATTLE

High casualty rate

Catastrophic defeat

Pyrrhic victory

Tactical blunder

Appalling conditions

TIGER BY THE TAIL: POLLILUR

1780

Antagonists: Army of Mysore under Tipu Sultan, "Tiger of Mysore," vs. East India Company army of Scots and native sepoys under Colonel William Baillie

Casualties: British: over 2,000; Mysorean (victors): unknown

In the history of the British people, there is nothing finer or more terrible than Baillie's resistance to the overwhelming army which surrounded him. Cannonaded on his left, his front, and his right, scorch'd with the fire of musketry and rockets, and harassed by incessant charges of horsemen, he struggled on.

David Leighton, *Vicissitudes of Fort St. George,* 1902

© Getty Images

Also known as the battle of Perambakkam or Perembacum, Pollilur in 1780 was the worst defeat that the British in India had yet suffered, a ghastly massacre resulting from indecision, ineptitude, and corruption in the body governing the East India Company's Indian conquests in Madras. For the handful of survivors, a fate worse than death awaited at the hands of the Tiger of Mysore.

By the late 18th century the East India Company controlled a broad swathe of Indian territory, almost completely enclosing the independent sultanate of Mysore, ruled by the fearsome and capable Haidar Ali. Haidar, having already fought one war with the British, was drawn into a second through his alliance with the French. Thanks to French support for the American revolutionaries, Britain and France were again at war and in 1779 British forces in India laid siege to the port of Mahé, a French trading post on the southwest coast of India. Haidar objected, sending troops to take part in the defense of Mahé and vowing vengeance when it fell.

"MOST FATAL AND SUPINE"

Haidar Ali possessed one of the most up-to-date and effective armies in India, trained and equipped with French help and also expert at the devastating use of rocket barrages. Yet the colonial government in Madras, the Council, riven with intrigue, incompetence, and corruption, failed to take the threat seriously. "The government of Madras at this period was lulled into the most fatal and supine security," wrote James Lindsay, a Scotsman serving with the colonial armed forces in Madras, "and affected to treat reports of Haidar Ali's hostile intentions as without foundation." In June 1779, while Madras vacillated, Haidar Ali mobilized what may have been the greatest army ever seen in South India, numbering some 90,000 men. The British had foolishly dispersed their meager forces around the country; one detachment, a force of 2,800 men under Colonel William Baillie, was stationed at Guntur on the Krishna River.

In August 1780, belatedly appreciating the gravity of the situation, the Madras Council tried to concentrate the nearest available forces, decreeing that they should rendezvous at Conjeerveram (modern Kanchipuram), south of Madras. Baillie was ordered to proceed there immediately, while the commander-in-chief of British forces, Sir Hector Munro, marched from Madras, reaching Conjeeveram on August 29th. Haidar sent his son, Tipu, with a force of 10,000 men, to intercept Baillie before he could meet up with Munro.

© Public domain

**DITHERING
SCOTSMAN**
Sir Hector Munro, whose
indecision contributed to
the disaster at Pollilur.

On September 6th Tipu's forces made contact with Baillie at Pollilur, just 14 miles (23 kilometers) from where Munro's forces were stationed with a store of supplies and guns at Conjeeveram. Munro could hear the fighting, but felt that he could not abandon his post. Receiving a desperate plea from Baillie, he despatched a thousand men as reinforcements.

For four days Baillie was harassed by Tipu's forces until, at first light on September 10th, he decided to make a bid for Conjeeveram, marching his men out onto the open plain. Immediately he was attacked by cannon on one side and cavalry on the other. Fighting bravely, Baillie's force of Scotsmen and native troops known as sepoys fought off one attack, and even briefly managed to take Tipu's gun battery, before a counterattack by Mysorean cavalry retook them. At 10:00 a.m., recorded John Lindsay, "A shout of joy was spread throughout the line," at the sight of a cloud of dust, assumed by the British to be created by Munro's force as it marched out from Conjeeveram to relieve them. But Munro had not moved—these were more Mysoreans. "It is impossible to describe the feelings of Baillie's devoted army," wrote Lindsay, "when they found that, instead of reaping a complete victory, they were surrounded upon all sides."

OUR DISASTER

The British force was massacred, suffering particularly under a barrage of rocket fire. One of the rockets hit a cartload of British ammunition, setting off a colossal explosion. Of the 86 European officers, 36 were killed and 34 wounded; the sepoys were killed or driven off, and a mere 200 Europeans, mostly wounded, were taken prisoner by Tipu. Baillie is reported to have told Haidar, "Your son will inform you that you owe the victory to our disaster rather than to our defeat." Nonetheless, Tipu was so proud of the victory that he chose it as the subject of a famous mural at his palace at Seringapatam, modern Srirangapatna, still preserved to this day.

As for Munro, his indecision was almost fatal. Having finally decided to march out to attempt a relief, he met fleeing sepoys bearing news of the defeat and retreated back to Conjeeveram, where he promptly ran out of the supplies he had been so concerned with safeguarding. Forced to ditch his heavy guns into a reservoir, he retreated to Madras in disorder.

Meanwhile, the captured British suffered terrible privations in the notorious dungeons of Mysore. Only a handful would ever return. A pathetic final letter to his father from Archibald Hope, taken prisoner at Pollilur at the age of just 19, bears testament to the sufferings of the unfortunate captives:

"About the middle of December when we had recovered from our wounds we were sent up here . . . which is the capital of Haidar's country . . . here we were put upon a scanty allowance hardly sufficient to support nature dragging on a miserable existence loaded with irons and every hardship that a close imprisonment and infamous usage for 22 months could inflict upon a set of the most unfortunate men that ever existed. About a month ago I was attacked with flux billuus, fever, and the liver. Youth and a good constitution struggled along with these three complaints but they are now almost overpowered and I am attacked with the fatal symptom (a hickup) as I find my end approaching I request that you will never send a son of yours to this country unless you wish to make him miserable."

BATTLE

High casualty rate

Catastrophic defeat

Pyrrhic victory

Tactical blunder

Appalling conditions

BLOOD IN THE SNOW: EYLAU

1807

Antagonists: French Grande Armée under Napoleon and Marshals Augereau, Murat, Davout, and Ney vs. Russian–Prussian alliance under Count von Bennigsen and General Anton L'Estocq

Casualties: French (victors): 25,000; Russians and Prussians: 15,000

What a massacre! And without a result!

Marshal Ney, February 9th, 1807

The Napoleonic Wars were a series of mostly colossal engagements between armies of tens of thousands, which eventually cost the lives of around 2 million soldiers in Europe. Napoleon's armies would experience some grim days and inflict some hideous butcher's bills, but few of their battles would combine terrible slaughter and atrocious conditions to produce such a perfect hell as Eylau, the aftermath of which left even Napoleon shaken and distressed.

In late 1806 Napoleon was in Poland pursuing Russian armies, but they twice slipped through his grasp. In early 1807 he caught up with the army of Leonty Leontyevich, Count von Bennigsen, outside the town of Eylau in East Prussia (now Bagrationovsk, near Kaliningrad). Both sides were expecting reinforcements, with Napoleon waiting for Marshals Louis Davout and Michel Ney on his right and left flanks, while the remnants of the Prussian army under General Anton L'Estocq would join their Russian allies. Eventually each army would total around 75,000 men.

The battle began on February 7th, but reached its climax on the following day. Overnight the temperature dropped from –5°C to –16°C. The bitter cold meant life was miserable for the troops, and made it difficult to prosecute a war. The weather would have terrible consequences during and after the battle. At such low temperatures clothing freezes, becoming heavy and rigid, horses struggle to find purchase on ice and hard frosted ground, swords are frozen in their scabbards, and muskets and cannon cannot be operated normally. Napoleon's battlefield surgeon Baron Dominique Jean Larrey reported that while he was operating on battlefield casualties inside a barn his attendant's fingers were so cold that he could not grasp the instruments.

After the inconclusive but bloody fighting of the 7th, Bennigsen had a chance to overwhelm the French by attacking early on the 8th before Davout and Ney arrived. He failed to do so, and around lunchtime Davout reached the field and fell on the Russian left. In an attempt to prevent Bennigsen from redirecting forces to meet the new threat to the flank, Napoleon ordered Marshal Pierre Augereau's corps to advance on the Russian center. However, it had been snowing on and off all day, and now a snowstorm blew up. According to Russian

IN THE BLEAK MIDWINTER

THE LITTLE CORPORAL
Napoleon rose from lowly artillery officer to become Emperor.

© Public domain

officer Denis Davidov, who wrote a memoir of the battle, "You couldn't see anything two steps away." Poor Augereau had pleaded with the Emperor only the day before to be excused command owing to his poor health; now his corps lost its way and turned up, to the surprise of all concerned, directly in front of the main Russian artillery battery, just as the weather cleared. "Seventy cannons belched total hell," wrote Davidov, "and a hail of grapeshot started to ring against their rifle barrels and hammer at the live mass of flesh and bone."

Russian troops poured forward to engage Augereau's shattered corps in a bayonet battle, Davidov records:

"There took place an engagement the likes of which had never been seen before. Over 20,000 men from both sides were plunging a three-faceted blade into each other . . . I was a personal witness of this Homeric slaughter . . . For about half an hour you didn't hear a cannon or a rifle shot . . . [only] some inexpressible roar of thousands of brave soldiers in hand-to-hand struggle, mixing and cutting each other up. Mounds of dead bodies were piled over with new mounds . . . this segment of the battle resembled a high parapet . . ."

MURAT'S RIDE

Meanwhile, the Russian right flank was advancing on Eylau, briefly threatening Napoleon himself. Supposedly, he turned to Joachim Murat, his dashing marshal of cavalry, and protested, "Well, are you going to let us be devoured by these people?" Murat summoned his cavalry reserve and cried, "Follow me!" before launching one of the most famous cavalry charges of the Napoleonic era.

Davidov described the spectacle:

"More than 60 squadrons galloped around to the right of the fleeing corps and rushed against us, waving their swords. The field was engulfed in a roar and the snow, ploughed over by 12,000 united riders, lifted and swirled from under them like a storm. Brilliant Murat with his carousel-like costume . . . was ablaze ahead of the onslaught with a naked saber . . ."

Murat's charge averted disaster for the French, and Davout made ground on the Russian left. Their lines were close to breaking when L'Estocq arrived with his Prussians to reinforce them. Hot on their heels, however, was Marshal Ney, who arrived on the field as the light was failing. Bennigsen finally ordered a withdrawal, technically giving the victory to the French, but it was at best a draw, and a bloody one. The French had suffered around 25,000 casualties, with many of the wounded freezing to death. Napoleon toured the battlefield, allegedly declaiming without irony, "If all the kings on earth could see this sight, they would be less greedy for wars and conquests."

The road away from Eylau offered fresh horrors to the French. As Davidov describes:

"The whole road was littered with debris without cease. We met everywhere hundreds of horses dying or obstructing the way which we followed, and ambulances filled with dying or dead soldiers and men of rank mutilated in the Eylau battle. The rush to evacuate had become such that besides the sufferers left in the carriages we found many that had been simply dumped on the snow without cover or clothes, bleeding to death."

IMPERIAL GRENADIERS
Grenadiers of the Imperial Guard advancing through a blizzard at Eylau.

BATTLE

High casualty rate

Catastrophic defeat

Pyrrhic victory

Tactical blunder

Appalling conditions

PENINSULAR PANDEMONIUM: ALBUERA

1811

Antagonists: British, Portuguese, and Spanish under Marshal Beresford and General Blake vs. French under Marshal Soult

Casualties: Allied (victors): 6,000; French: 8,000

... [T]he blood in that quarter was so profuse, that in several places, mingling with the rain, it ran in torrents like blood itself; but recollect, at this moment, it had, within the space of three-quarters of a mile, flowed from the veins of upward of 8,000 men, and exhausted many, the scene may be imagined, but I will not attempt to describe it.

King's German Legion Officer at Albuera

The Battle of Albuera was an inconclusive and relatively minor engagement in the Peninsular War, yet proved to be the bloodiest in relation to the number of troops involved. The grisliest passage of the battle was the result of an unfortunate series of circumstances that left an infantry brigade unprepared for the shocking assault of several units of cavalry, who inflicted terrible damage and were later accused of atrocities.

Napoleon's astonishing series of victories had brought much of continental Europe under his heel by 1808, and he used his hegemony to impose the so-called Continental System: a program of blockades and sanctions aimed at economically crippling the last great power that could still challenge France — Britain. But Napoleon's ambition and greed for conquest got the better of him and he turned on his own allies, the Spanish, seizing key forts and towns across the Iberian peninsula and staging a coup to replace the house of Bourbon with his brother Joseph.

© Public domain

BELLICOSE BLAKE
The Spanish commander whose insubordination almost lost the battle for the allies.

The Spanish responded with a general insurrection, which spilled over into Portugal, and the British seized on the opportunity to strike at a potential chink in the armor of Napoleonic Europe. Expeditionary forces were despatched, and in 1809 Arthur Wellesley — soon to be elevated to the peerage as the Duke of Wellington in order to ensure that snobbish aristocratic generals would take orders from him — took overall command of the allied forces of Britain, Portugal, and Spain in the Peninsular War. By 1811 Wellington was able to break out of Portugal and assault the fortresses governing the main routes into Spain at Ciudad Rodrigo and Badajoz. His subordinate, Marshal William Beresford, commanded the siege of Badajoz, but in May Beresford learned that the French general, Marshal Jean-de-Dieu Soult, had gathered a force of 23,000 men, including 4,000 cavalry, and was marching north to relieve the city.

Beresford commanded an army of 32,000 men, including a Spanish force under General Joaquín Blake. To prevent the French from reaching Badajoz he took up position at a low ridge near the village of Albuera, on the road from Seville. Here, on May 16th, he drew up his forces, expecting Soult to assault his center, but the clever French general had other ideas.

"CORDIAL ASSENT"

HUSSAR HURRAH
A British hussar taking two French officers prisoner at the Battle of Albuera.

© Getty Images

Spotting a hill opposite the allied lines, he marshaled the bulk of his army out of their sight, his superior cavalry forces having driven off the allied scouts. Thus, he was able to feint at Beresford's center while sending most of his strength in a surprise move to outflank the allies on the right.

Disaster threatened. Beresford sent orders to Blake to redeploy to meet the French threat. According to histories of the battle, the Spanish commander flatly refused until Beresford arrived in person to deliver the order. Beresford's own despatch to Wellington after the battle rather glosses over this rank insubordination, claiming that "the most perfect harmony has subsisted between us; and that General Blake not only conformed in all things to the general line proposed by your Lordship, but in the details, and in whatever I suggested to his Excellency, I received the most immediate and cordial assent and cooperation . . ."

In fact, Blake's hard-wrung "cordial assent" came too late, and only courageous resistance by the sole brigade of Spanish general José Pascual de Zayas stemmed the French onslaught. Beresford tried to rush British units to the right flank, but the leading brigade, under Lieutenant-General Colborne, had terrible luck. "Nearly at the beginning of the enemy's attack," Beresford relates, "a heavy storm of rain came on, which, with the smoke, from the firing, rendered it impossible to discern anything distinctly." Without a chance to form up to meet the charge, Colborne's brigade was savagely destroyed by French hussars and Polish lancers whom "the thickness of the atmosphere and the nature of the ground had concealed . . . Being thus attacked unexpectedly in the rear," Beresford writes, "[the brigade] was unfortunately broken, and suffered immensely."

CARNAGE OF THE COLORS

The carnage was extreme; three of the four battalions were more or less wiped out, with Colborne's brigade suffering 1,413 casualties out of 2,066 men. "The battlefield was covered with their dead," reported Marshal Soult, "and we took considerable numbers of prisoners." During the massacre there were two famous incidents as British troops bravely defended their colors. In one incident later discussed in Parliament, 15-year-old Ensign

Edward Thomas of the 3rd Foot, known as the "Buffs," fell defending the regimental colors. A Captain Stevens related Thomas's last moments in a letter to the ensign's aunt:

"I cannot refrain from tears, while I relate the determined bravery of your gallant little subaltern, who fell on the 16th instant, covered with glory; and it must in some measure alleviate the grief I know you will feel at his loss, to know he fell like a hero. He rallied my company after I was wounded and taken prisoner, crying out, 'Rally on me, men, I will be your pivot.' . . . He was buried with all care possible by a sergeant and a private, the only two survivors out of my company, which consisted of sixty-three men when taken into action."

Meanwhile, the king's colors with the same regiment were defended by Lieutenant Matthew Latham, who acted even more heroically. His ordeal was recounted by John Morrison, a surgeon who had served with the Buffs:

© Getty Images

MARSHAL SOULT
The French commander at Albuera, Marshal Jean-de-Dieu Soult.

"He was attacked by several French hussars, one of whom seizing the flag-staff, and rising in his stirrup, aimed a stroke at the head of the gallant Latham, which failed in cutting him down, but which sadly mutilated him, severing one side of the face and nose; he still, however, struggled with the dragoon [sic], and exclaimed, 'I will surrender it only with my life.' A second saber struck, severing his left arm and hand, in which he held the staff, from his body. The brave fellow, however, then seized the staff with his right hand, throwing away his sword, and continued to struggle with his opponents, now increased in number; when ultimately thrown down, trampled upon, and pierced by the spears of the Polish lancers, his last effort was to tear the flag from the staff as he thus lay prostrate, and to thrust it partly into the breast of his jacket . . ."

Amazingly, Latham survived, as Morrison relates:

" . . . in two hours afterward he crawled on his remaining hand and knees toward the river of Albuera, and was found by some of the orderlies of the army attempting to slake his thirst in the stream; he was carried into the convent, where his wounds were dressed, the stump of his arm amputated, and he ultimately recovered."

King George IV himself later footed the bill for reparatory surgery to Latham's face.

According to an officer of the 2nd Light Infantry Battalion, King's German Legion, the Polish lancers were guilty of perpetrating atrocities on the prisoners they took. One lancer stripped a captive of all his clothing and, declaring that he should have a mark to show he had been a prisoner of the Poles, drove his lance into the man's back. The officer also describes how the wounded, "whilst lying on the ground, were pierced through with spears," and relates the tale of "an officer of the 4th dragoons who had fallen into their hands" who:

" . . . was, as usual, stripped of his watch and money, of which I suppose he had rather a small stock, as there had been no pay issued for some time, on being asked if that was all, and replying in the affirmative, they deliberately cut off one or both of his ears, I believe both . . ."

DIE HARD Colborne's brigade was in tatters but Soult failed to press his advantage quickly enough. Beresford was able to re-form his lines and, as Soult describes, "the enemy line soon approached ours, and the fighting then became most terrible." A brigade under Hoghton held the ridge against the French advance but suffered horrific casualties, losing 1,044 out of 1,651 men. In one famous incident, Lieutenant Colonel Inglis of the 57th regiment lay on the ground severely wounded, but refused to leave his soldiers, calling out to them "Die hard, 57th!" This regiment was later known as "the Diehards."

Although Beresford was a solid commander and renowned for his great strength (engaged during the battle in personal combat by an enemy lancer, he disarmed the rider and threw him to the ground), he was not the most quick-thinking. The day was only won when one of his staff officers rode across to infantry General Lowry Cole and urged him to attack with or without orders. Cole's 4th Division finally turned back the French, though not without suffering terrible losses, and the battle petered out as Soult withdrew.

Soult and Beresford gave rather different reports to their respective commanders. "The [French] troops are covered in glory," wrote Soult, "As soon as I knew [my wounded had been escorted to safety], I maneuvered to join up with the other troops, and to complete the defeat of the enemy." Meanwhile, Beresford was writing to Wellington: "I have infinite satisfaction in communicating to your lordship that the allied army united here under my orders, obtained . . . after a most sanguinary contest, a complete victory." He may, however, have simply been acting under orders in recording the result in this way; Wellington, mindful of public opinion back in Britain, reportedly told one of his staff, "Write me down a victory." But in private he quoted Pyrrhus (see pages 21–4): "Another such victory will ruin us."

ALMOST OUTFLANKED

The French under Soult attempted to outflank the allied defensive line, but were held up first by Zayas, then Colborne, before British reinforcements beat off the French advance.

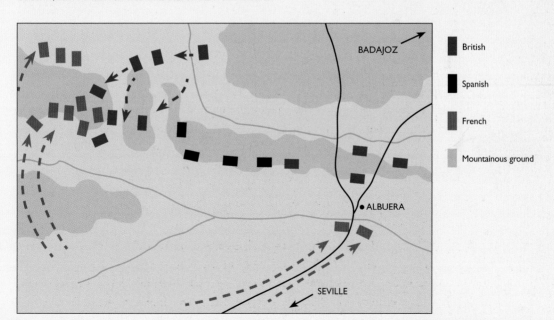

BADAJOZ

■ British

■ Spanish

■ French

■ Mountainous ground

● ALBUERA

SEVILLE

BATTLE

High casualty rate

Catastrophic defeat

Pyrrhic victory

Tactical blunder

Appalling conditions

MASSACRE ON THE MOSKVA: BORODINO

1812

Antagonists: La Grand Armée of France under Emperor Napoleon vs. Russians under Mikhail Kutuzov

Casualties: Russians: 44,000; French (victors): 50,000

Why was the battle of Borodino fought? There was not the least sense in it for either the French or the Russians.

Leo Tolstoy, *War and Peace*

© Oleg Golovnev | Shutterstock.com

Borodino marked the turning point of Napoleon's Russian campaign and entire career—after the terrible carnage of this battle his power ebbed away relentlessly and his eventual doom was sealed. On September 6th, 1812, two of the largest armies yet assembled in history met to produce the bloodiest single day of the entire Napoleonic Wars; the outcome represented perhaps the greatest Pyrrhic victory of all time. It was a battle devoid of subtlety, with all-out frontal assaults on fortified gun emplacements and massed batteries of artillery firing vast numbers of shots directly into immobile bodies of troops.

Napoleon's attempts to control all of Europe with his Continental System (see page 123) led him increasingly into conflict with the Russians, and he made the fateful decision to embark upon his 1812 invasion of Russia. The north–south alignment of rivers in Russia meant that Napoleon would have to rely on an immensely long and entirely land-based line of supply with long baggage trains, but the emperor was undaunted and set about collating a colossal force drawn from all the nations under his hegemony. Eventually he amassed a Grande Armée of 700,000 men from France, Poland, Italy, Iberia, and various parts of Germany, split into several armies. Napoleon himself took charge of the central army of 286,000 men, advancing toward Moscow in the hope of securing a quick and decisive victory by catching and destroying the main Russian army and marching unopposed to the capital to accept the Tsar's surrender. His logistical vulnerabilities necessitated the quickest possible campaign; he originally hoped to achieve victory within just three weeks.

Almost inadvertently the Russians brilliantly frustrated him. Infighting among the top generals prevented the Russian commander-in-chief Count Michael Barclay de Tolly from establishing a defensive line and instead his army was forced to retreat, denying Napoleon the major engagement he sought. By the time the Grande Armée had advanced to within 100 miles (160 kilometers) of Moscow, Tolly had been replaced by the venerable Russian general Marshal Mikhail Kutuzov, and Napoleon's army had been cut down by disease, desertion, and other travails. Kutuzov planned to

FOLLOW THE MOSKVA

© Popperfoto | Getty Images

RUSSIAN BEAR
Marshal Kutuzov, who commanded the Russians in what he called "the bloodiest battle of modern times."

BEFORE MOSCOW
A panoramic view of the Battle of Borodino, the Russians' final defense of Moscow.

make a stand by the banks of the Moskva River, 77 miles (124 kilometers) from Moscow, where reinforcements swelled his forces to around 120,000 men. Although he still could not match the ca. 140,000 men remaining to Napoleon, Kutuzov did have more guns, with 624 cannon to Napoleon's 587. Outside of their homeland Russian troops did not enjoy the highest reputation, but on home soil they could be relied upon to fight with almost suicidal courage. Opposing them Napoleon marshaled a multinational army: alongside 144 infantry battalions and 43 cavalry regiments from France, it consisted of around 50 more battalions and 30 more regiments from Poland, Italy, Spain and Portugal, Croatia, and various parts of Germany.

Kutuzov took up his defensive position around the village of Borodino on September 3rd. There is some debate over his original intentions; the conventional account is that he planned a line of defense astride the two main roads to Moscow, stretching from the Moskva on his right flank to the Utitsa forest on his left, with the Koloch stream in front of him (and the village of Borodino on its west bank), and that he drew up these lines so that the strongly fortified redoubt at Shevardino was left some distance to the west, in front of his lines, to break up the French approach and give advance notice of their arrival. Leo Tolstoy, writing in *War and Peace*, his fictional account of the 1812 campaign, argues that this is a post-hoc version intended to spare Kutuzov's blushes at being caught slightly unawares.

In fact, it seems more likely that the Russian line was originally drawn up with Shevardino as the anchor for the left flank, but a rapid reorientation was necessitated by the actions of September 5th, when a force of 40,000 French stumbled on the redoubt's 12,000 Russian defenders. After a ferociously bloody contest the French took the redoubt, but it cost them many casualties. The following day, when Napoleon reviewed one of the regiments responsible, he asked where its third battalion was—the colonel of the regiment pointed to the corpses in the redoubt.

AN ARTIFICIAL EARTHQUAKE

The Russians hastily improvised new fortifications to the east of Shevardino. At the center of their line was a *kurgan*, or burial mound, and atop this they constructed a great redoubt, filled with guns and commanded by an injured general named Raevsky. To the right of the Raevsky redoubt, just across the Koloch, the village of Borodino was occupied by Russian Jägers (light infantry). To its left, where the full force of the French advance would fall, the Russians' Second Army under Prince Piotr Bagration had to throw up a series of improvised earthworks known as *flèches* or *lunettes*. Although hastily constructed, the Russian line was formidable and the consensus opinion is that Napoleon made an uncharacteristic blunder when he adopted a plan of frontal assault. His own generals urged him to try an outflanking maneuver through the woods to the south, but the emperor was perhaps wary of risking a sizable portion of his force getting lost as it deployed, and almost certainly mindful of the need to strike at Kutuzov without allowing him any time to slip away again. Accordingly, Napoleon took up a position on the captured Shevardino redoubt and watched as his men advanced into a brutal clash of titanic forces.

At around 4 a.m. on the 7th, the French artillery commenced firing. The Russians replied, and Radozhitsky, an officer of Russian artillery, recorded that, "The rounds were so frequent that there were no intervals between them: they soon turned into one continuous roar like a thunderstorm, and caused an artificial earthquake." Soon after, French troops advanced on the Jägers holding Borodino, who were quickly driven out and retreated across the Koloch, only partially destroying the bridge before the French 106th Regiment, impetuously disregarding orders, chased after them. Unfortunately for the 106th, more determined resistance was awaiting them on the other side.

Meanwhile, the main French advance was against the Russian left flank, where the battle for Bagration's *flèches* would prove terrible and costly. Marshal Davout attempted to outflank the southernmost *flèche*, but his columns of troops were targeted by Russian artillery. Davout himself was knocked off his horse, causing a general panic that he was dead, but the best of his regiments, the "Terrible" 57th, bravely advanced through murderous firing to occupy the *flèche*.

Each time a French assault captured a *flèche*, the Russians would counterattack and retake it. Bagration himself reported that "the battle began so savage, desperate, and murderous that there are hardly any other examples like it. The enemy corpses were heaped in mounds and this place can justly be named the tombstone of the French." Among the leading

THE TOMBSTONE OF THE FRENCH

Russian units was Vorontsov's 2nd Combined Grenadier Division, which suffered so many casualties that, he wrote:

"An hour after the fighting began my division ceased to exist. Out of about 4,000 men, there was less than 300 at the evening roll-call and out of 18 staff officers only 3 survived, and only 1 of them was not wounded . . . If I were asked the following day where my division was, I would have responded . . . pointing my finger to our position and proudly declaring, 'Here it is.'"

© Public domain

RINGSIDE
A depressed Napoleon watches the battle unfold, in this iconic painting by Vasily Vereshchagin.

Bagration sent in his cavalry to try to turn the tide, and in one incident demonstrating the confusion that reigned on the field, a group of German infantry mistook Russian cuirassiers for the similarly uniformed Saxon cavalry. The Germans withheld their fire and allowed the Russians to approach, only realizing their fatal error when the Russian officer ordered his men to "Kill these German dogs!"

It would eventually require eight French assaults costing 30,000 casualties to capture the *flèches*, but Bagration himself was mortally wounded leading one of the innumerable counterattacks. He died a few days later.

A WALK INTO HELL

Arguably even more ferocious was the battle for the Raevsky redoubt. The redoubt itself was formidable; Lieutenant Bogdanov of the Pioneers recorded what he saw when was sent to deliver orders to Raevsky:

"The battery had 19 artillery pieces . . . It was necessary, despite the lack of time, to add two epaulments of ramparts and a moat on the flanks, and to cover the rear with double palisade with two passages with palisaded gateways in them . . . the fortification . . . was finished by half-past four in the morning."

Just a short time later Raevsky found himself trying to make out the French advance through a cloud of artillery smoke, which "hid the French so completely that we could see nothing of their array or ascertain what progress they were making." In fact, they were making rapid progress. In front of the redoubt the ground was pockmarked with foxholes, aka "wolfpits," occupied by Russian defenders. Captain François of 30th Line Infantry recorded the hectic French advance:

"A great number of Frenchmen fall into the wolfpits pell-mell with Russians who're in them already . . . Nothing could stop us . . . We hopped over the roundshot as it bounced through the grass."

Raevsky was taken by surprise, recalling that "one of my orderly officers was standing a little to the left of me, and after another volley he cried out, 'Your Excellency, save yourself!' I turned around and 15 yards away I saw French grenadiers pouring into my redoubt with fixed bayonets." He had just enough time to get on a horse and escape to his reserves.

The Russians poured in reinforcements to retake the redoubt, but the French deployed an artillery barrage against them. Prince Eugene, a Russian general, described his advance as "a walk into Hell . . . we went straight for the enemy mass, while the huge battery hurled its balls at us." The prince had three horses shot out from under him and his troops suffered terrible casualties, but eventually they forced the French to fall back.

Napoleon ordered Marshal Murat to lead a massed cavalry charge. French, German, and Polish cavalry advanced in regimental columns. A Russian officer wrote that "a cloud of dust swept down on us from the left like an avalanche and the closer it rolled the more monstrous its dimensions appeared." Baron Helldorf described how "the force of the onslaught of these mighty masses almost took our breath away . . . The French cavalry emerged from the dust with a gleam of armor, a rattling of their scabbards, and a flashing of the sun on the metal of those helmets of theirs with the horsetail switches. Drunk with victory, this majestic horde of cavalry pressed home its attack against our iron wall . . ." The infantry formed into squares to beat back the charge, and the Russian cavalry rushed in to meet their counterparts. The fight turned into a desperate melee: "What bloody fighting," wrote Fedor Glinka, "What a scrum!"

By now the battle seemed to have degenerated into a continuous, bloody exchange of artillery. "It seemed," wrote General Barclay de Tolly, "as if Napoleon had decided to eliminate us with his artillery." Cannon fire wreaked terrible carnage on columns of men. Russian Colonel Alexander Kutuzov reported that the French artillery "devastated our ranks," but "failed to produce any disorder among the men. The ranks were simply closed up again and soldiers maintained their discipline as coolly as if

DRUNK WITH VICTORY

they had been on a musketry exercise." General Paskevich wrote that his infantry division "lost half of its men under that dreadful artillery fire that wiped out entire ranks but, as the French acknowledged themselves, we held ground with remarkable courage."

A LOT OF MISCHIEF

The Russians, once more in control of the central redoubt, were using their position to pour cannon fire into the French. Marshal Joachim Murat laconically recorded that "the big redoubt . . . caused us a lot of mischief each time it found a favorable occasion." By now, however, its earthwork ramparts had been so blasted and beaten down that it was vulnerable to attack by cavalry. Cuirassiers under General Caulaincourt launched a famous assault. Murat describes how he "overthrew everything he met in front of him" but "died gloriously in that redoubt." A Colonel Griois gave a more emotive account:

"It would be difficult to convey our feelings as we watched this brilliant feat of arms, perhaps without equal in the military annals of nations."

© Oleg Golovnev | Shutterstock.com

EMPEROR OF DEATH
Napoleon surveys the carnage of the Borodino battlefield, which he described as "the most terrible battle I have fought."

"However," wrote Murat, "the Russians formed several masses of infantry composed of the Russian Guard and of their reserve. Supported by a great number of cavalry, the enemy was marching to re-take the [position] . . ." He quickly assembled a colossal battery of 80 pieces of artillery and ordered a rolling fire of grapeshot, "which stopped the movements of the Russians. The emperor was able to convince himself of the hardship inflicted by our artillery on the enemy when he surveyed the field of battle yesterday."

By this time, wrote Heinrich von Brandt, an officer of the Vistula Legion, "The redoubt and the area around it offered an aspect which exceeded the worst horrors one could ever dream of . . . The approaches, the ditches and the earthwork itself had disappeared under a mound of dead and dying, of an average depth of 6 to 8 men, heaped one upon the other."

The redoubt finally fell at around 3:30 p.m., and with the French now in possession of both the central fortification and the *flèches* to the south, and the Russians retreating, the time seemed ripe for Napoleon to throw his final reserves into the fray. He had held back the elite Imperial Guards for just such an eventuality, but now, suddenly mindful that he was a very long way from home and could ill afford to hazard all on a single throw of the die, Napoleon seems to have lost his nerve, refusing to commit them. "I will most definitely not," he is supposed to have replied, "I do not want to have [the Guards Corp] blown up. I am certain of winning the battle without its intervention."

Despite Napoleon failing to press his advantage, the French knew they had mauled the Russians very badly, and so were all the more astonished when they saw Kutuzov drawing up the remnants of his army in relatively good order in a new line farther to the east. But after 15 hours of desperate combat both sides were exhausted and the battle petered out by 6 p.m. Kutuzov decided to withdraw, leaving Napoleon technically the victor, although the little emperor was so despondent that he could only communicate his orders by writing.

© Public domain

CHARGING CHASSEUR
Géricault's famous painting shows an officer of the Imperial Horse Guards, flashing his saber.

The aftermath of Borodino was grisly. "Never did [a battlefield] present so horrible an appearance," wrote the Comte de Ségur. "Everything concurred to make it so; a gloomy sky, a cold rain, a violent wind, houses burnt to ashes . . . soldiers roaming in all directions amidst the dead." Eugène Labaume reported that the little spaces between the mounds of wounded "were covered with debris of arms, lances, helmets, or cuirasses, or by cannonballs as numerous as hailstones after a violent storm." Some 120,000 cannonballs and 3 million musket shots had been expended that day.

Particularly affecting were the 39,000 dead or cruelly mutilated horses. François Dumonceau described how:

"One could see some [horses] which, disemboweled, nevertheless kept standing, their heads hung low, drenching the soil with their blood, or, hobbling painfully in search of some pasture, dragged beneath them shreds of harness, sagging intestines, or a fractured member, or else, lying flat on their sides, lifted their heads from time to time to gaze on their gaping wounds."

The Grande Armée had suffered between 30,000 and 40,000 casualties, including 36 generals, while the Russians had 45,000–50,000 dead and wounded, including 23 generals. Napoleon himself claimed, "Of the fifty battles I have fought, the most terrible was that before Moscow." Kutuzov, writing to the Tsar, described it as "the bloodiest battle of modern times," claiming that "the battle ended with the enemy failing to gain even a single step of the ground in spite of his numerical superiority."

For Napoleon the victory proved utterly hollow. Although the route to Moscow was now clear, he found the city abandoned when he got there and that very night it burned to the ground around his ears. There was no Tsar to offer his surrender and it was now apparent that his already starving army would have to attempt a long retreat through a harsh winter. By the time the Grande Armée returned to Imperial territory, there were fewer than 60,000 survivors from the 700,000 men who had originally set out. Napoleon's empire was now doomed, although he was still able to muster enormous armies for still greater bloodbaths.

BATTLE OF THE NATIONS: LEIPZIG

1813

BATTLE

High casualty rate

Catastrophic defeat

Pyrrhic victory

Tactical blunder

Appalling conditions

Antagonists: French under Napoleon, with Marshals Ney, Murat, Oudinot, Poniatowski, and others vs. allied armies of Russia, Austria, and Prussia under Prince Schwarzenberg, with Marshals Blücher, Bernadotte, and others

Casualties: French: 13,000 dead, 23,000 wounded, 15,000–30,000 prisoners, and 5,000 defected; allied armies (victors): 50,000–55,000 casualties

Yesterday the monstrous masses battled with one another. It was a spectacle such as has not been seen for a thousand years.

Prussian general August Neidhardt von Gneisenau

The greatest battle on European soil until World War I, featuring the largest assemblage of armies in the history of the Continent to that point, Leipzig is known as the Battle of the Nations because of the number of nationalities involved. The primary contestants were Russia, Austria, and Prussia against the French and their Polish and German allies, but soldiers of more than 20 nationalities were present on the battlefield, from Swedes and Britons to Finns and Tartars. The battle was Napoleon's first clear-cut and overwhelming defeat and changed the course of European history. It was also gory and intense, with a calamitous error dooming thousands of fleeing French to capture and massacre.

THE BATTLE FOR GERMANY

After his disastrous mauling in Russia, Napoleon hurriedly raised yet another army, bleeding France white for fresh conscripts. Meanwhile, Prussia defected from the "Continental System" in 1813 and joined Russia in launching a "war of liberation" to force Napoleon out of Germany and break up his coalition of German states. They frantically lobbied Austria to participate in yet another grand alliance against the French, and were joined by Jean-Baptiste Bernadotte, Crown Prince of Sweden and erstwhile Napoleonic marshal. Although Napoleon gained minor victories over Russian and Prussian armies in the early summer, he was forced to agree an armistice in June through shortage of trained men and adequate supplies. On June 4th Austria declared for the allies and Napoleon maneuvered round Germany in an attempt to defend his own allies and prevent more states from defecting.

The little emperor defeated the allies under Prince Schwarzenberg at Dresden, but one of his marshals was soundly beaten at Kulm. In early October Bavaria defected to the allies, and Napoleon felt that he had to defend Leipzig, the second city of his main remaining German ally, Saxony. Although the forces massing against him were overwhelming (the total allied strength would eventually come to 342,000 against Napoleon's 195,000), Napoleon possessed some potentially key advantages. Leipzig was situated at the confluence of four rivers, splitting the battlefield into a number of sectors. Since he controlled the center and the only intact bridges, Napoleon would have great internal lines of communication and mobility. His opponents, however, were politically and geographically disunited. National and political rivalries made it almost impossible to establish a unified command. Prince Schwarzenberg, noted for his tact, particularly given that he had three emperors (the Russian Tsar, the Austrian Emperor, and the Prussian Kaiser) looking over his shoulder, had been made nominal commander-in-chief, but in reality the allied forces were split into three independent armies. Scwharzenberg commanded the Austrian-Russian Army of Bohemia, Prussian Marshal Gebhardt von Blücher the Prussian-Russian Army of Silesia, and Crown Prince Bernadotte the Swedish-Russian-Prussian Army of the North. From his central position, and given enough tactical acumen and rapidity of deployment, Napoleon might be able to deal with his enemies individually, concentrating his forces locally to crush each one in turn. "We seem to have reached the crisis," wrote Napoleon on October 12th, "now all depends on fighting hard." Two days later he entered Leipzig.

That same day, the 14th, as the French deployed across Leipzig, Napoleon's flamboyant marshal of cavalry, Joachim Murat (also Napoleon's brother-in-law, who had been made king of Naples), ran into Schwarzenberg's advance guard at a village to the south. Both sides incurred heavy casualties, but the allies could afford these with reinforcements arriving all the time. The following day Napoleon completed his deployment, concentrating his forces to the southeast of Leipzig near the village of Seifertshain, hoping to launch an attack that would turn Schwarzenberg's flank. The daughter of the vicar of Seifertshain described the scene: "The view from the church tower showed us that the entire area toward Leipzig was covered with soldiers. The roads as far as we could see were black with marching troops, guns, ammunition wagons, pouring in endless streams toward the battlefield." A French sergeant-major gave a similar description: "When day broke, we could see nothing but the sky and soldiers."

Battle was joined in earnest on the following day in three theaters. South and southwest of Leipzig, Austrian troops attempted to take the villages of Connewitz and Lindenau, the latter guarding the vital escape route to the west for the French. In the southeast the main force of Napoleon's army faced Schwarzenberg. To the northwest, Napoleon had posted a smaller force under Marshal Marmont to hold off Blücher's advance.

The Austrian advance along the banks of the Pleisse met with fierce resistance from Polish units. The Austrian General Bubna described the scene:

NOTHING BUT SKY AND SOLDIERS

"The [Polish] resistance here had been desperate; their bodies lay thickly in the rubble of the houses, in the roads, and among the barricades of the bridge . . . Many, many of our comrades had shed their blood here. The wood was full of our dead and on the bank of the Pleisse there were thick rows of our men who had died in a musket fire at 12 paces."

In one bizarre incident the extremely short-sighted commander of the Austrian troops on the banks of the Pleisse, Merveldt, mistook some of the enemy for his Prussian allies and crossed over to greet them, accompanied by his staff. His reception was less than cordial; his horse was shot out from under him and he was captured and sent to Napoleon along with a copy of the allied plan for the battle, found in his pocket.

THE MONK ON GALLOWS HILL

The key position in the French lines to the southeast of Leipzig was a Grand Battery of 100 guns set up on Gallows Hill, under the command of Antoine Count Drouot, "the Monk." Drouot was renowned as the finest artillery general of his era alongside Napoleon, and his battery first destroyed or drove off the inferior allied battery opposing it, before raining fire on Prince Eugene's Russian II Infantry Corps. Eugene, having learned nothing from the carnage at Borodino, did nothing to lessen the impact on his troops, instead demonstrating his disregard for personal safety. "We saw him . . . blind and deaf to the dangers," wrote a Russian officer, "death and terrors around him, with his slim pale face framed by his dark brown locks riding like an angel of death through the ranks." His horse did not share its rider's luck, and was shot through with a cannonball. When Eugene later came to present his casualty list to his corps commander Barclay de Tolly, Tolly could not believe his eyes. "Perhaps a look at the dead on the battlefield where we fought will convince you," responded Eugene.

When Drouot's guns had blasted a hole in the allied lines, Murat was ordered to exploit it. Napoleon himself described perhaps the greatest cavalry charge of the Napoleonic Wars: "The King of Naples placed himself at the head of the cuirassiers and marched on the enemy's cavalry to the left of Wachau, while the Polish horse and the dragoons of the Guard charged to the right." Some 10,000 horsemen surged forward. They were eventually checked by a countercharge, led by Russian cavalry, including the Tsar's Lifeguard Cossacks. Watching them with admiration Alexander purred, "They are going in to fight as if they were coming to a wedding." The regiment later adopted the "Wedding March" as their regimental music.

Cavalry engagements were followed by fierce infantry contests over the villages of Liebertwolkwitz and Wachau. Marshal Oudinot instructed his generals to give the enemy "a kick in the rear," but Schwarzenberg's men gave as good as they got. By the close of day General Poniatowski was forced to inform Napoleon: "My VIII Corps . . . have lost a third of their men and many officers. All ammunition stocks have been used up . . . the cartridge pouches and the ammunition wagons are empty . . . we have not enough to maintain combat for an hour." Napoleon promoted him to Marshal of the Empire, prompting Poniatowski to declare, "Sire, we are all prepared to die for you." He would soon have the chance to make good his boast.

In the northern sector, on Blücher's left flank, Russian General Alexandre Andrault de Langeron found himself facing Polish general Jan-Henryk Dabrowski's two regiments. Though massively outnumbered, the Poles advanced on their enemy. Langeron later wrote that he believed he was facing Napoleon himself. Prussian Major Ernst Moritz Arndt described "the deep hatred that existed between the Russians and the Poles . . . [they] were soon involved in a hefty fight . . . It was the bitterest fight I have ever seen in my life."

The Prussians engaged in a vicious fight with the French under Marshal Marmont over the village of Möckern, which they were forced to take four times before finally holding it. During the third assault, a Prussian musketeer battalion rashly attacked the French battery and was driven back, losing three-quarters of its men and every one of its officers. A Prussian cavalry charge broke through, and forced Marmont into retreat. Prussian artillery came forward and started pounding the French; only a brave counterattack by General Joubert and his seven battalions stemmed the tide. Marmont wrote: "I do not know any praise too great for these deserving troops, so brave and devoted, even though they had a lot of casualties they still fought with great courage . . ." Only nightfall prevented Blücher from pressing his advance further.

After an exhausting day's fighting both sides took a day to lick their wounds and redeploy, yet the advantage was all to the allies. Napoleon should probably have started his retreat; instead he waited while a third

© Nicku | Shutterstock.com

MARSHAL FORWARDS
General Blücher was known for his aggressive tactics.

A BAD OMEN

allied army arrived, as Bernadotte's Army of the North swung round to approach from the northeast, almost completely closing the ring around Leipzig. Finally, preparations for the great retreat westward via Lindenau began. Colonel Griois, commander of the foot artillery of the Imperial Guard, recorded:

"On 18 Oct at 3 a.m. in early morning, an orderly officer brought me an order to set off with my guns . . . The start of our march had been marked by a series of explosions and a great fire as all the wagons and caissons which could no longer be moved due to lack of horses were being burned with their contents. This spectacle caused a deep depression in me for it reminded me of our retreat from Moscow. It was a bad omen."

That same day Napoleon sent the Austrian Emperor a ceasefire request, offering to surrender a string of important fortresses if he were allowed to withdraw. The offer merely emboldened the allies, and on October 18th battle was rejoined. Fighting was fiercest to the south, where a column under Barclay de Tolly contested for the village of Probstheida. A Prussian of the 12th Brigade recorded his experience of the battle:

PATRIOTIC POSTCARD
A postcard showing a scene from the Battle of Nations and the Prussian generals Blücher and Gneisenau.

"The first thing that hit our skirmishers—of which I was one—was an artillery crossfire. It didn't take long for us to be scattered. We re-formed . . . and rushed forward to take half the village. The surprised French fell back before us . . . We were about to seize the prize, when there came a shout . . . the French had brought up reinforcements and now advanced against us in superior strength. We were lucky to get out of the village alive."

Griois, now positioned to the west of Probstheida, set up his guns and "opened up a lively fire," but complained to General Drouot that "the enemy infantry were getting uncomfortably close . . ." He sent up the battalion of Velites de Florence ". . . and they soon taught the enemy to have some respect." Allied staff officer Maximilian von Thielen admitted that "the French were holding out with unparalleled stubbornness . . ."

In the north, around the village of Schönefeld, the fighting was equally fierce, with the French hammered by the largest artillery battery—with

220 guns—of the Napeolonic Wars. The French replied with 137 guns of their own. At this crucial juncture the Saxons defected to the allies. Napoleon complained that the French had been winning until "the Saxons, with sixty guns, went over to the enemy at one of the most vital points . . . and turned their guns on the French . . ." Baron de Marbot wrote:

RETRAITE DES FRANÇAIS, APRÈS LA BATAILLE DE LEIPSICK (LE 19 OCTOBRE 1813.)

IN RETREAT
French forces retreating from Leipzig.

"The Saxons . . . seeing the Prussian ensigns in the fields . . . ran toward them at top speed . . . Some French officers could not believe such treachery, and thought that the Saxons were going to attack the Prussians; so that General Gressot . . . rushed toward them to moderate what he thought was an excess of zeal, only to find himself confronted by enemies . . ."

Yet despite the defection, wrote British observer Sir Robert Wilson, "the allied troops could not carry a single one of the villages which the French [held]. The action was closed by night, leaving to the French, and especially to the defenders of Probstheida, the glory of having inspired a generous envy in their enemies." Meanwhile, Napoleon was steadily withdrawing, attempting the mammoth task of moving 150,000 troops and hundreds of cannon across the only remaining bridge over the Elster.

At 8 a.m. on October 19th Napoleon left Leipzig, after a difficult meeting with the King of Saxony, described by Graf von Hochberg as an "animated conversation." Shortly afterward, disaster struck, when a frightened corporal left in charge of the demolition unit for the bridge blew the charges while the bridge was crowded with men and equipment, and while 30,000 troops were still trapped in Leipzig. In his memoirs Baron de Marbot recounted hearing "the disastrous news of the destruction of the Lindenau bridge. The army had lost by this nearly all its artillery; half the troops were left as prisoners, and thousands of our wounded comrades handed over to the outrage of the hostile soldiery, hounded on by its infamous officers to the slaughter . . ." The fighting in Leipzig, where the walls and gates were still defended by troops hoping to cover the retreat of the French army, would be intense and brutal.

At Leipzig's northern Halle Gate there was more bitter Polish–Russian conflict. When Russian sappers broke into a house occupied by Polish defenders, a Prussian staff officer named Nostitz was sent "to prevent a massacre and to order the Russian soldiers, in his name, to spare any of the enemy who laid down his weapon." When he suggested to the Polish commander that he should surrender he was answered in no uncertain terms: "I will never surrender to a Russian!' he shouted. "Get out or I will shoot you!' The enraged Russians stormed up the stairs and into the upper floor. After desperate hand-to-hand fighting they bayoneted all the enemy.

A Major Friccius recorded French defenders being thrown out of the upper windows of houses as "terrible hand-to-hand fights took place." He described the fighting for one of the inner city gates as "A dreadful melee . . . a real slaughter . . . Suddenly a force of Frenchmen, with 8 to 10 officers at their head, burst out of the churchyard gate and attacked us in the right flank . . . It seemed that we were lost again. But they had seen the dreadful slaughter that had just taken place and the same panic that had paralyzed their comrades now seemed to grip them. Instead of attacking us, the officers handed me their swords! What a scene!"

MONUMENTAL WARRIORS
A detail of the memorial of the Battle of the Nations at Leipzig.

© InavanHateren | Shutterstock.com

Things became desperate for those French now trapped in Leipzig. Marbot describes how he could hear "the despairing cries of the unhappy French, who, unable to retreat, and without cartridges, were being hunted from street to street, and butchered in a cowardly manner by Prussians, Badeners, and Saxons." Thousands of Frenchmen tried to swim the Elster under fire, among them the unfortunate Marshal Poniatowski. Leading a last counterattack, he had received a bayonet thrust in the chest, while one horse had drowned under him as he crossed the Pleisse. Refusing the chance to surrender, and already weakened by loss of blood, he now tried to cross the Elster but was wounded several more times by snipers and slipped from his horse just a few yards short of the other bank.

Leipzig was a disaster for Napoleon. "The Great Colossus fell like an oak tree in a storm," claimed Blücher. By the end of the battle, Napoleon had lost over 70,000 men, over 300 guns, and vast quantities of materiel. The allies had suffered around 54,000 casualties. Napoleon's first words on entering the Senate in Paris were, "A year ago all Europe marched with us—today all Europe marches against us." Within the year he would be deposed and exiled.

© Public domain

MAYFLY MARSHAL
Poniatowski's last charge: the Polish prince was killed just a few days after being made a Marshal of France.

BATTLE

High casualty rate

Catastrophic defeat

Pyrrhic victory

Tactical blunder

Appalling conditions

THEY DIED LIKE MEN: ALAMO

1836

Antagonists: Texan volunteers under Lt. Col. William B. Travis vs. Mexican "Centralist" Army of President Antonio López de Santa Anna

Casualties: Texans: ca. 257 dead; Mexicans (victors): ca. 600 dead and injured

. . . [T]hey died like men, and posterity will do them justice.

Benjamin Briggs Goodrich, whose brother John fell at the Alamo

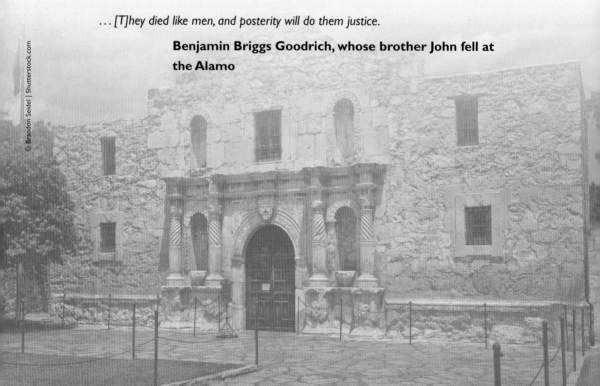

© Brandon Seidel | Shutterstock.com

"Remember the Alamo!" has become the traditional cry of Texans going into battle since the defenders of an old mission fort near San Antonio were overwhelmed by a vastly superior force of Mexicans. Heroic last stand or pointless suicide, there is no doubt that the defenders were brave and fought to the last man, inflicting casualties of at least two to one despite being vastly outgunned and outnumbered.

The territory of Texas was originally part of Mexico but its inhabitants revolted against the so-called "Centralist" rule of the Mexican president and commander-in-chief, Antonio López de Santa Anna, widely perceived as a despot infringing the God-given liberties of Americans. The old mission fort of San Antonio de Valero, known as the Alamo (from the Spanish for "poplar") since its occupation by Spanish troops in the early 1800s, held potential strategic value as it guarded the Old San Antonio Road from Mexico into Texas. In 1835 the fort was seized by troops of the Federalist Army of Texas, known as Texans, a force composed of American immigrants to Texas, Tejanos (Mexican Texans), and American volunteers. Although most of this force went home after capturing the Alamo, a small force remained in place under the command of James Clinton Neill. He viewed the role of the Alamo as a frontier picket for Texan territory, able to give vital advance notice of a Centralist invasion, and perhaps to buy time for Texas to prepare.

TORPID AND DEFENSELESS

Unfortunately for Neill, he had little to work with. His force consisted mostly of volunteers freshly arrived from North America, some of whom had been in Texas for less than a week. Although his chief engineer, Major Green Jameson, had boasted to Sam Houston (commander-in-chief of Texan forces) that he had set up the fort's cannons so well that its defenders could "whip 10 to 1 with our artillery," Neill was less optimistic. The men were in a "torpid, defenseless condition," he wrote on January 14th, 1836; "unless we are reinforced and victualled, we must become an easy prey to the enemy, in case of an attack."

Houston asked the head of the provisional Texan government, Governor Henry Smith, for permission to abandon the Alamo, but the energy and passion of Neill convinced Smith that the fort was worth defending. Neill's eloquent speeches and hard work in preparing the defenses of the fort inspired great zeal in his men, including a party of volunteers that had arrived on January 19th, led by Colonel James Bowie, an adventurer and noted knife expert. "I cannot eulogize the conduct & character of Col. Neill too highly," Bowie wrote to Smith. "No other man in the army could have kept men at this post, under the neglect they have experienced." Bowie and Neill vowed to "die in these ditches" rather than surrender the Alamo.

REPROACHFUL BONES

However, it was not Neill's fate to defend the Alamo. His continual pleas for reinforcements were finally answered by the despatch of a tiny company of just 30 cavalrymen under the command of Lt. Col. William B. Travis. Travis was reluctant to take the commission and even threatened to resign, but eventually followed orders, arriving on February 3rd. Five days later a party of American volunteers under famous frontiersman and former congressman Davy Crockett walked into the Alamo.

On February 14th, word reached Neill of a grave family illness and he left the fort. In his absence there was friction between the two remaining senior officers, Travis and Bowie. As a regular army officer, Travis was nominally superior, but they eventually agreed to split the command, with Travis retaining authority over his volunteers. Neill hoped to return within three weeks, and it was generally believed that although Santa Anna had mobilized an army, he would not threaten them until mid-March. To Travis's horror, the Centralist army arrived on February 23rd. Travis scribbled a message to the provisional government: "The enemy in large force is in sight. We want men and provisions. Send them to us. We have 150 men and are determined to defend the garrison to the last." When Santa Anna sent a courier demanding their surrender, Travis answered with a cannonball. Yet for all his bravado, there was little chance of the undermanned and poorly equipped fort holding out against the artillery of the besieging force. The following day Travis found himself in sole command when Bowie was struck down with a mystery illness described as "hasty consumption."

The Mexicans began shelling the fort, and as the siege wore on Travis became increasingly desperate for the provisional government of Texas, at that very moment meeting in convention, to send him reinforcements. On February 24th he wrote an open letter to the "people of Texas & all Americans in the world," pledging to "never surrender or retreat" and swearing "Victory or Death," yet also pleading, "in the name of Liberty, of patriotism & everything dear to the American character, come to our aid, with all dispatch." A small party of rangers arrived on March 1st but it was apparent that the politicos were too busy squabbling to send aid. Travis wrote to a friend: "If my countrymen do not rally to my relief, I am determined to perish in the defense of this place, and my bones shall reproach my country for her neglect."

The siege wore on for twelve days and the situation looked bleak for the Alamo. The walls were crumbling under the Mexican cannonade, it was apparent that relief would not be forthcoming and soon the defenders would be starved out. Yet on March 5th, despite the disbelieving objections of his senior officers, Santa Anna ordered a full-frontal assault on the fort. The next morning at 5 a.m. around 1,800 Mexicans equipped with ladders stormed the walls from all four sides simultaneously. Their advance was momentarily checked by a fearful blast of grapeshot and rifle fire, but they re-formed and came on once more. A vivid if potentially occasionally fanciful account was later garnered by William Fairfax Gray in an interview with "Joe," Travis's slave and one of the few people to survive the siege. According to Gray's record of the interview:

"Travis ran across the Alamo and mounted the wall, and called out to his men, 'Come on boys, the Mexicans are upon us, and we'll give them Hell.' He discharged his gun; so did Joe. In an instant Travis was shot down . . . On the third attempt the [Mexicans] succeeded in mounting the walls, and then poured over like sheep. The battle became a melee. Every man fought for his own hand, as best he might, with butts of guns, pistols, knives, etc. As Travis sat wounded on the ground General Mora, who was passing him, made a blow at him with his sword, which Travis struck up, and ran his assailant through the body, and both died on the same spot."

The defenders retreated to the barracks and vicious hand-to-hand fighting without quarter swallowed them up. According to Joe, Bowie "fired through the door of his room, from his sick bed. He was found dead and mutilated where he lay. Crockett and a few of his friends were found together, with twenty-four of the enemy dead around them." A last stand in the chapel ended when the Mexicans

THE MEXICANS ARE UPON US

JIM BOWIE
Texan folk hero Bowie was an adventurer and brawler before dying in the service of the Texan Federalists.

© Public domain

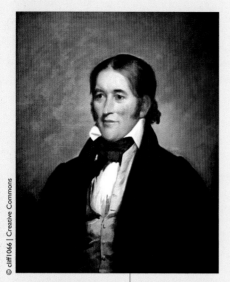

DAVY CROCKETT
The Tennessee-born frontiersman was known as the "King of the Wild Frontier."

blew off the doors with a cannon. The battle had lasted just 90 minutes.

Benjamin Briggs Goodrich, whose brother John was among the dead, reports that seven men survived and were brought to Santa Anna, who had them summarily executed. Slaves and female survivors were escorted out of the ruins, and some were set free. The American dead—possibly numbering as many as 257—were heaped up and burned. Mexican casualties were double this number.

There is no clear consensus on the military value of this heroic last stand. The popular belief, as related in the classic 1960 John Wayne film, that the defense bought time for Houston to raise an army, is fictional. Houston was involved in the Texan Republican Convention while the siege was underway. But the defense did delay Santa Anna's invasion of Texas, during which time the Convention declared independence and drafted a constitution, and without question it provided a lasting and potent symbol of the defense of liberty in the face of despotism akin to the Spartan stand at Thermopylae (see pages 10–16). Benjamin Briggs Goodrich, for instance, wrote proudly that Texan forces would gain revenge on Santa Anna: "We will meet him and teach the unprincipled scoundrel that freemen can never be conquered by the hirling [sic] soldiery of a military despot." Goodrich's boast was made good on April 21st, when Sam Houston's army utterly defeated the Mexicans at San Jacinto and Santa Anna was discovered, dirty and wet, hiding in the grass.

RETREAT FROM KABUL: GANDAMAK

1842

BATTLE

High casualty rate

Catastrophic defeat

Pyrrhic victory

Tactical blunder

Appalling conditions

Antagonists: British and Indian troops and camp followers under General Elphinstone vs. Afghan Ghilzai tribesmen under Akbar Khan and others

Casualties: British and Indian: ca. 16,500; Afghan (victors): unknown

... [A] most blind confidence, totally unwarranted, brought about the danger, and ... imbecility, unprecedented, completed the catastrophe.

Captain Julius Brockman Backhouse, Jalalabad, January 20th, 1842

The battle of Gandamak was the bloody, desperate, fatal last act of the retreat from Kabul of the British Army, one of the most ignominious and chastening episodes in British imperial history. It was the culmination of a long series of bad decisions, the result of incompetence, dithering, and arrogance on a monumental scale.

THE RUSSIANS ARE COMING

By the mid-18th century the extension of British control over India combined with the relentless advance of the Russian empire into Asia meant that Afghanistan was becoming a buffer state between the two rival empires. Since the fall of Napoleon, Russia had replaced France as the bogeyman for the British and there was disproportionate fear that Russian influence over the Afghans would open the way for an invasion of the subcontinent. Yet hamfisted handling of diplomatic relations with the ruler of Afghanistan, Emir Dost Mohammed, led him to entertain the Russians, which in turn convinced Lord Auckland, the British governor general of India, to engineer an excuse to invade Afghanistan and replace Dost Mohammed with an unpopular former ruler, Shah Shuja. In August 1839 a powerful army of British and Indian troops took Kabul and installed Shah Shuja; Dost Mohammed fled the country.

Although this was just the start of the First Anglo-Afghan War, the British naïvely thought it was over and that the country was secure. Many troops were withdrawn, and those remaining moved out of their secure fortress and into much less secure cantonments. Meanwhile, officers sent for their wives and families and attempted to replicate their life in India, even building a racecourse. One of the top political officers, Sir Alexander Burnes, was so complacent about the situation that he lived outside the cantonments in a house in Kabul. In fact, Shah Shuja was unpopular and resentment was building across Afghanistan and within Kabul itself, while the British severely weakened their own position by withdrawing yet more men and replacing the commander of British forces with the elderly and incompetent General William Elphinstone.

In November 1841 a riot in Kabul saw Burnes's house surrounded, and Burnes and others were murdered by the mob. Elphinstone, incapable of decisive action beyond blocking the initiative of junior officers, mounted no response, which emboldened the local emirs. Their attitude toward the British was further hardened by the arrival of the son of Dost Mohammed, Akbar Khan, to take charge of the Afghan revolt. Khan lured the head of the British delegation, Sir William McNaghten, to supposed peace talks on December 23rd, and allegedly murdered him with his own hands. Now desperate, the British agreed to leave the cantonments and march across the snowy mountain passes to Jalalabad, about 90 miles (145 kilometers) away. Along with the 4,500 troops (mainly Indian sepoys with British officers, although there was one British regiment, the 44th Foot), there were around 12,000 camp followers including the wives and children of many of the troops.

Khan had promised them safe conduct and taken a number of hostages, yet from the moment they left their quarters on January 6th, 1842, the British column was fired upon. Conditions were atrocious, and the freezing cold immediately began to take its toll. According to the account of Dr. William Brydon, who survived the ordeal, "Though [the first day's] March was not more than 5 miles [8 kilometers], a great number of women and children perished in the snow, which was about 6 inches deep."

LAST STAND
William Barnes Wollen's celebrated painting showing the last stand of the 44th Foot at Gandamak.

The next day Akbar Khan arrived, claiming that he was there to protect the column against further attacks. Extorting money and further concessions and hostages, he forced the column to camp early. By the next morning most of the soldiers were too cold to fight, yet as they made their way through the Khoord–Kabul pass Ghilzai tribesmen launched attacks from the heights all around. In an article titled "The English in Afghanistan," published just six months after the events, the Boston-based *North American Review* described what happened: "the Caboul forces commenced their retreat through the dismal pass, destined to be their grave. On the third day they were attacked by the mountaineers from all points, and a fearful slaughter ensued . . ."

The British 44th Foot fought a rearguard action as the column painfully inched through the pass, but over 3,000 casualties were left behind. The next day Akbar reappeared and demanded more hostages. Ironically, to be taken hostage was by far the best outcome—Akbar treated the hostages with great courtesy and almost all of them survived. On January 11th he demanded yet more, insisting that General Elphinstone and his next in command surrender themselves. But still the firing continued. According to one version, Akbar Khan was alternately ordering his men "Don't kill them," in Persian (which some of the British officers could understand) while telling them in Pashtun: "Shoot them!"

AWFUL SCENES

The retreat neared its terrible climax. According to Brydon:

"About an hour after dark an order was given to march, owing (I believe) to a note being received from General Elphinstone telling us to push on at all hazards, as treachery was suspected: owing to this unexpected move on our part, we found the abattis [a woven screen erected to block the way], and other impediments which had been thrown across the Jigdalak Pass, undefended by the Enemy, who, nevertheless, pressed upon our Rear, and cut up great numbers. The confusion now was terrible; all discipline was at an end . . ."

The account in the *North American Review* is even more graphic: "The troops kept on, and awful scenes ensued. Without food, mangled, and cut to pieces, each one caring only for himself, all subordination had fled; and the soldiers of the forty-fourth English regiment are reported to have knocked down their officers with the butts of their muskets."

AKBAR, THE KABUL EMIR
Akbar Khan, leader of the Kabul emirs and son of Dost Mohammad.

The British managed to knock a hole through the thorn abattis barricade with one of their last remaining guns, and some of the soldiers were able to press through. A group of six officers on horseback broke out toward Jalalabad, while the 44th Foot prepared to make a last stand on a hill near the village of Gandamak. Here, on January 13th, about 45 soldiers and 20 officers, almost out of food and ammunition, were surrounded. Hill tribesmen approached, feigning friendship and offering the chance to surrender. According to legend one British sergeant replied "Not bloody likely!" They were cut down almost to a man.

Of the six officers who broke out on horseback, only one made it to Jalalabad. The British garrison, awaiting the army of Kabul, was astonished to see one ragged figure approaching on an exhausted horse. It was Dr. Brydon, frozen, hungry, and severely wounded. Asked where the army was, he is said to have replied, "I am the army."

In fact, he was not the sole survivor, as a handful of others drifted into Jalalabad over the next few days and the hostages taken by Akbar were eventually returned or rescued.

A punitive British expedition was mounted and Kabul was retaken, but Shah Shuja was murdered in March and Dost Mohammed returned to the throne. The retreat from Kabul and the last stand of the 44th at Gandamak scarred the British imperial psyche and badly damaged the reputation of the British in India. In an extraordinary coda, British diplomat Sir Martin Ewans claims that in the 1920s a British missionnary in Kabul was introduced to two elderly women who had supposedly been on the retreat as British babies, and had been taken and raised by Afghans.

BATTLE

High casualty rate

Catastrophic defeat

Pyrrhic victory

Tactical blunder

Appalling conditions

INTO THE VALLEY OF DEATH: BALACLAVA
1854

Antagonists: British, French, and Turkish troops under Lord Raglan, including cavalry division under Lord Lucan, consisting of Heavy Brigade under Sir James Scarlett and Light Brigade under Lord Cardigan vs. Imperial Russian Army under General Liprandi

Casualties: British: ca. 400; Russian (victors): unknown

At the distance of 1,200 yards the whole line of the enemy belched forth, from thirty iron mouths, a flood of smoke and flame, through which hissed the deadly balls. Their flight was marked by instant gaps in our ranks, by dead men and horses, by steeds flying wounded or riderless across the plain.

William Russell Howard, *Times* correspondent

The Battle of Balaclava was a relatively minor engagement in the Crimean War between the British, French, and Ottoman Turks, and Russia. It resulted in a technical defeat for the British, yet it has become one of the most celebrated battles of all time, thanks to three famous incidents: the Charge of the Heavy Brigade; the Thin Red Line of the 93rd Highlanders; and the infamous Charge of the Light Brigade.

THE ROAD TO SEVASTOPOL

The Crimean War had been triggered by Russian encroachment on Ottoman Turkish territory, which was opposed by the British and French, who feared the balance of power would be tipped. In September 1854 an allied expeditionary force landed on the Crimean Peninsula and laid siege to the port of Sevastopol. The British force relied on a vulnerable line of supply running from the small port of Balaclava along the Woronzoff Road, and there was great alarm at the prospect that a Russian army under Prince Menshikov would sweep down and take Balaclava. Turkish forces had been sent to prepare fortifications along the strategically important Causeway Heights ridge, but their redoubts were poorly constructed.

RUSSIAN BEAR
Prince Aleksandr Menshikov, commander-in-chief of Russian forces for most of the Crimean War.

© Public domain

On October 25th, Menshikov sent an army under his deputy General Liprandi, to take Balaclava. The battlefield upon which they advanced from the east comprised, roughly speaking, two parallel valleys running east–west, the North and South Valleys, separated by the Causeway Heights. The North Valley was bounded on the north by the Fedioukine Hills. Balaclava lay to the south of the bottom end of the South Valley. The commander-in-chief of the British force, Lord Raglan, had an excellent view of the unfolding engagement from his position to the west, high on the Sapoune Ridge; his commanders in the field, on lower ground, could not see much past their own valleys and had no such appreciation of the overall situation.

Just a few British units stood between the Russian army and Balaclava: the Heavy and Light Brigades of Lord Lucan's cavalry division, and the 93rd Highlanders infantry regiment. The Russians installed cannon and troops in a strong position at the head of the North Valley and along the Fedioukine Hills, and quickly overwhelmed the Turks defending the redoubts on the Causeway Heights, giving them strong positions on three

HEAVY HORSE
The Heavy Brigade in action at Balaclava.

sides of the northern valley. As 3,000 Russian cavalry moved down from the Causeway Heights into the South Valley, they were met by the Heavy Brigade, numbering just 900. With desperate bravery, Major General Sir James Scarlett led his brigade in a charge against the Russians. Scarlett, his aide de camp Lieutenant Alick Elliot, and two others were so far in advance of the other troopers that the four of them initially took on the Russians on their own. Scarlett was wounded five times and Elliot fourteen.

The melee was intense, and the Russians threatened to envelop the Heavy Brigade until more British regiments slammed into their flank. Edward Hamley of the Royal Artillery was present at the battle and later wrote one of the definitive accounts. He describes how, "almost as it seemed in a moment, and simultaneously—the whole Russian mass gave way, and fled, at speed and in disorder, beyond the hill, vanishing behind the slope some four or five minutes after they had first swept over it." Lord Raglan sent Scarlett a message: "Well done."

Four squadrons of Russian cavalry had already detached from the main body and were bearing down on Balaclava, which lay apparently unprotected. In fact, hidden from view were the 93rd Highlanders. At the last minute they stepped out and formed what William Russell Howard, a correspondent for the London *Times*, famously described as a "thin red line tipped with steel" (although he originally used the word "streak"). They fired one or possibly two volleys, which was enough to send the Russians scurrying away.

WHAT AN OPPORTUNITY

Meanwhile, the Russian cavalry, turned by the Heavy Brigade, streamed back over the Causeway Heights and up the North Valley. To the watching Raglan and his staff it seemed like the perfect chance for Lord Cardigan, commanding the Light Brigade camped at the western end of the North Valley, to strike them in the flank and complete the rout. One of Cardigan's officers, Captain Morris of the 17th Lancers, thought so too, yet Cardigan refused to attack. Morris reportedly struck his thigh and lamented, "What an opportunity we have missed." Cardigan claimed that Lord Lucan had specifically told him not engage.

Many of the troopers in the Light Brigade shared his frustration — they had yet to see active combat in the campaign. This was due to the specific command of Lord Raglan, but the cavalry commander Lord Lucan had unfairly taken the blame, lampooned as Lord "Look-On." This was the background to what happened next.

From his position on the Sapoune Ridge, Raglan could see that the Russians were preparing to hitch up the guns they had captured on the Causeway Ridge and drag them off. Since they counted as trophies of war it was imperative to stop them, so he had General Airey draft to Lucan an order now notorious for being too vague: "Lord Raglan wishes the cavalry to advance rapidly to the front, and try to prevent the enemy carrying away the guns. Troop of horse artillery may accompany. French cavalry is on your left. Immediate."

© Public domain

To compound their error, Raglan and Airey entrusted the order to Airey's aide de camp, Captain Lewis Nolan of the 15th Hussars, described by Hamley as "the author of a book on cavalry tactics, in which faith in the power of that arm is carried to an extreme." Nolan was impetuous and his blood was boiling at the failure of the Light Brigade to tackle the Russian cavalry.

CALAMITOUS COMMAND
Baron Raglan, whose vague orders precipitated the Light Brigade debacle.

When Nolan delivered the order, Lucan, who could not see the activity on the Causeway Ridge, asked which enemy and which guns the order referred to. Nolan supposedly flung out his arm vaguely and insolently declared, "There is your enemy. There are your guns, My Lord." Unfortunately, he was gesturing toward the end of the North Valley, where the Russians were entrenched in force with their artillery battery.

Stung by Nolan's insolence, Lucan ordered the protesting Cardigan to charge up the valley at the Russian guns. So began the infamous Charge of the Light Brigade, "Cannon to right of them, Cannon to left of them, Cannon in front of them," as Alfred, Lord Tennyson wrote. Charging directly into the teeth of the Russian guns, and raked with fire from both sides, the brigade suffered murderous casualties both attacking and

INTO THE VALLEY OF DEATH

retreating, although they did overrun the Russian guns and scatter an infantry regiment. Lord Lucan initially led the Heavy Brigade in a following charge, but quickly halted as the toll of fire mounted. Captain Nolan had joined his friend Morris to take part in the charge, but quickly realized that a horrible misunderstanding had arisen. He tried to ride across the front of Cardigan to warn him, but was one of the first to be killed.

By the time the brigade reached the Russian guns at the head of the valley only half their number were still mounted and fighting. A timely intervention by French cavalry to clear the Fedioukine Hills helped to cover their retreat down the valley, but the remnants were attacked by Russian cavalry. According to William Russell Howard:

CANNON IN FRONT
The remnants of the Light Brigade reach the Russian guns after their suicidal charge.

" . . . they were breaking their way through the columns which enveloped them, when there took place an act of atrocity without parallel in the modem warfare of civilized nations. The Russian gunners, when the storm of cavalry passed, returned to their guns. They saw their own cavalry mingled with the troopers who had just ridden over them, and to the eternal disgrace of the Russian name the miscreants poured a murderous volley of grape and canister on the mass of struggling men and horses, mingling friend and foe in one common ruin. It was as much as our Heavy Cavalry Brigade could do to cover the retreat of the miserable remnants of that band of heroes as they returned to the place they had so lately quitted in all the pride of life."

Lord Cardigan was one of the first to make it back to British lines. On meeting Sir George Cathcart, he is reported to have said "I have lost my brigade." He was not far wrong. Of the 673 mounted men, only 195 were still able and on horseback, with 247 men killed and wounded and 475 horses killed. Their suicidal assault achieved nothing; the Russians were left in control of their positions and the guns were not retaken.

BIRTH OF THE RED CROSS: SOLFERINO

1859

BATTLE

High casualty rate

Catastrophic defeat

Pyrrhic victory

Tactical blunder

Appalling conditions

Antagonists: French and Piedmontese armies under Emperor Napoleon III and King Vittorio Emanuele II vs. Austrians under Emperor Franz Josef I

Casualties: Combined total of French and Piedmontese (victors) and Austrians: ca. 6,000 killed, 40,000 wounded

Here is a hand-to-hand struggle in all its horror and frightfulness; Austrians and Allies trampling each other under foot, killing one another on piles of bleeding corpses, felling their enemies with their rifle butts, crushing skulls, ripping bellies open with saber and bayonet . . .

Henri Dunant, *A Memoir of Solferino*

Solferino was a key battle in the struggle for the unification of Italy, yet it is more famous today for the horrors of the battlefield carnage, which inspired the creation of the Red Cross and the Geneva Conventions on warfare.

ABSOLUTELY NOTHING NECESSARY

After the defeat of Napoleon, Italy was once more divided between competing states and occupying "foreign powers." In the north the Austrians controlled Lombardy and Venetia, while its northwestern territories belonged to the House of Savoy, whose kingdom encompassed Sardinia and Piedmont, and could be known as either. One of Napoleon's most enduring legacies was the kindling of nationalist fervor in many parts of Europe, with Piedmont bearing the torch for a unified Italy. Sharing this sentiment was the ruler of France, Napoleon III (nephew of Bonaparte), who had been in his youth a member of the Carbonari, a quasi-Masonic secret society dedicated to a liberal nationalist agenda.

An initially disastrous effort by Piedmont to wrest control of Lombardy from Austria had led, in 1848, to the abdication of Carlo Alberto in favor of his son Victor Emmanuel II. Ten years later, however, Napoleon III signed a treaty with Piedmont promising to come to the latter's defense if Austria attacked. The plan was for Piedmont to provoke Austrian aggression, whereupon the allies would seize Lombardy for Piedmont, which in turn would give up Nice and Savoy to France. The Piedmontese began mobilizing and in March 1859 the Austrians obligingly threatened retaliation; the plan was in motion.

SOLFERINO SMOKES
Napoleon III directing operations at Solferino.

© Public domain

Unfortunately, the logistical and organizational abilities of the French military failed to live up to the grandiose ambitions of the French emperor. Napoleon III ordered his troops to cross the Alps into Piedmont without bothering to make sure they had any of the necessary equipment. When Marshal Canrobert, the general in charge of the expedition, arrived in Lyon on April 23rd to take command, he found the order to cross the frontier waiting for him. Alongside it was a telegram from the commander of his advance guard, complaining, "The troops of my division are without blankets. It is cold. We have neither tents nor water-bottles, nor camp equipment, nor cartridges. There is no hay. Absolutely nothing necessary for the organization of a division has been sent here." Canrobert in turn complained to the French War Ministry, only to receive a telegram from the Emperor himself: "I repeat my order that the frontier is to be crossed forthwith."

Fortunately for the allies, the Austrian army was equally poorly prepared for a modern war, adhering firmly to battlefield tactics from the Napoleonic War era. Of particular note at the Battle of Solferino was the poor reconnaissance and intelligence ability of the opposing armies (despite the novel availability of balloon reconnaissance and telegraphic communications). Neither side had any idea of the immediate presence of the other until the last minute.

© Public domain

BONAPARTE'S HEIR
Napoleon III was Bonaparte's nephew, becoming first president and last emperor of France.

The Austrian field commander, Field Marshal Ferenc Gyulai, initially enjoyed great superiority in numbers and should have taken the initiative by crushing the Piedmontese army before the French arrived. He failed to do so, instead falling back in the face of the allied advance and coming off worse in a fierce encounter at Magenta on June 4th. Despite their operational incompetence, the French were renowned as the finest soldiers in Europe for their sheer élan, their speed and aggression making up for their tactical shortcomings.

The Austrians retreated to Venetia where they had a well-established network of supporting fortresses. At this point the young Austrian emperor Franz Josef arrived, dismissed Gyulai and took charge. Instead of letting the allies attack his fortifications, a position of strength, the emperor was swayed by rash council and took the offensive. Two colossal armies— around 120,000 Austrians with 500 cannon versus around 130,000 French and Piedmontese, with 400 cannon—were on a collision course.

On the morning of June 24th both sides were moving to take up positions on high ground around the village of Solferino, home to the tall medieval tower known as the Spia d'Italia (the Spy of Italy). Neither side seemed aware of the proximity of the enemy, and the first that Napoleon III knew of the Austrian position was at 7 a.m. that morning when a messenger brought him the news as he was moving his headquarters. The Austrians had gained the heights first, and Napoleon decided that he would have to strike the center of their line in force to break it apart. This meant attacking Solferino, high ground that was by now well defended with dug-in troops, fortified houses, and artillery batteries.

The battle that ensued combined the medieval ferocity of hand-to-hand combat with the explosive violence of machine-age warfare. Present at the allied headquarters in the village of Castiglione was a Swiss businessman, Henry Dunant. His account, *A Memoir of Solferino*, graphically depicts the horror and carnage of the battle:

"The Austrians, from their vantage points on the hills, swept the French with artillery fire and rained on them a steady hail of shells, case- and grape-shot . . . Facing the thunder of these batteries, roaring and spitting forth death upon them, the French rushed forward like an opposing storm sweeping from the plain, to attack the positions they were determined to secure . . . Every mound, every height, every rocky crag, is the scene of a fight to the death; bodies lie in heaps on the hills and in the valleys . . . No quarter is given; it is a sheer butchery; a struggle between savage beasts, maddened with blood and fury. Even the wounded fight to the last gasp. When they have no weapon left, they seize their enemies by the throat and tear them with their teeth."

THE BIRTH OF THE RED CROSS

The sheer ferocity of the French assault eventually drove the Austrians back and after a day of desperate fighting in intense heat, the battle closed at around 5 p.m. with a terrific thunderstorm. The Austrians withdrew, and eventually agreed a peace deal with the French that more or less realized the allied war aims. Piedmont was significantly enlarged and the process by which Italy would be united under the House of Savoy was irreversibly set in motion.

For Dunant, however, the end of the battle simply marked the start of a new horror—the appalling inadequacy of provision for dealing with the estimated 40,000 casualties. The organizational and logistical deficiencies of the French military meant that not only were there no dedicated medical or ambulance units, let alone sufficient medical supplies, but that there was barely a drop of water or crumb of food for the exhausted and suffering soldiers. Dunant describes one horrific but typical scene:

" . . . the harassed cavalrymen returned to throw themselves on the ground and sleep all night without having taken any nourishment. As they made their way back, they again passed many wounded men crying out for water. A Tyrolean lying near their bivouac kept calling to them, but there was no water to give him. The next morning they found him dead, with his mouth full of earth and foam on his lips. His swollen face was green and black, and he had been writhing in fearful convulsions; the nails on his clenched hands were twisted backward."

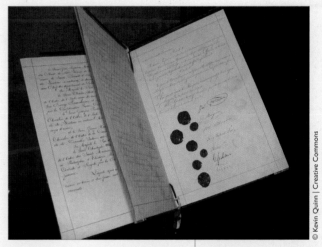

© Kevin Quinn | Creative Commons

Dunant organized volunteers in a relief effort at Castiglione, paying for supplies out of his own pocket, but the scenes he had witnessed stirred him to propose a much grander scheme, leading to the birth of the International Committee of the Red Cross. Eventually his proposals would lead to the Geneva Conventions on warfare.

GENEVA CONVENTIONS
The original Geneva Conventions, drawn up as a result of Dunant's campaigning.

BATTLE

High casualty rate

Catastrophic defeat

Pyrrhic victory

Tactical blunder

Appalling conditions

SLAUGHTER AT SHARPSBURG: ANTIETAM

1862

Antagonists: Confederate Army of Northern Virginia under General Robert E. Lee vs. Union Army of the Potomac under General George B. McClellan

Casualties: Confederate: 10,361; Union (victors): 12,401

A frightful struggle was now going on in the woods half a mile or so to our left. It appeared to us as if all the demons of hell had been unloosed—all the dogs of war unleashed to prey upon and rend each other; long volleys of musketry vomited their furious discharges of pestilential lead; the atmosphere was crowded by the exploding shells; baleful fires gleamed through the foliage, as if myriads of fireflies were flitting through the boughs, and there was a fringe of vivid, sparkling flame spurting out along the skirt of the forest, while the concussion of the cannon seemed to make the hills tremble and totter.

Alexander Hunter, *A High Private's Account of the Battle of Sharpsburg*

The single bloodiest day in American military history, the Battle of Antietam, also known as the Battle of Sharpsburg, saw Lee's Confederate Army of Northern Virginia achieve a draw against McClellan's Army of the Potomac, which was twice its size. In military terms it was technically a victory for the Union side, but it was also a day of tactical blunders, missed opportunities, and unnecessary carnage on their part. In political terms it proved to be arguably the most decisive battle of the American Civil War.

In the Civil War, the Confederate South was vastly outmatched in manpower and industrial output by the Unionist North. The Confederacy's only hope, as Robert E. Lee saw it, was to win a decisive victory on Union territory that would turn public opinion and force the US government to accept Confederate independence. Such a victory would have the added benefit of demonstrating to the vacillating European powers of Britain and France that the Confederacy could triumph and thus gain diplomatic recognition and possibly even economic and military intervention. This was the rationale behind Lee's Maryland campaign, which saw him cross into Union territory on September 5th "to give battle," but before doing so he believed he had time to pursue lesser strategic goals, dispersing his men to forage and sending a significant detachment of his limited forces to besiege the federal arsenal at Harper's Ferry.

Unfortunately for Lee, a copy of his orders fell into the hands of the Union general George B. McClellan. McClellan had been put in charge of the Army of the Potomac, which had been badly mauled by Confederate forces in the previous months, a mauling that Lee had assumed would buy him time. In fact, McClellan succeeded in reinvigorating his command with remarkable speed, and by September 7th his reinforced army was ready to take the field. McClellan, however, was an overly cautious commander lacking strategic and tactical initiative (his inaction would later lead Lincoln to describe the Army of the Potomac in sarcastic terms as "McClellan's bodyguard"). He failed to capitalize on the intercepted intelligence and didn't follow up the advantage gained from an encounter

MCCLELLAN'S BODYGUARD

BLOODY ANTIETAM
A late 19th-century lithograph showing the Battle of Antietam centered on the struggle for Burnside's Bridge.

BATTLE OF ANTIETAM.

© Public domain | Creative Commons

with one of Lee's divisions at South Mountain on September 14th. Lee was allowed time to gather most of his forces along the Sharpsburg Heights, a ridge of high land between the Potomac River and the Antietam Creek. On the 16th some of the men from Harper's Ferry arrived, although others were still on the way, and that same day Union forces arrived, but did not advance, giving Lee another day to organize. At this point Lee had fewer than 40,000 men and McClellan had over 80,000, but the Union general believed he was outnumbered thanks to Lee's skillful use of the complex terrain.

MILLER'S FIELD AND BURNSIDE'S BRIDGE

McClellan devised a plan of attack for the 17th, intending broadly that coordinated attacks on the Confederate flanks would draw in troops, whereupon a strong Union advance would break through the weakened center. In fact, he overextended his line, sent in his divisions piecemeal and the attacks were uncoordinated, allowing Lee to shift forces to meet threats individually. In particular, he didn't manage to take advantage of his numerical superiority, even failing to commit his reserves.

The bloodiest fighting occurred to the north on the Confederate left flank, where Major Generals Joseph Hooker, Joseph Mansfield, and John Sedgwick successively threw themselves at T. J. "Stonewall" Jackson's corps. Desperate fighting saw Miller's cornfield change hands fifteen times at the cost of 10,000 casualties to both sides. Union general Jacob D. Cox described what happened when Union forces attacked through the field:

" . . . the main line, which had come up on the left, leaped the fence at the south edge of the corn-field and charged across the open at the enemy in front. But the concentrated fire of artillery and musketry was more than they could bear. Men fell by scores and hundreds, and the thinned lines gave way and ran for the shelter of the corn."

Hooker's report on the battle graphically depicts the carnage inflicted on Confederate troops spotted in the cornfield, and blasted with grapeshot:

"In the time I am writing every stalk of corn in the northern and greater part of the field was cut as closely as could have been done with a knife, and the slain lay in rows precisely as they had stood in their ranks a few moments before . . . It was never my fortune to witness a more bloody, dismal battle-field."

Meanwhile, to the south Major General Ambrose E. Burnside should have crossed the Antietam Creek in force and outflanked the Confederates to the right, circling round behind Lee's headquarters in the town of Sharpsburg and cutting off the Confederate retreat. Had he succeeded, the Army of Northern Virginia would have been destroyed, but instead he allowed his entire corps of 12,000 men to be held up throughout the morning by a single brigade defending a narrow bridge (later named in his honor), and then halted for two hours once he was across. In the center there was a ferocious battle over a sunken lane aptly called Bloody Lane, where poorly coordinated frontal assaults by Union forces were repeatedly repulsed by outnumbered Confederates.

Eventually the weight of numbers began to tell, particularly on the Confederate right where Burnside was at last advancing, but then came a dramatic turn of events. Alexander Hunter, taken prisoner as one of only three survivors from his unit of 46 Confederate muskets, describes in his *Account of the Battle of Sharpsburg* how, as he was escorted to the Union rear, news reached him of a turn in the tide of the battle:

OLD STONEWALL COMES UP

"At last a prisoner, a wounded Rebel officer, was being supported back to the rear, and we asked him, and the reply came back; 'Stonewall Jackson has just gotten back from Harper's Ferry, those troops fighting the Yankees now are A. P. Hill's division . . . Well, we felt all right, if Old Stonewall was up, none need care about the result.'"

In fact, Jackson had been present at the battle from the start, but Hill's arrival swung the battle as he took Burnside in the flank and drove him back. The battle ended with the Confederates occupying their initial positions—the mass of Union dead seemed to have achieved nothing. For Hunter, reaching the Union rear, there was another surprise in store: the Union reserve—10,000 fresh troops—simply waiting around. "Had those men advanced early in the day, instead of being held back," he wrote, "it would have been a black day for the South, and the Yankees would have gained a glorious victory, for we had no reserves, and A. P. Hill

© Public domain | Library of Congress

PRESIDENT AND GENERALS
Lincoln visiting the Union generals at Antietam.

was miles away in the morning." Instead, the Unionists had suffered over 2,000 killed and 9,500 wounded, against Confederate losses of 1,500 dead and 9,000 wounded, missing or captured.

The next day McClellan was reinforced with two fresh divisions, but Lee withdrew to Virginia unhindered and was not pursued. Lincoln promptly removed McClellan from command, yet Lee's retreat allowed the Union to claim a victory and gave the president the political capital to make the Emancipation Proclamation. This in turn made it impossible for Britain, the leading abolitionist power, to come in on the Confederate side, and signaled Lincoln's intention to destroy utterly the social system of the South. America's future was now fixed.

BURNSIDE'S BRIDGE
A view of the troublesome bridge four years after the battle.

THE LAST FULL MEASURE OF DEVOTION: GETTYSBURG

1863

BATTLE

High casualty rate

Catastrophic defeat

Pyrrhic victory

Tactical blunder

Appalling conditions

Antagonists: Confederate Army of Northern Virginia under Robert E. Lee vs. Union Army of the Potomac under George Gordon Meade

Casualties: Confederate: 28,000; Union (victors): 23,000

On they came, up to the very mouths of the cannon, up the hill sides, along which were stone fences in all directions. Our riflemen lay behind them, and as the rebels played upon us at Fredericksburg, so we poured a sheet of flame into their faces as they came within range, and hundreds were piled up as quickly as grain would fall before the reaper's iron hand.

An account of Pickett's Charge from the *Philadelphia Inquirer*

Gettysburg was the bloodiest battle of the Civil War and sounded the death knell for Lee's hopes of gaining a decisive victory that would affect public and political opinion in the North, despite being messy and inconclusive.

THE THING BEGAN

Although Lee's Maryland campaign of 1862 had come to naught (see page 167), his resounding success at Chancellorsville in May 1863 convinced the Confederacy to back another invasion of Union territory. For once Lee enjoyed near parity in numbers with his Union opposition, the Army of the Potomac, with nearly 72,000 men against 94,000. In June Lee moved into Pennsylvania, shadowed by the Army of the Potomac under Joseph Hooker, who was replaced just three days before Gettysburg by Major General George Gordon Meade. The Confederates hoped that the Union army would attack them, since the war had shown that attacking was generally far more costly than defending; the impending battle would prove this true. A concise account by General E. P. Alexander, Chief Of Artillery under Confederate General James Longstreet, explains how, on July 1st, the battle started:

ROAD TO BATTLE
The Gettysburg Road, with recreated timber fortifications.

" . . . we considered the enemy very slow in moving upon us, and took our time everywhere to give him opportunities to attack, if he desired, and that the concentration which was ordered at Gettysburg [a major road junction that allowed Lee to concentrate his forces] was intended as an offer of battle to him. In making this concentration [Confederate General A. P.] Hill's corps unexpectedly came in collision with [Union Major General Joseph] Reynolds' corps, and the thing began. Reynolds' corps was not expected there, and our information of the enemy's movements was incomplete on account of the absence of all of the cavalry, or nearly all, with General [J. E. B.] Stuart [commander of Lee's cavalry], who, instead of being between us and the enemy, was on a raid around him."

This initial, unplanned encounter had enormous consequences. The Union forces were badly mauled and pushed out of Gettysburg, but this defeat proved the salvation of the Union army, which was forced back onto highly defensible positions running from two hills in the south named Big and

Little Round Top, north along the Cemetery Ridge to Cemetery Hill, and then hooking round to the east on Culp's Hill. Lee drew up his forces on facing ground and prepared to attack.

The second day of the battle proved decisive precisely because it ended as a stalemate. Either through poor planning or poor execution, Lee's attacks were uncharacteristically badly coordinated and were repulsed with heavy casualties. Despite the huge tactical blunder made by Union Major General Daniel Sickles, who advanced his corps out in front of the Union lines in an unsupported salient, and was duly massacred, the day ended without Lee having secured the victory. For the Confederates, with their limited supplies of manpower and materiel, occupying the weaker ground, this was a poor outcome. Alexander, for instance, argues that "the battle was lost by the delays and faults of detail in the execution of the second day's efforts."

The third day brought one of the most famous, controversial, and disastrous actions of the Civil War, Pickett's Charge. In an act of desperation, supported by vain hopes that the Union center was by now weakened and demoralized, Lee ordered Longstreet to launch his corps in a frontal assault on the Cemetery Ridge. Major General George Pickett was given the honor of leading the charge, and Alexander assembled 160 guns to fire off one of the largest artillery bombardments of the Civil War, which was met with a similarly ferocious Union response. According to a contemporary account in the *Baltimore Sun*: "Horses were shot down by scores, gun carriages were demolished, pieces dismounted, caissons exploded, whole batteries were swept away, and cannoniers and officers killed and wounded in numbers almost incredible."

Longstreet was reluctant to give the final go-ahead, recognizing that the charge was suicidal. "I don't want to make this charge," he complained to Alexander, "I don't believe it can succeed. I would stop Pickett now, but that General Lee has ordered it and expects it."

PICKETT'S CHARGE

HANCOCK'S DEFENSE
Union General Hancock under fire during the Confederate bombardment prior to Pickett's charge.

© Adam Cuerden

The attack went ahead, Pickett's column leading the way with another on each side.

Advancing across half a mile of open ground, the Confederate charge was rent by grapeshot and then blasted with continuous volleys of musket fire. The *Philadelphia Inquirer* described how "the dead were lying literally in heaps, many hit in all manner of degrees, from a clean shot through the head to bodies torn to pieces by exploding shells." The two supporting columns soon turned back, and just a fraction of Pickett's division reached the Union line. When the survivors stumbled back to their own lines, as many as 10,000 out of the 13,000 or so attackers had been cut down.

Lee retreated to a defensive position and waited another day, hoping that Meade would go on the offensive and expose the Union troops to the dangers of attack, but he did not take the bait. During the night of July 4th, in a heavy downpour, the Confederates withdrew toward Virginia, having lost 28,000 men to the Union's 23,000. Lee would never regain the strategic initiative, and coupled with simultaneous Union gains in Mississippi, Gettysburg marked the beginning of the end for the Confederacy.

© Public domain

GENERAL MEADE
George Meade was made commander of the Union Army of the Potomac just days before Gettysburg.

IN THE CHAMBER POT: SEDAN

1870

BATTLE

High casualty rate

Catastrophic defeat

Pyrrhic victory

Tactical blunder

Appalling conditions

Antagonists: Prussian Third and Meuse Armies led by Prussians, under Field Marshal Helmuth von Moltke vs. French Army of Châlons under Emperor Napoleon III, Marshal Patrice de Mac-Mahon, General Félix de Wimpffen, and General Auguste Ducrot

Casualties: Prussians (victors): 8,000; French: 17,000 casualties and 100,000 prisoners

There were heaped up bodies everywhere, yet one looked in vain for a single intact, undamaged corpse; the men had been mutilated by the fire ...

Sergeant Oskar Becher, Prussian 94th infantry

In the second half of the 19th century the Prussian chancellor Otto von Bismarck pursued an agenda of German unification. Having successfully defeated the Austrians, thanks to the military innovations of Helmuth von Moltke, head of the general staff, winning territory in northern Germany, Bismarck moved on to the next phase of his grand plan. The only way to unify all the remaining German states was through a war against a common enemy—the French. In July 1870 Bismarck successfully goaded the foolishly belligerent French under Napoleon III into declaring war. The Franco-Prussian War would shape the fate of Europe for the next hundred years, and its climactic battle was Sedan, a calamitous defeat for the French marked by inept and delusional command, suicidal bravery, and a foretaste of the horrors of industrialized warfare.

INTO THE MOUSETRAP

Although French soldiers were brave and capable, and equipped with an infantry rifle—the long-ranged, breech-loading "chassepot"—superior to the Prussian "needle-gun," they were badly led and poorly served by the same logistical and operational incompetence that marked all of the Second Empire's military adventures (see Solferino, pages 161–5). Most significantly, the French artillery establishment had fatally passed up the chance to adopt the most up-to-date artillery available, so that the Prussians with their modern breech-loading steel cannon outranged and outgunned their French counterparts.

THE KAISER
Thanks in part to Prussian success at Sedan, Wilhelm I of Prussia became first Kaiser of Germany.

© Public domain

These factors set the pattern for the Franco-Prussian War—stout defense by French infantry dug into trenches and armed with chassepot rifles inflicted heavy casualties on Prussian assaults, but superior Prussian staff work and artillery drove back the French at a series of battles. By mid-August one French army was besieged in the fortress town of Metz, while another, the Army of Châlons, under Marshal Patrice de Mac-Mahon, was clumsily maneuvering northeast, intending to relieve them. Moltke sent the Prussian Third and Meuse Armies to intercept Mac-Mahon, who by this time was saddled with the Emperor Napoleon III himself.

On August 30th the Meuse Army defeated the French at Beaumont, and Mac-Mahon pulled back to

Sedan to regroup. It was a poor decision. Although a fortress town, Sedan was ringed by high ground, which would make the superior Prussian artillery the decisive factor. "Now we have them in the mousetrap," Moltke crowed. Moltke launched the Prussian assault on September 1st, intending to pin the French in place while he deployed troops to encircle Sedan and achieve his favorite strategy, the *Kesselschlacht*, or "pocket battle" (i.e. envelopment), like Hannibal at Cannae (see pages 26–32). Mac-Mahon was wounded early in the morning and appointed Auguste-Alexandre Ducrot as his replacement. With the Prussian bombardment pulverizing his men, Ducrot realized the gravity of the situation, famously remarking, "We are in the chamber pot and about to be shat upon." He ordered a withdrawal to the west.

Unfortunately for the French, Ducrot was promptly relieved of his command by the arrival of General Félix de Wimpffen, who seemed out of touch with reality. Wimpffen countermanded the retreat, leaving the French in disarray, and the Prussian artillery continued to pound them, having completed the encirclement of Sedan by midday. With suicidal bravery the French cavalry, led by the Chasseurs d'Afrique, made repeated charges in an attempt to break out, but in the face of rapid-firing breech-loading rifles and cannon, the age of the cavalry charge was over.

The first charge was driven back with fearful casualties, a Prussian observer noting the terrible damage inflicted by the heavy guns: "One looked in vain for a single intact, undamaged corpse; the men had been mutilated by the fire . . ." Yet when Ducrot sought out General de Gallifet, the new commander of the Chasseurs (the previous one having been killed), to ask whether they could try again, Gallifet replied cheerfully, "As often as you like, *mon général*, so long as there's one of us left." Watching from a nearby height, the Prussian king Wilhelm famously admired the courage of the doomed Chasseurs, exclaiming "Ah! *Les braves gens*!" ("The brave men!").

The battle was clearly lost and Napoleon III ordered his generals to surrender, yet Wimpffen seemed delusional. "Your Majesty may be quite at ease," he wrote in a note to the emperor, "within two hours I shall have driven your enemies into the Meuse." A last breakout attempt failed with massive casualties, and in the late afternoon Napoleon personally ordered Wimpffen to surrender, riding out himself to meet the Prussian king, only for Bismarck to intercept him on the road.

UNDER THE THUNDERBOLT

The French had already suffered 17,000 casualties and had 20,000 men taken prisoner, for the loss of just 8,000 Prussians. Now the remaining 100,000 and all their guns and materiel were captured. Napoleon went into exile and the Second Empire was replaced by the Third Republic. "From time to time in History," wrote Victor Hugo in *L'Année Terrible*, "Divine logic makes an onslaught. Sedan is one of those onslaughts. Thus on the 1st of September, at five o'clock in the morning, the world woke under the sun, and the French army under the thunderbolt."

GERMAN OFFENSIVE, AUGUST–SEPTEMBER 1870

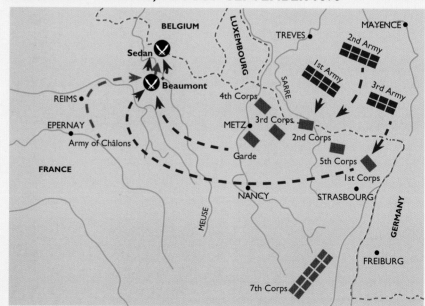

- German forces
- French forces
- **Battle**
- --- Border

OUT-MANEUVERED
German forces crossed the Sarre and forced the French to hole up in Metz. The 3rd Army was dispatched to intercept the French Army of Châlons to the west, defeating it at Beaumont. Mac-Mahon fell back to Sedan where the French were surrounded and trapped.

CUSTER'S LAST STAND: LITTLE BIGHORN

1876

BATTLE

High casualty rate

Catastrophic defeat

Pyrrhic victory

Tactical blunder

Appalling conditions

Antagonists: US 7th Cavalry under Lieutenant Colonel George Custer vs. Lakota Sioux, Northern Cheyenne, and Arapaho warriors under Sitting Bull and Crazy Horse

Casualties: US Cavalry: 268 dead (including Custer's entire command) and 55 wounded; Native Americans (victors): ca. 40–140

The battleground looked like a slaughter pen, as it really was, being in a narrow ravine. The dead were much mutilated.

Account of Muggins Taylor, US Army scout, from the *Cincinnati Daily Gazette*, July 6th, 1876

One of the most famous battles in history was an inglorious affair in which five companies of US cavalry were led to a gruesome death for no clear reason, as part of an expeditionary force enforcing a brutal land grab in clear violation of a treaty. Even at the time the incident was seen as controversial. An editorial of July 6th, 1876, in the *Boston Evening Journal* described how "Gen. Custer directly and without a particle of excuse, so far as we now know, charged into the very jaws of destruction . . ."

STRONG AS WE WERE

Little Bighorn is the most celebrated of the series of battles and skirmishes comprising the Plains Indian Wars, in which the nomadic culture of the horse and buffalo peoples of the Great Plains was crushed by the encroaching agricultural and industrial culture of the United States. The Indians were corralled in reservations and forced to give up their nomadic lifestyle, but even concession to imposed treaties gave them little protection. In 1868 the Lokata Sioux signed a treaty confining them to a reservation in the west of present-day South Dakota, but many bands of Lakota, Cheyenne, and other peoples refused to be party to it; their continued nomadic roaming put them into conflict with the US authorities. This conflict escalated when an 1874 expedition led by Lieutenant Colonel George Custer discovered gold in the Black Hills, sacred to the Lakota and located within the reservation. The Indians were ordered to report to the reservation by January 1876, so that the Black Hills could be occupied and annexed, but the order was ignored. Three expeditionary forces were sent into southern Montana to locate and round up "hostiles."

DASHING BUT DISTURBED
General George Custer, recognized as a dashing cavalry officer but deemed unstable by his commanding officer.

In the rich hunting grounds around the Rosebud, Bighorn, and Yellowstone rivers, groups from several Indian nations came together to form roving bands or "villages" of several thousand individuals, especially around the time of the religious festival known as the sun dance. At a sun dance ceremony at Lame Deer, Montana, in early June, Lakota Sioux leader and holy man Sitting Bull received a vision of soldiers falling upside down into his village, which he interpreted to mean that his people would soon win a great victory. By late June around 8,000 Plains Indians, including around 1,800 warriors, were gathered in a village moving along the Little Bighorn

River. There were rumors of American soldiers approaching, but, as Low Dog, an Oglala Sioux, later recalled, "I did not think anyone would come and attack us, so strong as we were."

In fact, US forces were closing in on them. On June 21st over a thousand men had reached the junction of the Yellowstone and Rosebud to the northeast of the Indians, and the following day Custer's 7th Cavalry, nearly 500 strong, was detached from this force and sent up the Rosebud to swing round and catch the village from the south, while the rest of the troops approached from the north. Custer, a Confederate veteran of the Civil War, had a mixed reputation. According to the *Boston Evening Journal*:

"Gen. Custer was preeminently the embodiment of the phrase, 'a dashing cavalry officer.' His bravery was perfect, his energy was remarkable though not always sustained, and when under wise direction few officers were more effective and brilliant. But he was not well balanced, and Gen. Grant, whose judgement of army officers at least will never be questioned, deposed him from the chief command of the expedition against the Indians . . ."

By June 25th Custer had reached Wolf Mountain, and his scouts brought word of the large Indian village nearby. With apparently breathtaking arrogance Custer decided his meager force was up to the task of dealing with the village without the rest of the force from the north, and planned an attack. Perhaps he feared that the mobile Indian village would slip out of his grasp, or perhaps he did not want to share the glory. When the scouts brought word that the village had detected his presence, Custer acted still more rashly, dividing his forces without proper intelligence of the enemy. Three companies comprising 140 men under Major Marcus Reno were sent to cross the Little Bighorn and approach from the south to drive the Indians out of their camp, while he led the bulk of the force, 210 men, around to the north to catch the flushed-out "hostiles." A third force of 125 men under Captain Frederick Benteen was sent in via another angle.

The plan went disastrously wrong. Reno's approach met with fierce resistance and he was routed and sent packing back over the Little Bighorn

A DASHING CAVALRY OFFICER

© Public domain

INDIAN SCOUT
Photographic portrait of "Curley," a scout with Custer's 7th Cavalry.

with heavy casualties. Retreating up the bluffs he was met by Benteen, who had returned having encountered no hostiles. Together they set off to find Custer, whose last communication read: "Come on. Big Village. Be Quick." Following the sound of gunfire they saw the dust and smoke of a battle but were driven off by approaching warriors and besieged on a hilltop for nearly 36 hours. Finally, on the evening of June 26th, the village moved off to the south.

The next day the rest of the US forces arrived to find the naked and mutilated corpses of Custer's command strewn about the ridges to the east of the river. The scout Muggins Taylor reported that "Custer, his two brothers, nephew, and brother-in-law were all killed, and not one of his detachment escaped. Two hundred and seven men were buried in one place . . ." Archaeological evidence shows that the four companies of his command were defeated individually, with about 40–50 men surviving long enough to retreat to what is now called the Last Stand Site. Some tried to break out, but all were caught and killed. In all, the 7th Cavalry lost 268 men; Indian casualties are unknown, although estimates range from 40 to 140.

The news of the massacre shocked America and more troops were sent against the rebel Indians. Within the year most of the "hostiles" had surrendered and the Black Hills were taken by the US without compensation.

FINAL SHOT
A contemporary lithograph imagines Custer's heroic last stand.

GORDON THE HERO: KHARTOUM

1884–85

BATTLE

High casualty rate

Catastrophic defeat

Pyrrhic victory

Tactical blunder

Appalling conditions

Antagonists: Anglo-Egyptian garrison under Major General Charles Gordon vs. Mahdist "dervishes" under Muhammad Ahmad

Casualties: Anglo-Egyptians: 7,000; Mahdists (victors): unknown

December 14th, 1884: Now mark this: if the Expeditionary Force does not soon come, the town will fall; and I have done my best for the honor of our country. Goodbye.

Journal of Charles Gordon

The Siege of Khartoum was another of the great and grisly colonial adventures that enthralled the Victorian public. The defense of the city and its eventual fall just days before the arrival of the relief force made a hero out of the man leading the garrison, Charles Gordon, and brought down the government of William Gladstone. For the garrison itself there was little glory—just a drawn-out siege culminating in a massacre.

CHINESE GORDON TO THE RESCUE

In 1882 Britain took control of Egypt from its nominal Ottoman overlords, inheriting with it a brewing storm to the south, where the Sudan was in a ferment. Religious leader Muhammad Ahmad had declared himself to be the Mahdi (a prophesied Muslim redeemer), and was leading a holy war to take control of the territory. Tens of thousands of his followers, known to the Victorians as dervishes, occupied most of the Sudan by the end of 1882 and defeated British-led Egyptian armies sent against them the following year. The British government under Gladstone was unwilling to meet the expenses of involvement in a foreign adventure, and decided to evacuate the Egyptian presence at Khartoum, the Sudanese capital. To oversee the evacuation they turned to eminent Victorian troubleshooter and colonial adventurer, Charles Gordon.

VICTORIAN HERO
A Victorian imagining of the death struggle of General Gordon.

© Public domain | Library of Congress

Gordon had distinguished himself in service, in locations from Crimea to Uganda to India, but he was best known for his exploits as a military commander in China in the 1860s, earning him the popular nickname "Chinese Gordon." In 1873 he was appointed governor of a province in the far south of Sudan and won further fame mapping the area, opening up the course of the Nile as far as Uganda and fighting the slave trade.

An evangelical Christian who read only the Bible, he was noted for his ascetic lifestyle. In *Eminent Victorians*, Lytton Strachey describes him as "an English gentleman, an officer, a man of energy and action, a lover of danger and the audacities that defeat danger, a passionate creature . . . The easy luxuries of his class and station were unknown to him . . ." However, Gordon also had a fierce temper: "There were moments when his passion became utterly ungovernable; and the gentle soldier of God, who had spent the day in quoting texts . . . would slap the face of his Arab aide-de-camp in a sudden access of fury, or set upon his Alsatian servant and kick him till he screamed."

In 1884 Gordon was sent to Egypt, reappointed Governor General of Sudan, and sailed up the Nile, arriving in Khartoum on February 18th. He had available to him a few gunboats and a force of around 7,000 men of doubtful reliability. At once Gordon set about evacuating the thousands of Europeans and Egyptians in Khartoum, but he resisted orders to evacuate the entire garrison and abandon the city altogether, claiming that he had insufficient boats available. This may have been true, but it also seems likely that he had independently decided that the Mahdists had to be stopped in the Sudan or they would threaten all of Egypt. Perhaps he counted on popular sentiment to force the British government's hand and send him the reinforcements he continually demanded. Gladstone steadfastly refused.

In May the Mahdi arrived with around 50,000 men and laid siege to Khartoum. Gordon was now trapped, but he had prepared the city for a siege, boosting its fortifications and laying landmines of his own devising. He reckoned that he had supplies to last five months, and used his gunboats to raid for more. Meanwhile, his despatches stoked support back home; Gladstone's intransigence made him increasingly unpopular. Eventually, Queen Victoria herself intervened. "It is alarming," she wrote to Lord Hartington, the Secretary of State for War, "General Gordon is in danger; you are bound to try to save him . . ." Still, Gladstone resisted, finally agreeing to raise a relief force in August, after Lord Hartington threatened to resign.

VICTORIA IS ALARMED

The relief expedition under General Sir Garnet Wolseley, however, took time to organize. It was not dispatched until October and then advanced up the Nile with agonizing slowness. Gordon grew gloomy at his prospects and feared treachery; on December 14th a friend in Cairo received a letter saying, "Farewell. You will never hear from me again. I fear that there will be treachery in the garrison, and all will be over by Christmas."

In fact, he held on until January, while Wolseley attempted to increase his pace. On January 17th, 1885, the relief force defeated Mahdists at Abu Klea. At Khartoum the Mahdi was prompted into decisive action. On the night of January 25th–26th he launched an assault with 50,000 men; according to many sources the gates of the city were opened by the treachery Gordon feared. Swarming into the city, the Mahdists massacred the entire 7,000-strong garrison and around 4,000 of Khartoum's residents. Gordon, observing the invasion from his rooftop, is said to have changed into his uniform, armed himself, and gone out onto the street. Despite supposed orders from the Mahdi that he should not be harmed, he was quickly butchered and his head stuck on the end of a pike. The relief force arrived two days later, but with nothing to relieve, Wolseley ordered the city abandoned and returned to Cairo. The Mahdi would die later that year of typhus, but not until 1898 did the British regain control of the Sudan. Gordon passed into history as a Victorian hero, "Gordon of Khartoum," while Gladstone bore the brunt of public recriminations; his government fell in March 1885.

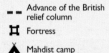

—— Advance of the British
relief column

☒ Fortress

▲ Mahdist camp

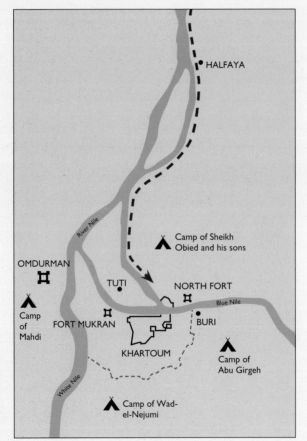

**UP THE NILE
WITHOUT A PADDLE**
Disposition of forces at
Khartoum, where Gordon
had precious few men and
boats to attempt to hold the
city and its outer defenses.

BEARS LED BY DONKEYS: TANNENBERG

1914

BATTLE

High casualty rate

Catastrophic defeat

Pyrrhic victory

Tactical blunder

Appalling conditions

Antagonists: Russian Second Army under Alexandr Samsonov vs. German Eighth Army under Paul von Hindenburg and Erich Ludendorff

Casualties: Russians: 30,000 dead, more than 130,000 prisoners; Germans (victors): 10,000–20,000

We had not merely to win a victory over Samsonof. We had to annihilate him.

General Paul von Hindenburg, *Summary of the Battle of Tannenberg*

The original Battle of Tannenberg was a catastrophic defeat for the Teutonic Knights at the hands of the Lithuanians and Poles in 1410. The Germans adopted this symbolic name to describe the immense victory they achieved against overwhelmingly more numerous Russian forces in 1914, in what was probably the greatest victory of World War I. For the Russians it was an appalling disaster which led to the utter destruction of 12 divisions, surrounded in a swamp and pounded mercilessly by artillery.

BAD BLOOD

The speed and success of the German advance in 1914 rang alarm bells among the Allies, with France begging Russia to waste no time in opening an Eastern Front. Accordingly, the Russian mobilization was hasty and botched, and although by August two colossal armies were advancing into German territory in East Prussia, they were hopelessly ill-equipped, badly trained, and poorly led. For instance, in 1914 the Russian army was short of a million modern rifles and a billion cartridges.

© Popperfoto | Getty Images

PRISON TRAIN
A German train loaded with Russian troops taken prisoner at Tannenberg.

The First Army under General Pavel Rennenkampf was to the north, while to the south General Alexandr Samsonov commanded the Second Army, made up of three corps totaling 12 divisions. Each army comprised about 400,000 men, setting some 800,000 in total against the sole German force defending the homeland from the east, the Eighth Army, which numbered 200,000 men, under Max von Prittwitz. Between the two Russian armies lay the Masurian Lakes, a scattering of lakes and swamps. The Russian plan was for Rennenkampf to engage the Germans, while Samsonov swung round to the south of the Lakes and surrounded the Germans—a classic double envelopment on a colossal scale, which would destroy the Eighth Army and open the way to Berlin.

There were a number of flaws with this plan. For one thing, Rennenkampf and Samsonov were supposedly bitter enemies, with bad blood between them dating back to the Russo-Japanese War of 1904–05. Apparently Rennenkampf had failed to support Samsonov's division when it was routed by the Japanese with massive casualties, and the story was that when the two men met at a railway station a few days later Samsonov slapped Rennenkampf in the face, triggering an all-out brawl. In fact, this tale, which was later claimed to have played a pivotal role in the battle, was an invention.

All too real, however, were the logistical and operational failings of the Russian Army, and above all the disastrous state of their communications. As early as August 18th, the Germans discovered from captured troops that the Russians used unencrypted, easily intercepted radio transmissions for sending orders. Almost from this point on the Germans had a better idea about the whereabouts and intentions of the Russian forces than their own commanders.

Nonetheless, first blood went to the Russians, when the Germans suffered partial defeat to the First Army at Gumbinnen on August 20th. Rennenkampf failed to press his advantage, however, and the main consequence of the battle was that von Prittwitz lost his nerve and called for the abandonment of East Prussia, which led to his replacement by retired General Paul von Hindenburg, who had spent much of the past few years planning for precisely this campaign. His chief of staff was to be the brilliant German general Erich von Ludendorff.

A DANGEROUS SCHEME

Hindenburg later recalled his staff's assessment of the situation, formulated with the aid of intercepted Russian signals: "The Russians were thus planning a concentric attack against the Eighth Army . . . What, indeed, could we do to meet this dangerous enemy scheme?" The answer was a scheme of their own, hatched in the main by one of von Prittwitz's staff officers, Max Hoffmann. Hoffmann's plan was daring and brilliant, calling for the concentration of all available German forces on the encirclement of Samsonov in the south, while leaving only a screen of cavalry as a simple ruse to prevent Rennenkampf being apprised of the situation. It was extremely risky, relying on the inertia of Rennenkampf, and making use of the network of railways in the area to facilitate rapid large-scale redeployment of forces from the north to the south. Hindenburg approved the plan—he knew that "Samsonov's Army now already extended farther west than was originally intended," and intended to seize the chance: "We had not merely to win a victory over Samsonof. We had to annihilate him."

Meanwhile, Samsonov was advancing through foreign territory without having been issued with any maps, and poor logistics meant his troops were exhausted, half-starved, and dressed in rags. He had little idea of Rennenkampf's whereabouts, and no inkling of the trap into which he was marching.

MAGNIFICENT WORK

One German corps moved eastward, turning back the Russian I Corps on Samsonov's left flank before circling south of his main force, consisting of XIII, XIV, and XXIII Corps (twelve divisions in total). Reinforcements brought in by rail helped the Germans meet the main thrust of the Russian advance in the west, while the divisions pulled away from facing Rennenkampf achieved a forced march to crash into the Russians from the north, chasing off the VI Corps on Samsonov's right flank.

The encirclement was almost complete, with the Germans having committed practically every soldier that could be mustered from East Prussia. The battle began on August 26th. Things went well, yet the German command were haunted, Hindenburg recalled, by the possibility that "Rennenkampf might fall upon us like an avalanche from the northeast at any time." If the First Army moved south it would be the Germans who were encircled. The crucial moment came when aerial reconnaissance brought intelligence (which proved to be false) that Rennenkampf's cavalry were on the move. Ludendorff called for Hoffmann's plan to be scrapped just as it was swinging into action, and this is when Hoffmann apparently invented the tale of the feuding Russian commanders. There was no way, he assured Hindenburg, that Rennenkampf would come to Samsonov's aid. Whether this all really happened or not, the battle proceeded according to plan. Hindenburg wrote that "By the evening [of the 26th] magnificent work had been done."

Over the next four days the Germans continued to do magnificent work. German artillery achieved a high level of accuracy thanks to the use of spotters in airplanes—the first ever large-scale use of tactical airborne reconnaissance—and their barrages wreaked terrible carnage on the Russians. Although the troops fought bravely and with increasing desperation, the Germans were able to counter their every move thanks to intercepted radio messages. According to one story, Ludendorff remarked

"The Russian soldiers fight like bears," to which Hoffmann replied, "Yes, General, but these bears are led by donkeys."

As the situation deteriorated Samsonov lost control. In his summary of the battle, Russian general Vasily Gurko wrote: "Destitute of any information concerning the other troops under his control, Samsonov lost all power of directing operations . . ." By the 29th, wrote Hindenburg, "a large part of the Russian Army saw itself faced with total annihilation . . . The ring round thousands and thousands of Russians began to close."

Three Russian corps found themselves trapped in what Hindenburg described as "a great cauldron, in which we were engaged in the work of destruction." Attempting to flee, the Russians blundered into bogs and swamps, or drowned trying to raft across lakes. Of the 150,000 troops caught in the trap, only 10,000 would escape. Gurko relates that, "Caught in the ring, although the Germans did not know it, was General Samsonov and his personal staff." The Russian commander met a sorry end, as Gurko reports:

"Samsonov, accompanied by five other staff officers, was guiding himself through the thick forest toward the Russian frontier . . . all that could be heard was the trampling of the undergrowth and an occasional voice as members of the little party called out to each other in order to keep together. General Samsonov, who suffered from heart trouble, and found his breathing more and more difficult, lagged behind. There came a time when everybody had been called and all had answered but Samsonov. General Postovski, the Chief of his Staff, immediately called a halt and in the thick darkness led a search for the missing general. It was fruitless."

German search parties later found Samsonov's body—he had committed suicide.

By August 31st the Russian Second Army had ceased to exist. Hindenburg referred to "a day of harvesting" as German forces rounded up troops and equipment. Some 30,000 Russians had been killed, and the Germans took over 130,000 prisoners and captured over 500 guns. It took 60 trains to transport all the captured equipment back to Germany.

BATTLE

High casualty rate

Catastrophic defeat

Pyrrhic victory

Tactical blunder

Appalling conditions

DISASTER IN THE DARDANELLES: GALLIPOLI
1915–16

Antagonists: British Empire troops under General Sir Ian Hamilton, including Anzacs under Sir William Birdwood, vs. Turkish divisions under German field marshal, Liman von Sanders, including Second Division under Mustafa Kemal

Casualties: Allies: 240,000; Turks (victors): at least 300,000

. . . [T]he sight in the trenches that we take is awful. We wear our respirators because of the awful smell of the dead. I'll never get the sight out of my eyes, and it will be an everlasting nightmare. If I am spared to come home I'll be able to tell you all about it, but I cannot possibly write as words fail me. I can't describe things.

Letter from a soldier at Gallipoli, 1915, from the UK National Archives

© Sufi | Shutterstock.com

Gallipoli was a disaster for both the British Imperial Navy and Army, a colossal blunder that stranded hundreds of thousands of men on the rocky hillsides and narrow beaches of a Turkish peninsula. Subjected to terrible conditions, the suffering of troops from almost every corner of the British Empire, most notably the Australian and New Zealand Army Corp (the Anzacs), was exceeded only by that of their Turkish counterparts. The campaign consisted of a series of tactical blunders by ill-equipped and/or incompetent commanders, except for the brilliant final act—the retreat.

Gallipoli is a narrow finger of land jutting south from the European coast of what is now Turkey (during World War I it belonged to the Ottoman Empire). Its eastern coast forms the western side of the Dardanelles, the narrow straits leading from the Mediterranean to the Sea of Marmara, Istanbul (formerly Constantinople), and the Black Sea. In 1915 the Dardanelles seemed to the young First Lord of the Admiralty, Winston Churchill, as though they might hold the key to unlocking the stalemate in the war in Europe. The Western Front had ossified into a line of trenches impenetrable to assault, but Churchill hoped that forcing the straits would allow Allied forces to take Constantinople, drive the Ottoman Empire (allied with the Germans) out of the war, supply hard-pressed Russia, and strike at the German–Austrian alliance through what he would later come to call "the soft underbelly of Europe."

Accordingly, he convinced the War Minister, Lord Kitchener, to support his proposal over the objections of senior naval officers, and also secured French cooperation. On March 8th, after bombardments and commando assaults on the Turkish forts guarding the entrance to the Dardanelles, the Navy tried to force the straits, with disastrous results. The passage was heavily mined and the Turks had guns on either side of the straits. Three battleships were sunk and another three crippled, and the naval force withdrew with its tail between its legs on March 18th. It was now apparent that taking the strait would

A MUCH TOUGHER NUT

FLAGSHIP FAILURE
HMS *Queen Elizabeth*, the flagship during the British Navy's failed attempt to force the Dardanelles prior to the Gallipoli landings.

© IWM via Getty Images

depend entirely on a land campaign to occupy the Gallipoli Peninsula and silence the guns on at least one side of the Dardanelles.

The man who was to command the campaign, the newly installed head of the Mediterranean Expeditionary Force Sir Ian Hamilton, was on board HMS *Phaeton* inspecting the peninsula while the naval attempt was underway. On March 18th he wrote to Lord Kitchener: " . . . am now steaming . . . to inspect the Northwestern coast of the Gallipoli Peninsula . . . Here, at present, Gallipoli looks a much tougher nut to crack than it ever did over the map in my office." He appended a PS, describing his impression of the naval attempt to force the Straits: "The scene was what I believe Naval writers describe as 'lively'."

NOT TO ATTACK, BUT TO DIE

Hamilton now formulated an ambitious plan to launch the first major amphibious operation in modern warfare. The peninsula is rugged and mountainous, with a spine of high hills interlaced with dry gullies prone to flash floods, and few accessible beaches. Clever ruses and diversions misled the German commander of Turkish forces, Field Marshal Liman von Sanders, into failing to reinforce the two divisions stationed on the peninsula itself, but these proved sufficient.

IAN HAMILTON
Sir Ian Hamilton, head of the Imperial Mediterranean Expeditionary Force and commander-in-chief at Gallipoli.

The plan of attack called for two landing areas: five beaches labeled X, Y, V, W, and S toward the southern tip of the peninsula, where British and French forces would land; and landings farther north by the Anzacs under Sir William Birdwood. The landings by the 29th Division on S and Y beaches on the western coast were unopposed but lack of initiative on the part of Major-General Aylmer Hunter-Weston meant the chance was missed to outflank the Turkish defenders at the southern tip, who gave the landings at W and V beaches a torrid reception. At W the heroic assaults of the Lancashire Fusiliers earned the regiment six Victoria Crosses; at V there was wholesale slaughter. A naval pilot flying over the beach half an hour after the assault began reported that the sea was red with blood up to 147 feet (45 meters) from the shore.

Meanwhile, a strong northerly current had caused the Anzacs to drift too far north, missing their beach landing. As they scrambled ashore they found themselves on a narrow strip of sand facing steep hills. Amidst general confusion units dumped their gear on the beach and charged inland, trying to reach the strategically vital summit of Chunuk Bair. At first it seemed as though they had caught the defenders napping, but in charge of the Turkish 2nd Division was a quick-thinking and resourceful colonel, Mustafa Kemal (later to become the father of modern Turkey as Kemal Atatürk). Disregarding the chain of command, Kemal rode at once to the summit of Chunuk Bair and surveyed the situation, then threw his closest division into the fray to stop the Anzacs by any means necessary. His instructions were blunt: "I am ordering you not to attack but to die."

© Public domain

LANDING PARTY
A boat crammed with men of the Lancashire Fusiliers en route to Cape Helles, Galipoli.

The Anzac charge was turned back agonizingly short of the summit and soon the division found themselves hemmed into a tiny patch of ground around the landing point, which became known as Anzac Cove. The Anzac commander pleaded for his men to be extracted immediately, but was told to dig in. The travails of the Anzacs over the next eight months became legendary, helping to form Australian national consciousness.

The Anzacs clung on grimly, suffering weeks of deadly sniper fire that accounted for at least one general, among others. On May 2nd a ferocious Turkish attack was repelled with enormous Turkish losses, leaving a pile of 4,000 corpses that quickly started to rot. An armistice had to be arranged so that they could be removed. Turkish and Anzac lines were, in places, less than 59 feet (18 meters) apart.

CORPSE FLIES

Conditions on the southern tip of Gallipoli were just as bad. Thousands of unburied corpses in no-man's-land spawned plagues of rats and billions of corpse flies. Dysentery and typhoid ravaged the troops. In an interview in the British National Archives a Gallipoli veteran recalled:

"I well remember the very first time we went up these trenches. A lot of the parapets . . . had been built up—it sounds awful—with dead bodies, which were partially buried under earth . . . just as we entered the trench . . . there, half-buried, was a body. And a hand was sticking out . . . we got so callous . . . that every time when men went . . . they always used to shake hands with it."

Allied forces gained ground agonizingly slowly, suffering terrible losses. Henry Hanna, a Dubliner who had joined a "Pals" regiment (a battalion made up of men who had enlisted and served together) that was sent to Gallipoli, related a typical passage of action:

"Next item was our bayonet charge, headed by Hickman. He was killed, Jack Boyd and Willie Boyd and young Kener also, and some others. Lax was wounded and Drummond . . . I was lying quite close to a chum called Cecil Murray . . . he was badly hit. I asked him where he was hit. He showed me his left hand, which was in pulp, and, while speaking to him, he was hit three times in the body. The groans were heartrending. Then a young chap called Elliott . . . was shot in front of me . . . he jumped about three feet [a meter] when hit; he started trying to crawl back to our lines, and just got above me when he was hit again. He died in a few minutes . . ."

MISSED BY MINUTES

The morass at Gallipoli cost Churchill his job, but British high command agreed to send Hamilton reinforcements for a misguidedly ambitious offensive in August. Secretly landed British troops and Ghurkhas would join a carefully coordinated, multipronged assault in August. Inevitably, the plans went awry, despite many acts of heroism, such as the audacious Anzac assault that captured the supposedly impregnable position known as Lone Pine. The Ghurkhas successfully took a height called Hill Q, only to be driven off by "friendly" artillery fire. Most galling of all was the inertia of the IX Corps under the appropriately named Lieutenant-General Sir Frederick Stopford, who landed at Suvla to the north. Anzacs to the south watched in disbelief as the IX Corps, despite landing unopposed, stopped to cook meals and play soccer. Stopford dithered on the beach for nearly three days until Hamilton arrived to urge him into action. His forces finally reached their objective, the heights of Tekke Tepe, 36 hours late, to find that Turkish reserves had arrived just minutes before. The British were thrown back with heavy losses.

ANZAC ASSAULT
Australian troops charging a Turkish trench near Anzac Cove.

© Public domain

Perhaps the worst incident of the August offensive was during the battle for Scimitar Hill on August 21st. As successive waves of attackers were cut down by Turkish defenders, the brush caught fire and hundreds of wounded soldiers lying on the battlefield were burned alive.

Scimitar Hill marked the final failure of Allied offensives, and Hamilton was called home. His replacement, Sir Charles Monro, called for evacuation. The British General Staff reluctantly agreed; their report of November 22nd advised: " . . . the General Staff have arrived at the conclusion that . . . withdrawal is likely to prove more advantageous than retention of our positions." Kitchener came to look for himself and immediately assented. The evacuation of the troops from December 1915 to January 1916, accomplished under the noses of the Turks without the loss of a man, turned out to be the one great success of the campaign.

ADVANTAGEOUS WITHDRAWAL

The Gallipoli campaign had been a disastrous failure with shockingly high casualty rates: 52 percent for the Allies, 60 percent for the Turks. Some 559,000 Allied personnel had been committed: 420,000 British and Empire troops, 80,000 French, 50,000 Australians, and 9,000 New Zealanders, with 250,000 casualties. Of the 50,000 killed, only 10,000 have known graves. The Turks' lossses were even graver: 300,000–400,000 casualties, including 87,000 dead.

BATTLE

High casualty rate

Catastrophic defeat

Pyrrhic victory

Tactical blunder

Appalling conditions

BLEED FRANCE WHITE: VERDUN

1916–17

Antagonists: German army under General Erich von Falkenhayn vs. French defenders under Henri Phillipe Pétain

Casualties: Over 722,000 in total. French (victors): at least 392,000; Germans: at least 330,000

They must be crazy to do what they are doing now: what a bloodbath, what horrid images, what a slaughter. I just cannot find the words to express my feelings. Hell cannot be this dreadful. People are insane!

Last note in the diary of Alfred Joubaire, French soldier at Verdun

Verdun was an old fortress town in northwest France, on the River Meuse where it is crossed by the road to Paris. A symbol of national pride due to its role in the Franco-Prussian Wars and its importance as far back as the early Middle Ages, it would earn a grimmer place in history as the venue for the most awful battle of World War I, becoming one of the most blood-soaked patches of ground in history.

BLEEDING THE FRENCH TO DEATH

After the initial German advances of 1914 the Western Front had ossified into a stalemate of opposing trenches. Sticking out from the French lines into German territory was a salient around Verdun, a town encircled by wooded hills and steep-sided valleys. Despite being heavily fortified, and having successfully resisted the initial German advance, the area was considered by the French high command to be poorly defensible in the light of the ease with which the German artillery had destroyed the similar Liège forts in Belgium, and most of the guns and garrison had been removed.

Not everyone in the French army agreed, and local commanders protested but were dismissed by the French commander-in-chief, General Joffre: Verdun was not thought to be an important target for the Germans. He was wrong. His German opposite number, Erich von Falkenhayn, had decided it was the perfect place to inflict a lethal wound on the French, given the symbolic importance of the fortress. He believed that if the Germans could capture it, the French would sacrifice unlimited manpower to get it back, claiming, according to legend, that the effort would "bleed France white." In fact, there is no surviving record of von Falkenhayn having used the actual word *weissbluten*, but in the event both sides would shed oceans of blood.

ERICH VON FALKENHAYN
Commander of German forces at the start of World War I and architect of the Verdun offensive.

The assault on Verdun had been planned in secrecy since late 1915, and was scheduled to start on the night of February 11–12th. However, bad weather enforced a delay of ten days, during which the French were able to rush two divisions into the front line and reinforce their defenses. A network of 60 forts and fortified outposts surrounding Verdun, along with the topography of the area, made it a fiendishly dangerous battleground.

In the early hours of February 21st, over 1,200 German guns laid down the heaviest bombardment yet seen in history, lasting over 9 hours and firing nearly 2 million shells. As the guns fell silent the troops advanced south on both sides of the Meuse, which bisected the battlefield roughly north–south. The two most tactically important forts on the right bank were Fort Douaumont and Fort Vaux, but the former was disastrously lost to the Germans with barely a shot on February 25th after a mix-up with the French orders left one of the gates unguarded. The French flooded the area around Fort Vaux with troops, delaying the Germans long enough to set up formidable artillery around the appropriately named Dead Man's Hill, on the left bank of the Meuse, which pounded the Germans every time they tried to advance. General Henri Phillipe Pétain, an exponent of defensive warfare, was put in charge of the defense of Verdun.

HEAVY METAL
A Prussian howitzer
used at Verdun.

The Germans decided they needed to take out the French artillery on Dead Man's Hill, but this in turn was covered by gun emplacements on Côte (Hill) 304. On May 3rd the German attack on Côte 304 began, with 500 guns aiming at a field of just 1.2 square miles (2 square kilometers). A French soldier described the horror of being under a bombardment: "It is as if you are tied to a pole and threatened by a man with a hammer. First the hammer is swung backward in order to hit hard, then it is swung forward, only missing your skull by an inch, into the splintering pole. In the end you just surrender . . ."

German and French forces exchanged pointless and costly attacks and counterattacks over Fort Vaux. It eventually fell to the Germans after a French sally to attack Fort Douaumont was repulsed with the loss of most of their men, leaving Vaux almost undefended. The Germans moved in and the French lost yet more trying to retake it. In June, a German attack on the village of Fleury involved the first use of phosgene gas, with 110,000 poison-gas shells fired by 230 guns. The attack failed anyway.

THE STENCH OF VERDUN

In July, the Battle of the Somme diverted German resources, but French offensives continued, with equally little result. By mid-July more than 23 million shells had been fired. Between August and September the battle degenerated into an exhausting quagmire with ill-defined front lines, fought over a landscape of colossal shell holes. The testimony of a captain in the French army captures the horror of the combat: "I have returned from the most terrible ordeal I have ever witnessed . . . Four days and four nights—ninety-six hours—the last two days in ice-cold mud—kept under relentless fire, without any protection whatsoever except for the narrow trench, which even seemed to be too wide . . . I arrived with 175 men, I returned with 34 of whom several had half turned insane . . ."

The trenches became, in the words of Frenchman Henri Barbusse, "a network of elongated pits in which the nightly excreta are piling up. The bottom is covered with a swampy layer from which the feet have to extricate themselves with every step. It smells dreadfully of urine . . ."

Many of the troops suffered from dysentery, often because faulty supply lines meant they had to eat emergency rations of salted meats, which in turn made them crazed with thirst. An eyewitness described how: "One soldier was going insane with thirst and drank from a pond covered with a greenish layer near Le Mort-Homme [Dead Man's Hill]. A corpse was afloat in it . . ." The sole road into Verdun, along which traveled reinforcements and supplies, came to be known as the Voie Sacrée, the Sacred Way. It had to be continuously rebuilt to repair shell damage, yet nonetheless carried during the course of the battle 6,000 vehicles, 25,000 tons of supplies, and 90,000 soldiers—it was said 66 percent of the French army was passed along this road during the siege.

TRENCH TERROR
A French trench on the frontline at Verdun.

© Roger-Viollet | Getty Images

Blocked latrines and the stench of decomposing corpses combined to create a horrendous and indelible smell that haunted men of both sides. One soldier described how: "you could never get rid of the horrible stench. If we were on leave and we were having a drink somewhere, it would only last a few minutes before the people at the table beside us would stand up and leave. It was impossible to endure the horrible stench of Verdun . . ."

In October 1916, a French offensive successfully retook Fort Douaumont, but German machine-gunners at Vaux repulsed successive waves of attackers. The German command decided to abandon it anyway, pulling out and blowing it up. Further horrifically costly assaults behind rolling artillery barrages drove the Germans away from Verdun itself, and in many accounts December 19th, 1916, is recorded as the end of the Battle of Verdun.

In reality, however, fresh and equally intense fighting broke out again in the autumn of 1917, when the commander of Maas Gruppe West, General von François, convinced the German high command to allocate him troops for yet another assault around Dead Man's Hill. An account by Lieutenant General August Fortmüller encapsulates the Pyrrhic nature of advances on the Verdun front: " . . . 15 French officers and 853 men, along with much materiel, were captured. The cost had been heavy; the Germans had lost 18 officers and 1,157 men." When the attacks abated the new German commander-in-chief, Ludendorff, wrote, "I was happy that the fighting there had come to an end and was not content that I had allowed the attacks. As before on the Eastern front, I had an aversion to victories with a disproportionally high cost in blood."

In August 1917, the French prepared a final assault to restore the fronts to their pre-February 1916 positions. With aerial spotters marking the positions of German reserves, French artillery launched a bombardment that lasted for three weeks. French forces made slow but steady progress against ferocious German resistance, culminating in a final attack on November 25th. French casualties are estimated

IN MEMORIAM
War cemetery at Verdun.

at around 390,000 dead, missing and wounded, while the Germans lost 142,000 dead and missing and 187,000 wounded. These figures exclude the continued fighting in 1917, so the real cost may have been higher still. At least 130,000 corpses were unidentifiable and many more were never recovered. The Battle of Verdun, according to some sources, had cost more dead per square foot than any battlefield in history.

A TERRIBLE SPECTACLE: THE SOMME

1916

BATTLE

High casualty rate

Catastrophic defeat

Pyrrhic victory

Tactical blunder

Appalling conditions

Antagonists: British Fourth and Fifth Armies under overall command of Sir Douglas Haig, with French Sixth Army, vs. German Second Army under Fritz von Below and First Army under Max von Gallwitz

Casualties: British and French (victors): 620,000; German: 500,000

... [T]hey just mowed us down ... And it seemed to me eventually there was just one man left, I couldn't see anybody at all, all I could see was men lying dead, men screaming ... and I thought what can I do, I was just alone in a hell of fire and smoke and stink.

Private Don Murray, Somme veteran

© kette | Shutterstock.com

Featuring the worst single day in British military history, the Battle of the Somme has become emblematic of the pointless carnage of World War I. Debate still rages about whether the troops were lions led by donkeys, but the terrible scenes enacted on the Somme battlefield undoubtedly rank among the most shocking in the history of war.

SEVERAL VESUVIUSES

In 1916 the Western Front crossed the valley of the Somme River in northern France, and here the British and French sectors of the line met. Accordingly, it was chosen as the place to mount a joint British–French operation, intended to punch through the German lines so that they could

be rolled up, striking a decisive blow. The operation was originally intended to feature greater French involvement and take place later in the year, but the German offensive at Verdun meant that the main burden fell on the British, with an earlier start date of July 1st. The British Army had lost much of its original strength by this point in the war, so the ranks featured a high proportion of new recruits known as "Kitchener's Army" after the recruiter-in-chief, Lord Kitchener.

MATERIEL REMAINS
World War I British army helmets and kit on the ground in front of a Somme battlefield.

The operation was preceded by an immense artillery bombardment, with allied artillery pounding the German lines for a week, firing over a million and a half shells. German-born American journalist and war correspondent Karl Henry von Wiegand described the impact of the bombardment from the German point of view:

"There was a roar as if several Vesuviuses were in eruption and a number of Niagaras adding to the din. The earth trembled and shook under mighty blows; the very air vibrated intensely . . . It was the famous *'trommelfeuer,'* or 'drumfire,' of hundreds of big guns. The British were 'drumming' the German trenches in the adjoining sector . . . Probably close to 1,000 shells a minute were raining and exploding on the German trenches. We stood awe stricken."

A German staff officer described to von Wiegand the effects of shell bursts: "Men sometimes go insane, sometimes their eardrums burst; their eyes are burned out by the withering blasts of explosions; they are suffocated and their lungs burned out by gaseous fumes. God! It's awful!"

The bombardment was supposed to destroy the German positions, kill most of their men, and cut the wire defenses that blocked no-man's-land. In his diary Haig wrote: "June 30th: The weather report is favorable for tomorrow. With God's help, I feel hopeful. The men are in splendid spirits. The wire has never been so well cut, nor the Artillery preparation so thorough." The truth was rather different. "Our artillery hadn't made any impact on those barbed-wire entanglements," Corporal W. H. Shaw of the Royal Welsh Fusiliers later recalled. The German commander von Below, despite little support from his high command, had observed the intensive preparations for the assault and wisely ordered his men to construct deep-lying concrete bunkers. The German troops weathered the bombardment and waited for it to cease before emerging to take up their positions at the machine-gun emplacements.

At 7:30 on the morning of July 1st the whistles blew and the British men went over the top. British tactics were horribly outdated. In his postwar book *Prelude to Victory*, General Sir Edward Spears wrote:

"My memory was seared with the picture of the French and British attacking together on the Somme on July 1st 1916, the British rigid and slow, advancing as at a military parade in lines which were torn and ripped by the German guns, while the French tactical formations, quick and elastic, secured their objectives with trifling loss. It had been a terrible spectacle. As a display of bravery it was magnificent. As an example of tactics its very memory made me shudder."

German machine-gunners cut down wave after wave of assaults. "We never got anywhere near the Germans," Corporal Shaw recalled. "Our lads were mown down. They were just simply slaughtered . . . yet we kept at it, making no impact on the Germans at all. And those young officers, going ahead, they were picked off like flies." By the end of the first day, the British had lost 57,450 officers and men; 19,240 of them killed, 2,152 missing, the rest wounded. Some 60 percent of the officers involved had been lost.

Particularly savage were the terrible casualties suffered by the "Pals" brigades, battalions made up of men who had enlisted together after Kitchener had agreed that those who "joined together" should "serve together." Of the 32 battalions that lost 500 men or more on July 1st,

A TERRIBLE SPECTACLE

20 included Pals units. Writing in his 1989 book *Britain and the Great War*, J. M. Bourne notes, "In the industrial north of England, on Tyneside and in Ulster whole communities were plunged into mourning. The 10th West Yorks lost 22 officers and 688 men, the Accrington Pals 21 officers and 585 men, the 4th Tyneside Scottish 19 officers and 610 men."

SOMETHING WRONG

The wholesale slaughter had achieved little, although the French effort to the south achieved some of its objectives. The Somme campaign would last for 144 days, involving 12 separate battles, and ending on November 18th, when the 51st Highland Division took Beaumont Hamel, one of the objectives that were supposed to have been achieved on Day One. The end of the campaign saw the first appearance of tanks on the battlefield, but by the time the final breakthrough was made it was too late in the year to take advantage.

The ferocity of fighting on Day One and throughout the campaign was indicated by the number of Victoria Crosses (the highest British military honor) awarded: 9 on July 1st and a further 41 during the whole campaign. The experiences of the Somme left an indelible mark on a whole generation of survivors. Corporal Joe Hayles of the Rifle Brigade remembered:

OVER THE TOP
British soldiers crossing no-man's-land at the Somme front lines.

"There was a terrible smell. It was so awful it nearly poisoned you. A smell of rotten flesh. The old German front line was covered with bodies—they were seven and eight deep and they had all gone black. These people had been lying since the First of July. Wicked it was! I'll never forget it. I was only eighteen, but I thought, 'There's something wrong here!'"

By the end of the campaign there had been 420,000 British casualties, 200,000 French, and 500,000 German. The front line had advanced 6.2 miles (10 kilometers).

Today, the mainstream view is that Haig and his staff were incompetent old fogeys who sent young men to the slaughter: "lions led by donkeys." This view has been challenged, however. The highest echelons of the

© IWM via Getty Images

officer class were far from immune to the cost of battle: Haig lost 58 of his fellow generals, killed or fatally wounded while leading from the front. At the Somme, three generals died in the first few days. The battle was a brutal learning experience for the British Army, which changed as a result, and the campaign was a victory of sorts, eventually achieving its objectives and costing more German lives than British.

Yet even at the time there was widespread dismay at the slaughter and scepticism of Haig's command. Prime Minister David Lloyd George witheringly described Haig as "brilliant to the top of his boots," while in late July 1916 Winston Churchill circulated a paper to the British Cabinet directly attacking Haig: "We have not advanced 3 miles [5 kilometers] in the direct line at any point . . . In personnel the results of the operation have been disastrous; in terrain they have been absolutely barren . . . from every point of view the British offensive has been a great failure."

Haig dismissed the attack, putting it down to sour grapes and noting acidly in his diary, "I expect Winston's judgement is impaired from taking drugs." But criticism mounted. In a letter of July 29th Haig's chief of staff in London, General Sir William Robertson, warned him, "The powers that be are beginning to get a little uneasy in regard to the situation . . . They will persist in asking whether I think a loss of say 300,000 men will lead to really great results."

Haig insisted that the campaign had "shaken the faith of the Germans [and] impressed on the world, England's strength and determination, and the fighting power of the British race." He remained in place as commander-in-chief, a fact attributed by critics to his friendship with the king. The view of many in the rank and file, however, was summarized by W. Hay, who had been a private in the Royal Scots Battalion:

"We were between the devil and the deep blue sea. If you go forward, you'll likely be shot, if you go back you'll be court-martialled and shot, so what the hell do you do? It was hell, it was impossible, utterly impossible. The only possible way to take High Wood was if the Germans ran short of ammunition. They couldn't take it against machine-gunners, just ridiculous. We always blamed the people up above. We had a saying in the Army, 'The higher, the fewer.'"

They meant the higher the rank, the fewer the brains.

BATTLE

High casualty rate

Catastrophic defeat

Pyrrhic victory

Tactical blunder

Appalling conditions

ITALIAN FOR DISASTER: CAPORETTO

1917

Antagonists: Italian Second Army under General Luigi Capello and Commander-in-Chief Luigi Cadorna vs. German and Austrian armies under General Otto von Below

Casualties: Italian: 300,000 (mostly taken prisoner), plus another 350,000 unable to fight; Austrian–German (victors): unknown

He yelled at me, "Go or they'll get us!" I asked, "But what about the others?" "Go! Go! Everyone go! Run!" We hopped on the running board of our staff car in which I saw some of the officers of my unit. All around the car was a cowardly mass of humanity grabbing onto the car screaming wildly "Go! Go!" Even our honor—gone.

Attilio Frescura

Possibly the least known but most awful front of World War I was the Italian–Austrian front that ran through the Alps. Here, the Italian Commander-in-Chief Luigi Cadorna had overseen a long series of incredibly wasteful offensives along the River Isonzo, known as the Eleven Battles of the Isonzo. The Twelfth Battle would be the only one in which the Austrians, with vital German help, were on the offensive, and for the Italians it would constitute one of the most catastrophic defeats of any nation in World War I.

WAR IN THE MOUNTAINS

The terrain of the Italian–Austrian border and the relatively primitive nature of both armies combined to make the Italian–Austrian war in the mountains one of the grimmest theaters in the whole conflict. Positions were set up on high mountains in freezing temperatures, and poor training, equipment, logistics, supply, and leadership meant that conditions were often squalid and brutal. Italian soldiers in particular suffered harsh penalties for disobedience and desertion, yet the lengthening butcher's bill incurred by campaigns that yielded minuscule gains led to desperately low morale, which in turn contributed to the high number of soldiers who surrendered or deserted. By the autumn of 1917, Italians on the Isonzo front had seen 146,000 of their comrades killed and many more injured and captured, with the casualty rate accelerating to an appalling 60% in the Tenth Battle of Isonzo, and desertions had jumped from 650 soldiers per month in 1915 to 5,500 per month.

RIVER OF DEATH
The Soča River in Slovenia, known as the Isonzo in Italian; its valley was the scene of twelve terrible campaigns.

© bepsy | Shutterstock.com

The Austrians had suffered equally badly, and unlike the Italians they were failing to replace the wasted men and materiel. The Tenth and Eleventh Battles of Isonzo had stretched their resistance to breaking point, and the Austrian high command called in German assistance. Ludendorff sent six divisions, and German planners put together an offensive that would utilize the most modern and effective tactics, including creeping bombardments (*feuerwalze* in German) advancing just ahead of the infantry, massed columns concentrated at weak points, targeted artillery and gas bombardments, and specific targeting of enemy command and control. A key element was surprise, with forces mobilizing

VON BELOW
The commander of German troops during the Caporetto offensive, Otto von Below.

WHAT ARE WE DOING UP HERE?

under cover of darkness, yet in fact the Italians had ample warning that German and Austrian forces were massing for something. The Germans had spotted a weakness in the Italian lines—a salient near Mount Nero, a peak almost impossible to storm, but which could be isolated by attacking around its base and striking at Caporetto.

Unfortunately, the Italian response was complacent and inadequate. In a memoir of the battle, the chief of the British Red Cross in Italy, G. M. Trevelyan, related that some of the worst troops in the Italian army had been sent to Caporetto, where they made plain their lack of appetite for the fight:

"I know from what I have been told by those who were in Caporetto in the last weeks before the disaster, that the soldiers made no secret of their intentions, and that many of their officers lived in fear of their own men, locking themselves up carefully at night. Indeed, certain of these troops refused to accept the usual gifts distributed by patriotic agencies among the men at the front, grounding their refusal on the fact that they regarded themselves as no longer in service."

At 2 a.m. on October 24th a short, sharp bombardment and gas attack preceded rapid deployment of German–Austrian forces. Helped by the cover of a dense fog, they quickly overran forward Italian positions. In the Plezzo valley Italian-issue gas masks had proved ineffective and the entire 87th Regiment was killed. The Italian defense crumbled with terrible speed, compounded by a series of tactical mistakes. Very little of the Italian artillery ever fired, thanks to a combination of poor communication and German targeting of central command posts. One of the corps commanders in the area continually shifted his headquarters, making it impossible for anyone to reach him. Some posts were defended pointlessly while others were abandoned prematurely, only for commanders to order futile counterattacks to retake them. Many of the bridges over the Isonzo were not blown, while the bridge at Caporetto was blown too early, trapping two divisions on the wrong side.

Retreat became a full-scale rout. Units streamed off the mountains and across the bridges. In some places officers tried to turn men back if they still had their weapons, which merely encouraged others to ditch their rifles. Attilio Frescura related the frantic scene he encountered as he attempted to deliver a message to a lieutenant-colonel: "He ordered me and several others to stop the wave of runaways that was flooding the area and sweeping everyone away with them . . . the battle had moved to the roads, but the battle was lost . . ."

Cadet Giovanni Comisso described chaos on the roads: "I saw a crowd of soldiers and officers all mixed together; unarmed, none of them had their equipment; with a blank look in their eyes . . . 'But where are you coming from?' 'We ran out of ammunition. In the end we were fighting with rocks.' 'And headquarters? And the General?' 'We haven't heard anything from them.'"

Alpinists dug in high on Mount Nero watched the action unfolding below and, horrifyingly, behind them. Lt. Cesco Tomaselli described the scene on the evening of the 24th:

"Night fell, one of those cloudy and gloomy nights in which even the air tastes like misfortune. When it stopped snowing and the sky cleared, the defenders of Kozliak and Pleka [Italian-held positions] realized only then that they were the only defenders on Mount Nero. Behind them, everything was ablaze. Down in the basin, Dreczenca was burning, throwing off sparks and clouds of reddish smoke; the reflection of the flames lit up the sides of the mountain. On the hills on the other side of the Isonzo, on Kolovrat, at Luico, toward Mount Matajur, rockets flashed, followed by the brief bursts of machinegun fire. 'Lieutenant, if our side is retreating, what are we doing up here?' It was terrifying."

IGNOMINIOUS SURRENDER

Worst hit was the Italian Second Army, but when its commander, General Luigi Capello, requested permission to withdraw, Cadorno refused for nearly a week. Finally, on October 30th, he relented and ordered a withdrawal across the Tagliamento. Yet this was only a small river, and by the time what was left of the Italian army had crossed over, so had the Germans. By now, around 70 percent of the Italian army was hors de combat, with 40,000 dead and wounded, 280,000 taken prisoner, and 350,000 men separated from their units. The Italians had lost two thirds of their artillery and 3,000 machine guns. Eventually, the Italians pulled back to the Piave, not far from Venice, and the Germans and Austrians ran out of steam, having outrun their own supply lines after surprising themselves with the speed of their advance.

Cardona, who would eventually carry the can for the debacle when he

© Petr Moravek | Shutterstock.com

BONE YARD
Italian military cemetery and memorial in Slovenia, near Caporetto (modern-day Kobarid).

was replaced in November, got his recriminations in early. On October 29th he issued an infamous communiqué to the Italian people, blaming the "lack of resistance of some units of the 2nd Army, who cowardly retreated without fighting, or ignominiously surrendered to the enemy." Accusations of Communist incitement to mutiny among the troops would later be peddled by the Italian Fascists as the cause for the defeat, which was so monumental that Caporetto became a byword for disaster for many decades afterward. In fact, the blame lay mostly with the generals and their failure to learn the lessons of two years of hard fighting, which left the Italian army demoralized and unprepared for a modern, coordinated offensive.

THE GREAT CAPITULATION: SINGAPORE

1942

BATTLE

High casualty rate

Catastrophic defeat

Pyrrhic victory

Tactical blunder

Appalling conditions

Antagonists: British, Indian, and Australian forces under Arthur Percival vs. three Japanese divisions under Tomoyuki Yamashita

Casualties: British Empire: 9,000 killed and 130,000 captured; Japanese (victors): 3,500 killed

Private Tanner stood 6ft 2in, and had proved himself in the fighting to be a very brave soldier—when he heard the order [to surrender], he stood there unashamedly with tears streaming down his cheeks. His were not the only tears that sad day. I felt as though my bowels had been painlessly removed, my mind refused to work properly, and I was unable to grapple with the situation.

Len Baynes, Fall of Singapore veteran

Churchill famously described the Fall of Singapore as "the worst disaster and largest capitulation in British military history." Singapore was strategically vital to British domination of South East Asia and would inevitably be a target for the Japanese after they entered the war in December 1941. It had strong naval and air defenses, but its security depended on the defensibility of the Malay Peninsula, and this would prove to be the Achilles heel of "Fortress Singapore," with a colossal force of defenders falling to a Japanese force less than a third of the size, without putting up much of a battle. The Japanese conquest of Malaya, the culmination of which was the Fall of Singapore, was a campaign of shocking speed and even more shocking savagery.

SHOVE THE LITTLE MEN OFF

At the outbreak of war, the British in the Far East believed in the myth of white superiority over the "little yellow man." The top brass had recognized that the defense of Singapore began in Thailand, where the line must be held to prevent the Japanese penetrating down the Malay Peninsula. Even after the immediate success of the Japanese strategy of targeting the British airfields so as to guarantee Japanese air superiority, racist complacency was still the order of the day. After the Japanese landed at Kota Bharu aerodrome, in Malaya, Sir Shenton Thomas, the governor of Singapore, supposedly remarked to a military officer, "Well, I suppose you'll shove the little men off."

The Japanese were terrifyingly brutal. They had been ordered not to take prisoners as they advanced, and all soldiers had been issued with a pamphlet that said: "When you encounter the enemy after landing, think of yourself as an avenger coming face to face at last with his father's murderer. Here is a man whose death will lighten your heart."

© Mondadori via Getty Images

ADVANCE ON SINGAPORE
A Japanese tank advances down the Malay Peninsula during the Singapore offensive.

On December 9th, 1941, the RAF in Singapore lost most of its planes in a Japanese raid on the island's airfields, and the loss of air power was to prove crucial the very next day. Task Force Z, a flotilla including two of the Royal Navy's finest ships, the newly built modern battleship *Prince of Wales* and the veteran battle cruiser *Repulse*, was steaming north to intercept the Japanese forces attempting a landing on the Malay coast. On December

10th the task force was attacked by Japanese torpedo bombers and both the capital ships were sunk. Among the 800 men lost was the commander of the force, Admiral Sir Tom Phillips. Churchill recorded in his memoirs his reaction to the devastating news: "I put the telephone down. I was thankful to be alone. In all the war I never received a more direct shock."

The man in charge of land forces in and around Singapore was Lieutenant General Arthur Percival. He suffered a series of defeats by the Japanese, starting at the Battle of Jitra in Malaya on December 11th–12th, followed by three more reverses culminating in the fall of Kuala Lumpur on January 11th. In their hectic advance the Japanese used all means available, even traveling by bicycle. Their methods were horrific; they murdered both wounded and uninjured soldiers who surrendered, burning some to death after dousing them with petrol. Locals who helped the British forces were tortured and murdered.

WAR CRIMINALS ON A BICYCLE

British and Australian forces withdrew to Singapore on January 31st, 1942, and the causeway linking them to the mainland was blown up. Despite their numerical superiority over the oncoming Japanese, the defenders were already doomed. The story of the huge guns of the naval defenses that pointed the wrong way became legendary. A Singapore veteran, Len Baynes, who served with No.1 Commando, recalled:

"Singapore's only big guns were still concreted in to positions facing out to sea. Their main defensive weapons were therefore hardly used. This was at a time when nearly every army in the world was training paratroops, and our potential enemy had been advancing through the Chinese mainland for years . . ."

In fact, the big guns in question had only ever been intended as naval defenses. Given that the Japanese did not attempt to take Singapore by sea, they could be said to have been effective. Other guns could rotate 360 degrees but artillery placements were not the issue. The real problem was that Churchill had overruled a scheme, known as Operation Matador, to increase the military resources available for the defense of South East Asia. According to Singaporean military historian Dr. Ong Chit Chung:

"The battle for Malaya and Singapore was lost, even before the first shot was fired, in the corridors of power at Whitehall when the political leadership refused to provide these resources. The blame rests entirely on

Churchill, who overestimated the impregnability of the British fortress of Singapore and underestimated the Japanese threat and refused to implement Operation Matador . . . all the guns and fortifications in the world would not have ensured the landward defense of Singapore. Churchill took a calculated gamble—and lost."

THE HONOR OF THE BRITISH EMPIRE

Churchill's strategic blunder was compounded by Percival's tactical ones. Rather than concentrate his superior forces against the most obvious point of attack, he spread them out along a 70-mile (113-kilometer) front, having overestimated the strength of the Japanese. Shortly before the final attack, Churchill ordered Percival not to surrender until "after protracted fighting among the ruins of Singapore city . . . commanders and senior officers should die with their troops. The honor of the British Empire and the British Army is at stake." In fact, Singapore relied on the mainland for most of its drinking water, and with the population swollen with refugees there was little hope of Percival withstanding a siege.

PERCIVAL
Lieutenant-General Arthur Percival, commander of British Imperial forces in Malaya at the time of the Japanese attack.

On February 8th the attack began, with Japanese forces crossing the Johor Strait. Most of Percival's men were too far away to influence the battle. It was all over quickly, and on February 15th he gave the order to surrender. Baynes recalls the feelings of dread that gripped the troops as they waited for their captors to arrive:

© Public domain-

". . . our thoughts dwelt on what we had heard of the way the Japanese dealt with prisoners. We had been told of soldiers' bodies found with their hands tied together with barbed wire and riddled with bullets, and that they liked torturing their captives before disposing of them . . . Our comrades out on the lawn had been shot down in cold blood. We did not discuss these things as we waited in silence, each kept his thoughts to himself."

The Japanese murdered the patients at the Alexandra Military Hospital and took some 130,000 men prisoner. Many would be used as forced labor in the construction of the Burma–Thailand railway and nearly 10,000 would die in the process. The large Chinese population in Singapore suffered terrible cruelty at the hands of the Japanese, and it is estimated that around 50,000 of them were murdered.

WHEN THE EARTH BREATHED FIRE: STALINGRAD

1942–43

BATTLE

High casualty rate

Catastrophic defeat

Pyrrhic victory

Tactical blunder

Appalling conditions

Antagonists: German Sixth Army under General Friedrich Paulus vs. Soviet 62nd Army under Lt. Gen. Vasily Chuikov and Stalingrad, Southwest and Don Front army groups under Marshal Georgy Zhukov

Casualties: Axis: ca. 850,000; Soviets (victors): ca. 1.13 million

These five months experienced in Stalingrad were the equivalent of five years in our subsequent lives … the earth in Stalingrad breathed fire for days.

Captain Nikolay Aksyonov, Stalingrad veteran

(*The Motherland Calls*, Battle of Stalingrad monument) © photo.ua | Shutterstock.com

Possibly the most terrible battle in history, the siege of Stalingrad was epic in every way, from the numbers involved to the suffering inflicted. To the Soviets, who successfully encircled and crushed a supposedly superior German force, it was a latter-day Cannae with the Nazis as the Romans; to the Germans it was a despicable *Rattenkrieg* (rat war).

OPERATION BLUE

By the spring of 1942 the German army's thunderous advance into Russia and frantic Russian counterattacks had stabilized into an eastern front stretching from Leningrad in the north to the Black Sea in the south. Russian success had depended on the ferocious winter conditions, but with better weather the Germans were confident that they could overcome anything the Red Army could muster. At the same time the entry of America into the war, and its unexpected emphasis on dealing with the European Axis powers before Japan, meant that Hitler needed a bold strategic move that would trigger the collapse of Soviet resistance.

The obvious place to strike a killer blow against the Soviets was Moscow, but the capital was heavily fortified. Hitler believed strongly in the strategy of targeting resource areas, and his preferred option was to strike at the south, aiming for the oilfields of the Caucasus while also cutting off Soviet access to the breadbasket areas of Ukraine and the wheat transport lines up the Volga. The strategic key to all this was Stalingrad, a major industrial city with massive propaganda value since it bore the Soviet leader's name.

Operation Blau ("Blue") involved splitting the Axis Army Group South in two, with Army Group South B, comprising the Sixth Army under Friedrich Paulus and the Fourth Panzer Army under Hermann Hoth, detailed to move east and take Stalingrad. The operation was delayed from May to the end of June by other operations, but progress was so quick that initially Hitler thought the Panzer Army would not be needed and ordered it south, only to change his mind when it got caught in a colossal traffic jam with the Sixth Army, as both tried to use the few decent roads in the area.

Now that it was clear that the Germans were headed for Stalingrad, the Soviets tried to organize a defense, scrambling units across the Volga to the city, which sat on the west bank. These units would comprise the 62nd Army under Lt. Gen. Vasily Chuikov.

The German advance was preceded by a titanic bombing campaign. First the Luftwaffe attacked the Soviet shipping that linked the forces in the city to their supply lines to the east, destroying 41 ships in 6 days in late July. Then the German army's air support arm, Luftflotte 4, which in August and September 1942 was the most powerful air command in the world, annihilated the city itself. Over a thousand tons of explosives were dropped, and on August 23rd a firestorm leveled much of Stalingrad. Little was left standing; in the Voroshilovsky district, for instance, 90 percent of living space was destroyed. The human toll of this savage pounding was immeasurably worsened by Stalin's callous refusal to allow the city's civilian population to be evacuated.

Despite all this, the Germans encountered ferocious resistance when they entered the city. The 16th Panzer Division found itself facing a lone Soviet antiaircraft regiment made up of young women volunteers with no training in dealing with ground targets, yet they were matched shot for shot. Each antiaircraft battery had to be individually destroyed. With real Red Army units in short supply at the start of the battle, the gap was filled by workers' militias drawn from factory staff, even as their comrades continued to produce tanks in factories that were on the front line, which they would then man themselves. Tanks were literally driven from the factory floor into battle, sometimes without paint or even gunsights.

© Getty Images

BLASTED CITY
A Russian soldier signals across a battle-scarred square during the siege of Stalingrad.

The city's defenders were motivated by fierce patriotism and burning hatred for the invaders, inflamed by the atrocities they committed. "One sees the young girls, the children, who hang from the trees in the park," sniper Vasily Zaytsev told a Soviet researcher not long after the battle; "this has a tremendous impact." A Major Pyotr Zayonchovsky told of finding the remains of a captured Russian "whose skin and fingernails on his right hand had been completely torn off. The eyes had been burnt out and he had a wound on his left temple made by a red-hot piece of iron. The right half of his face had been covered with a flammable liquid and ignited."

Yet zeal alone could not overcome the superiority of the Germans' training, equipment, and air support. By September the life expectancy of a Soviet private arriving in Stalingrad was less than 24 hours. Officers could expect to survive for three days.

HUGGING THE GERMANS

Chuikov developed a tactic he called "hugging" the Germans, which meant pressing his front line as close to the enemy as possible to neutralize the Axis advantage in tank, artillery, and air support. The Germans had to fight not just street to street and house to house, but for every room. Every cellar, basement, and sewer was defended, and the Germans joked about capturing the kitchen while still fighting for the living room. "In this street fighting, hand grenades, machine guns, bayonets, knives, and spades are used," said Chuikov. "They face each other and flail at each other. The Germans can't take it."

Some areas saw inconceivably desperate battles. For instance, on September 13th Railway Station No. 1 at Mamayev Kurgan changed hands 14 times in 6 hours. The historian Antony Beevor relates the tale of two bodies dug up at Mamayev Kurgan in 1944: a German and a Soviet soldier, who had apparently been simultaneously stabbing each other in the chest with bayonets when they were buried by an exploding artillery shell.

GERMAN POW
A young German soldier turned prisoner of war, with his Red Army guard.

Another location that became legendary was a house overlooking a square that was heavily fortified by Russian defenders, and which came to be known as Pavlov's House after the sergeant in charge of its defense. Chuikov later said, only half-jokingly, that more Germans died trying to capture Pavlov's House than died capturing Paris. One story was that, in order to clear the field of fire for their machine and antitank guns, the defenders had periodically to run out and kick over piles of German corpses.

It took three months for the Germans to push through to the river bank, but although they had captured 90 percent of the city two pockets of Soviet resistance remained. Factory workers from the unoccupied sectors would run out onto the battlefield to service damaged tanks, and despite having no training would join the crews to replace the dead and wounded.

Even as the Germans continued painfully on to the river, the Soviet commander-in-chief for the region, Georgy Zhukov, had been planning a huge pincer movement to envelop the besieging forces. To the west and south, the flanks of the German Sixth Army were guarded by allied Axis divisions—Romanians and Italians. On November 19th the Soviets launched Operation Uranus, which saw multiple army groups brush aside these divisions and swing round behind Paulus's forces. On November 22nd the two arms of the Soviet pincer met at Kalach; Paulus was surrounded.

Army commanders urged Hitler to allow Paulus to attempt a breakout, but the Nazi dictator had already pledged in a speech of September 30th that the German army would never leave Stalingrad. Göring convinced him that the Luftwaffe could create an "air bridge" to keep the encircled troops supplied, but the ambitious operation was a huge failure. There were too few aircraft and logistical confusion. One aircraft arrived bearing 20 tonnes of vodka and summer uniforms for the freezing and malnourished soldiers. Pilots reported that the soldiers were too hungry and weak to unload the aircraft, and back in Germany General Zeitzler, wanting to show solidarity with the plight of the trapped men, restricted himself to the same rations. After a few weeks he was so thin that Hitler became annoyed and personally ordered him to start eating properly.

On December 12th, the German counteroffensive, Operation Winter Storm, attempted to break through from the south to rescue the besieged force, but it was stopped well short of its objective. It was now clear that the Sixth Army was doomed, and Paulus pulled his men into Stalingrad city center, where a grim reprise of the original siege was played out but with the roles reversed. German units fortified their positions for house-to-house fighting, for instance by fixing wire nets over the smashed-out windows to prevent the Soviets from throwing in hand grenades, but the resourceful Russians fixed fish hooks to the grenades so that they would catch on the nets.

Running low on ammunition and weak from starvation, cold, and illness, the Germans fought on. Hitler refused Paulus's plea to be allowed to surrender. On January 30th he promoted Paulus to Field Marshal, on the basis that since no Field Marshal had ever been taken alive, Paulus would take the hint and either fight to the death or commit suicide. Broken and disgusted, Paulus declined to comply (he was supposed to have

URANUS AND WINTER STORM

said "I have no intention of shooting myself for that Bavarian corporal") and surrendered the following day. He met with little sympathy from his Russian captors. "They could have easily shot themselves," said Major General Ivan Burmakov. But Paulus and his staff chose not to do that. "They had no intention of dying — they were such cowards. They didn't have the courage to die." Thousands of Germans and Axis allies fought on, convinced that the Soviets would kill them anyway, and indeed illness and mistreatment meant that of the 90,000 Germans taken prisoner only 5,000 ever returned to Germany.

The Battle of Stalingrad had lasted for 199 days. Including the prisoners of war who died in captivity, some 850,000 Axis soldiers lost their lives at Stalingrad, along with another 600,000 or so in the surrounding regions. The Soviet death toll is harder to estimate because the Stalinist authorities suppressed the truth, but it is believed that around 1.13 million died, bringing the total death toll at Stalingrad to around 2 million.

Even the Reich minister of propaganda, Joseph Goebbels, admitted, "The news from Stalingrad had a shock effect on the German people." This was the turning point of the war on the Eastern Front, the most important theater in World War II in Europe. As British historian Eric Hobsbawm concluded: "From Stalingrad, everyone knew that the defeat of Germany was only a question of time."

FATEFUL FIELD MARSHAL
Friedrich Paulus, commander of the German Sixth Army.

THE MOUNTAIN AND THE MONASTERY: CASSINO

1944

BATTLE

High casualty rate

Catastrophic defeat

Pyrrhic victory

Tactical blunder

Appalling conditions

Antagonists: Allied forces, including Americans, British, French, New Zealanders, Indians, and Poles vs. General Heinrich von Vietinghoff's German 10th Army and General Eberhard von Mackensen's 14th Army

Casualties: Allied (victors): 115,000; German: unknown

The Stalingrad of the Italian Front

Description of the Cassino campaign by General Anthony Farrar-Hockley, who served with 1st Airborne in Italy

© Panaccione Robertino | Shutterstock.com

The series of battles for the town of Cassino and the neighboring heights of Monte Cassino is generally regarded as the most ill-advised and strategically incompetent campaign in the European theater of World War II. Four separate battles would subject forces from over half a dozen Allied countries to gruelling and bloody combat in terrible conditions.

The Cassino campaign epitomized the rigors of fighting in Italy, a battleground described by the eminent military historian, Richard Holmes, as "little short of hell." The long Italian peninsula lent itself to the strategy of hooking around defensive lines by landing behind them, but the buildup to the Normandy landings diverted the amphibious resources needed for this approach. Instead, any Allied advance from Sicily up the Alps would have to force its way over rivers and ridges in what Holmes describes as "heartbreaking sequence," while also contending with boiling summers and freezing winters. And to what end? Italy was of little strategic value and was essentially a sideshow to the main event being prepared in France, making the terrible sacrifices endured there even more depressing, and the blunders of the generals even less forgivable.

THE GUSTAV LINE

South of Rome the Germans had set up a band of defenses called the Gustav Line. A key stronghold on this line, controlling the road to Rome, was the town of Cassino and the heights to its north, dominated by the brooding monastery of Monte Cassino, combining to form "a vile tactical puzzle" in the words of military historian John Ellis. Crack troops had been sent to defend the area, and they had made good use of the terrain in setting up mortars and artillery. Holmes describes it as "one of the strongest natural defensive positions in military history."

The Allied commanders appeared to have little appreciation of this. The initial attack on Cassino was merely a diversion, drawing troops away from an intended landing zone at Anzio, with the expectation that once the beachhead had been secured the Germans would abandon the Gustav line and withdraw north of Rome. In January 1944 the US 36th Texas Division attempted to cross the Gari south of Cassino but walked into a nightmare of mines, entrenched machine-gun positions, and crack defenders. At least three heavy machine guns covered every point of the crossing and the attempt failed with heavy casualties. A French force, experienced in mountain fighting, fared better in the heights to the north, but the Germans defenses held.

The attacks did succeed in drawing German forces away from Anzio, where the US VI Corps under Major General John Lucas landed with little resistance. Rather than break out from his beachhead, however, Lucas stayed where he was. Churchill complained, "Instead of hurling a wildcat onto the shore all we got was a stranded whale." In fact, the Allied strategy was flawed: the Germans did not abandon the Gustav Line, making it impossible for Lucas to strike at Rome, and Anzio turned into a grim, Anzac Cove-style siege. It became apparent that the Allies would now have to launch attacks on the Gustav Line at Cassino to draw pressure off Anzio. As Richard Holmes puts it, "the tail had begun to wag the dog."

On February 2nd the US 34th Division started the main push to capture Monte Cassino, but found that the steep terrain and German mortars wreaked havoc on their ranks. Of the 3,200 men of the US 135th and 168th Infantry Regiments, only 840 remained when they were relieved on February 12th. An eyewitness account described the grim state of the survivors:

BODY BEARERS
Polish troops carrying a fallen comrade at Monte Cassino.

"It was more than the stubble of beard that told the story; it was the blank, staring eyes. The men were so tired that it was a living death. They had come from such a depth of weariness that I wondered if they would quite be able to make the return to the lives and thoughts they had known."

Allied commanders decided to try and bomb their way out of trouble, and on February 15th, as the prelude to the Second Battle of Cassino, the monastery on Monte Cassino was controversially and probably pointlessly leveled by bombers. Having not previously been used by the Germans, its ruins were promptly occupied and fortified by German defenders. The second assault was repulsed with heavy casualties, and a third battle was begun on March 15th. New Zealand troops took the main role in both these battles, and although they fought bravely they had to contend

MILITARILY STUPID

with mortars, artillery fire, and snipers coming from higher ground. A contemporary report in the *NZEF Times* describes the soldiers as "men who have spent hours in direct heavy shell fire against German strongpoints often 200 yards or less from them. All these incidents have been part of their everyday life—hunted by snipers on the slopes above them in daylight, mortared and shelled in the darkness."

© Pilecka | Creative Commons

POLISH PRICE
The Polish war cemetery at Monte Cassino, seen from the abbey.

Belatedly realizing quite how tough a nut Cassino was to crack, Allied commanders brought in extra divisions and launched a concerted operation called Diadem on May 11th–12th. With multiple points of attack the German position was made untenable, although the battle for the monastery heights themselves was brutal nonetheless. It finally fell to Polish troops who entered the ruins on May 17th.

Lieutenant General Mark Clark's US Fifth Army now had the chance to break out of the Anzio beachhead and he was ordered to cut off the German withdrawal from Cassino, which would have captured valuable men and materiel. Clark preferred to go for the glory of liberating Rome, and let the Germans escape to set up a fresh defensive line to the north (the Gothic Line). American military historian Carlo D'Este called his decision "as militarily stupid as it was insubordinate." According to some estimates, the Allies suffered almost 115,000 casualties during the Cassino campaign. German losses are unknown, although at the German cemetery at Cassino (for soldiers lost from various parts of Italy), 20,000 men are buried.

THE GREEN HELL: HÜRTGEN FOREST

1944–45

BATTLE

High casualty rate

Catastrophic defeat

Pyrrhic victory

Tactical blunder

Appalling conditions

Antagonists: Elements of German Seventh Army under Erich Brandenberger vs. American First Army under Courtney Hicks Hodges

Casualties: Americans: 30,000; Germans (victors): 28,000

Passchendaele with tree bursts.

Ernest Hemingway's description of the Battle of Hürtgen Forest

One of the least known yet grimmest battles of World War II, Hürtgen Forest was the longest battle ever fought by the US Army, and probably their worst conflict in the entire European theater. No less than ten divisions of the US Army would suffer the "green hell" of Hürtgen, a thickly wooded plateau cut into many ridges and valleys by numerous streams, situated on the Belgian–German border near Aachen.

THE GREEN INFERNO

The stunning success of the Allied advance across France and the speed with which the Germans were pushed back to their own border triggered wildly over-optimistic assessments of the course of the war by Allied commanders in the late summer of 1944. For instance, post exchange officers sent word to the States to stop all Christmas packages, assuming that the war would be over by Christmas. In fact, the speed of the advance had caused the leading units to outstrip their logistical support, while the Germans made full use of the Siegfried Line, a fearsome band of defenses protecting the homeland, composed of pillboxes and fortifications with overlapping fields of fire. The Allied advance was about to come to a standstill.

The Siegfried Line ran straight through the middle of Hürtgen Forest, 50 square miles (80 square kilometers) of thickly wooded ridges. Unbeknownst to the American First Army, which was advancing on it, the forest had been deemed of vital strategic importance by the Germans since it controlled access to a series of major dams. General Erich Brandenberger had been told to hold it at all costs, and the Siegfried Line defenses were manned by troops who knew the local geography and were defending their homeland. The scene was set for a bloody struggle, in the most atrocious conditions imaginable. "Go outside on the coldest, wettest, most miserable day you can find, throw in some snow, ice, fog, and mist. Then dig a cold, wet, lonely, muddy hole and live in it like an animal for weeks at a time, that's what the Hürtgen was like," recalls Bob Hyde, a machine-gunner with 28th Infantry Division.

George Morgan, who served with the 22nd Infantry, described how, "The forest up there was a helluva eerie place to fight . . . Show me a man who went through the battle . . .

WOODLAND WAR
American troops on the move in Hürtgen.

and who says he never had a feeling of fear, and I'll show you a liar . . . Everything is tangled. You can scarcely walk. Everybody is cold and wet, and the mixture of cold rain and sleet keeps falling." General James M. Gavin, who commanded the 82nd Airborne in the later stages of the battle, described it as "an eerie scene, like something from a low level of Dante's *Inferno.*" He particularly mentioned the pillboxes: "Although I had seen heavy pillbox fortifications in Sicily, they were nothing compared with those in the Hürtgen Forest."

Fighting in a forest was a huge tactical mistake by the Americans. "The German Command could not understand the reason for the strong American attacks in the Hürtgen Forest," wrote Generalmajor von Gersdorff, who had been Chief of Staff for the German 7th Army. "The fighting in the wooded area denied the American troops the advantages offered them by their air and armored forces, the superiority of which had been decisive in all the battles waged before." Worst of all, the trees transformed incoming artillery and mortar rounds into terrible "tree bursts"—lethal showers of splinters and metal that lacerated troops below. American soldiers soon learned to "hug a tree" when a round was incoming, as normal foxholes provided no protection.

The first to enter the forest were Ninth Division, who began fighting on September 14th. Gavin describes them as just "the first of a steady procession of American units which in subsequent weeks would learn to equate the Hürtgen with gloom, misery, wounds, and death." Repelled with heavy casualties, the same division tried again on October 6th. By late October they had gained just 3,000 yards (2,750 meters), at a cost of one and a half casualties per yard. The official report read: "The real winner appeared to be the vast, undulating, blackish-green sea that virtually negated American superiority in air, artillery, and armor to reduce warfare to its lowest common denominator." A captain complained: "We are taking 3 trees a day, yet they cost 100 hundred men apiece."

A new assault was planned for November, with an experienced and well-rested unit, the 28th Division, given the difficult task of crossing the Kall River gorge to take Schmidt; at this time of year, says Gavin, "heavy autumn rains and dense fogs and mist plagued the attackers. Soon there would be snow. The infantry could expect little air support." The attack started on November 2nd, and met with initial success because

THE LOWEST COMMON DENOMINATOR

the Germans were in the process of exchanging the defenders of Schmidt. The next day the Americans were driven back with terrible losses. Division headquarters, unaware of what was going on, continued to send pointless orders insisting on fresh attacks, and called the regimental commander to account for himself in person. When he arrived, exhausted and twice wounded by artillery fire, the division commander, General Norman Cota, fainted at the sight of him.

A further four divisions were committed to the terrible battle, which petered out in December but did not officially end until February 1945. John R. Weiner, who served with the 4th Infantry Division at Hürtgen, described the savage toll of the fighting:

"The death and destruction was unbelievable. Dead bodies were stacked, like logs, awaiting recovery. Whole sections of forests were sheared off 50 to 60 feet [15–18 meters] above ground by incoming artillery tree bursts. D Company, full strength being 193 men, was reduced to 8 men, a sergeant, and 7 privates. I was one of 110 replacements. Three months later there would be 10 of us left."

In the end it was determined that the Hürtgen was strategically worthless; the Americans should simply have bypassed it to strike at the real targets—the dams beyond the forest. In the event, the final German counterattack, the Battle of the Bulge, diverted attention and resources from Hürtgen. Over 30,000 casualties had been largely in vain. It was, concluded General Gavin, "a ghastly mistake . . . a battle that should not have been fought."

THE MEAT GRINDER: IWO JIMA

1945

BATTLE

High casualty rate

Catastrophic defeat

Pyrrhic victory

Tactical blunder

Appalling conditions

Antagonists: 3rd, 4th, and 5th Marine Divisions and other units of the Fifth Amphibious Corps, under Lieutenant General Holland M. "Howlin' Mad" Smith, vs. Japanese defenders under Lieutenant General Tadamishi Kuribayashi

Casualties: US Marines (victors): 26,000 casualties, including 6,800 dead; Japanese: 19,000

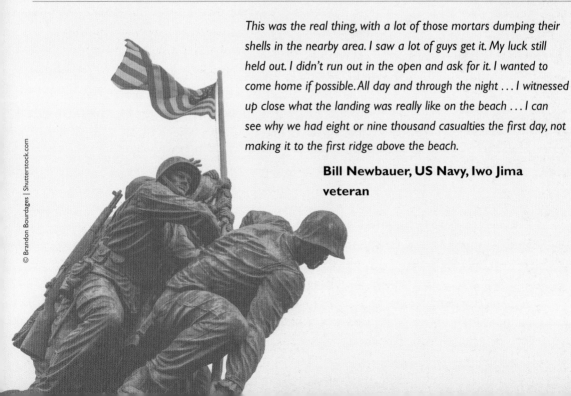

This was the real thing, with a lot of those mortars dumping their shells in the nearby area. I saw a lot of guys get it. My luck still held out. I didn't run out in the open and ask for it. I wanted to come home if possible. All day and through the night ... I witnessed up close what the landing was really like on the beach ... I can see why we had eight or nine thousand casualties the first day, not making it to the first ridge above the beach.

Bill Newbauer, US Navy, Iwo Jima veteran

The war in the Pacific had a special horror of its own, with both sides stoking mutual loathing and hatred to genocidal levels. The tide of war had turned against Japan after the Battle of Midway in 1942, after which the Americans began an arduous process of assaulting strategic Pacific islands. After the Battle of Leyte Gulf in October 1944—the largest naval battle in history—any hopes of a Japanese counterstrike were finished, but the Japanese made it clear that every last soldier would fight to the death. This suicidal "banzai" resistance made the conquest of island strongholds savage and bloody. At Saipan, for instance, 99 percent of the 27,000 defenders were killed and American troops were horrified to see mothers with their babies leap to their deaths over cliffs rather than submit. In this febrile atmosphere the conquest of Iwo Jima would stand out as the bloodiest and most intense fight of them all.

PORK CHOP

Iwo Jima, meaning "sulfur island," is a volcanic island of 13 square miles (21 square kilometers), at the end of the Bonin chain of islands to the south of Japan's Honshu island. It had great symbolic importance as the first bit of traditional Japanese territory to be invaded, and was deemed strategically important because of its short runway, which could provide a base for emergency landings for large bombers returning from raids on Japan, and for fighter-escort cover for those raids. Unaffectionately nicknamed the "pork chop" because of its shape, the island is a grim and desolate landscape of volcanic sand, ash, and pumice, reeking of sulfur, with a volcanic peak, Mount Suribachi, rising at the southern tip.

MAD MARINE
Lieutenant General Holland M. "Howlin' Mad" Smith, commander of the American assault on Iwo Jima.

© Public domain

By 1945 the US Marines had honed their amphibious assault capabilities, but Iwo Jima would prove to be the sternest test the corps had ever faced. The battle would be the bloodiest engagement in the history of the Marine Corps. The Japanese defenders, under the leadership of Tadamichi Kuribayashi, had prepared a network of caves and tunnels dug deep into the island, and this enabled them to ride out the two months of "softening up" by air and naval bombing. According to the Navy Department Library, "the island would suffer the longest, most intensive shelling of any Pacific island during the war." For the three days immediately preceding the first attack, six battleships lay just off the shore and pounded the island with their big guns, achieving little more than making the beaches impassable to many of the Marines' vehicles.

On February 19th the amphibious assault was launched and the landings were met with an eerie calm, but as soon as the naval bombardment halted to allow the Marines to advance, the defenders emerged from their underground bolt-holes and began to inflict savage casualties. By the end of the first day, nonetheless, the Marines had secured their initial objectives, including encircling the base of Mount Suribachi. By the end of the next day the southern third of the island including the all-important airstrip was under American control, and after three more days of intense combat the 28th Marines reached the summit of Suribachi and twice raised the US flag. The second attempt was photographed by Joe Rosenthal, becoming one of the most iconic images of the war and providing the model for the Marine Corps memorial at Arlington Cemetery.

With the fall of the southern sector and the loss of the mountain and the airfield, the Japanese knew that the island was now indefensible. Yet they were determined to make the Americans pay in blood for every square foot. Kuribayashi concentrated his resources on the central and northern sections, where caves, fortifications, and pillboxes connected together to form an almost impenetrable defense. One of the most heavily defended areas was a section with three high points, which came to be known as the "Meat Grinder." On some days American forces advanced just a few hundred feet, yet they pressed on. By March 9th the 3rd Division succeeded in cutting the island in two, by which time the invading forces had been greatly cheered by the first emergency landing by a B-29 bomber on March 4th, underscoring the strategic rationale behind the costly invasion.

For the Japanese defenders, life became increasingly intolerable. Conditions in the cave shelters must have been horrific. Gareth W. Rosson served on Iwo Jima after the war in 1946–47 and was part of a detail clearing out some of the caves. He described a typical scene:

"This cave is on the N. E. end of the island on the main road . . . The opening was only 5 feet [1.5 meters] high and 3 feet [1 meter] wide . . . The room was HOT around 105°F [40°C] with a terrible smell. There were 5 or 6 Japanese soldiers, fully clothed, on the floor on the other end

THE MEAT GRINDER

of the room. Their bodies were dried like leather. We didn't go down to the next level due to the stench and heat."

Rather than surrender, remaining pockets of defenders would stage "mini-banzai" attacks—hopeless assaults on fortified positions. On March 10th Japanese naval troops staged a banzai attack on the 4th Marine Division, with the loss of 700 men, while another such attack on March 26th marked the end of the battle. According to one estimate, just 212 of the island's 21,000 defenders survived to be taken prisoner.

ALL ASHORE
American landing craft and armored vehicles on a beach during the Battle of Iwo Jima.

The tiny island had taken 36 days to subdue. There have since been questions over the true strategic value of Iwo Jima, but by the end of the war 2,400 B-29 bombers carrying 27,000 crewmen had made unscheduled landings on the island. The US Marine Corps suffered more casualties than the Union forces at Gettysburg, and the invasion forces won 27 Medals of Honor, more than were awarded for any other single operation during the war, accounting for more than a quarter of those awarded to the Marines in World War II. "Among the Americans who served on Iwo Island," Admiral Chester W. Nimitz famously wrote, "uncommon valor was a common virtue."

BATTLE

High casualty rate

Catastrophic defeat

Pyrrhic victory

Tactical blunder

Appalling conditions

THE TOILET BOWL: DIEN BIEN PHU

1954

Antagonists: French paratroopers and foreign legionnaires under Colonel Christian de Castries vs. Viet Minh forces under General Vo Nguyen Giap

Casualties: French: more than 20,000, plus an unknown number of Indochinese auxiliaries; Viet Minh (victors): ca. 23,000

The Viets are everywhere. The situation is very grave. I feel the end is approaching but we will fight to the finish.

Radio message of Colonel Christian de Castries, commander of French forces at Dien Bien Phu

The siege of Dien Bien Phu was a catastrophe for French colonial rule of Indochina and a disaster for the French military. In an analysis of the battle commissioned by the Marine Corps University Command and Staff College, Major Harry D. Bloomer writes, "At Dien Bien Phu the French violated nearly all of the principles of war at every level of war—strategic, operational, and tactical."

OPERATION CASTOR

Dien Bien Phu was the Vietnamese translation of the French name for the village of Muong Thanh, an obscure spot in a valley in far northwest Vietnam near the border with northern Laos. Equipped with a small airfield, it was chosen by the commander of French forces in Indochina, General Henri Navarre, as a promising spot from which to thwart the operations of the Viet Minh, the Communist nationalist force led by Ho Chi Minh. The French and the Viet Minh had been fighting since 1946, with oscillating fortunes. In 1952, for instance, Navarre had scored a major victory by setting up a fortified camp at Na San and supplying it by air. The Viet Minh had attacked it using their traditional "human wave" tactic (frontal assault by densely concentrated infantry), and had been beaten off with heavy losses. Navarre hoped to replicate this success at Dien Bien Phu, which controlled the road from Vietnam into northern Laos, at the time the object of Viet Minh operations. It was also vital to control of the opium trade, which the French were keen to sustain since they relied on the income to subsidize their military presence in Vietnam. Navarre named the plan Operation Castor, neglecting to inform the French government about it until six hours after it had begun.

Unfortunately for Navarre, Dien Bien Phu presented a very different prospect from Na San. Where the latter had seen the French installed on high ground from which their artillery could pick off Viet Minh targets, the former was in the bowl of a valley surrounded by ridges and mountains. The French made the classic error of underestimating their opponents, calculating that their artillery and air support could easily pick off any Viet Minh positions in the surrounding heights, and working on the basis of intelligence that suggested the Viet Minh general, Vo Nguyen Giap, intended to commit just a single division to the region.

The first French troops parachuted in on November 20th, 1953, and within three days there were 9,000 French troops and Indochinese auxiliaries there. By the end of November six parachute battalions were in place and

Viet Minh forces in the area had been easily chased off. At this point the commander on the ground, Colonel Christian de Castries, compounded the errors of Navarre by setting up seven fortified strongholds around a central command post next to the airstrip, but failing to position them where they could achieve mutual support and cover. The southernmost post, code-named Isabelle, was isolated 3 miles (5 kilometers) to the south of the others, and accounted for one-third of the defenders available.

In 1953 Ho Chi Minh ordered Vo Nguyen Giap "to throw all available forces against the Expeditionary Corps" at Dien Bien Phu. A major international conference on the future of Indochina was being convened and Ho Chi Minh wanted to secure a victory that would strengthen his hand at the negotiating table. The Viet Minh planned an operation involving the use of human-wave attacks to be launched on January 26th, but at the last minute Giap had second thoughts. It would be far better, he argued, to take a slower, more methodical approach. "In striking surely and advancing cautiously," he wrote, "we could keep complete initiative, attack the enemy . . . only when we were sufficiently prepared and sure of victory."

Accordingly, a breathtakingly arduous logistical operation was set in train to lug heavy artillery through rainforest and mountains, and set up firing points all around Dien Bien Phu, in places even tunneling through mountaintops. The Communist Central Committee mobilized 33,500 *dân công* (patriotic workers) to support the 50,000-strong Viet Minh contingent, and deployed over 17,000 horses and 2,724 modified bicycles known as *xe thô* to carry ammunition and 20,584 tons of rice to the front.

On March 13th, 1954, the hard work paid off as Giap launched a withering artillery assault on the French position and its 16,000 defenders. By the following day the airstrip was damaged beyond use, the planes that constituted much of the French force's airpower had been disabled, most of the French artillery had been neutralized, and one of the fortified outposts had been taken. The French artillery commander committed suicide. The French "air bridge" strategy was in tatters; from now on they could only be

A BIT LIKE VERDUN

FRESH MEAT
French reinforcements arrive by parachute.

© Gamma-Keystone via Getty Images

resupplied by air drops, and well-prepared antiaircraft emplacements on the heights around the valley meant that the drops would have to be done from a great height and at night.

The encirclement of Dien Bien Phu was complete by the end of March but after an air assault caused heavy casualties to Viet Minh troops in the open, Giap adopted World War I-style tactics, digging trenches and slowly but surely sapping closer to the French defenses. "It's a bit like Verdun, but Verdun without the depth of defense—and, above all, without the Sacred Way," Colonel de Castries wrote to General Cogny on March 22nd. In fact, according to Martin Windrow, author of *The Last Valley: DBP and the French Defeat in Vietnam*, owing to the scattered disposition of the strongholds and the lack of a continuous battlefront, it was more like "a series of individual, company-sized Verduns."

THE TOILET BOWL

The French were soon referring to Dien Bien Phu as *la cuvette*, "the toilet bowl." Outposts were cut off and taken one by one. In one incident on April 19th, troopers from a surrounded outpost, Huguette 6, staged a breakout to get back to the main command center. Of the 300 men originally stationed at Huguette 6, only about 60 reached safety. They were examined by a French army doctor, Dr. Grauwin, who declared: "They aren't wounded, but they have nothing left—they're dead men."

FRENCH TRENCH
Part of the defenses prepared by French paratroopers at Dien Bien Phu.

By April 22nd the Viet Minh controlled the airstrip, but still fresh French forces were airdropped into the killing zone. The air supply program was going horribly wrong. On April 13th Colonel de Castries reported to French high command: "In 24 hours we have sustained three [French] bombing attacks within our defensive perimeter. On the other hand the cargo of five C-119s, or a minimum of 800 artillery rounds, has been delivered to the enemy. No comment." By now, however, de Castries had been told by his commanders on the ground that they had no confidence in his leadership and that paratrooper Colonel Langlais would take over.

The French held out until May 7th when the last posts were overrun by a huge Viet Minh assault. Some 11,700 men were taken prisoner and 10,863 were marched off into the jungle. Only 3,290 were ever repatriated. The fate of the French forces' Indochinese auxiliaries is unknown. Viet Minh casualties had been heavy as well, with 8,000 dead and around 15,000 wounded, but the operation was a major strategic success. At the Geneva Conference of July 1954 the French agreed to pull out of Indochina, although the settlement reached merely prepared the ground for a longer and much more costly conflict to come.

BATTLE

High casualty rate

Catastrophic defeat

Pyrrhic victory

Tactical blunder

Appalling conditions

CALAMITY OF THE CUBAN BRIGADE: BAY OF PIGS
1961

Antagonists: Anti-Castro Cuban Brigade 2506 and the CIA vs. Fidel Castro's Cuban Communist army and militia

Casualties: Brigade: 114 killed, 1,190 captured; Castro's Cuban forces (victors): ca. 150 killed

So then I thought, "Well, they're getting the shit shot out of 'em, so now the task force will come in and support them." And they didn't. We made two or three passes up and down the beach. One time was real close. That's when I saw them, some of them were lying on the beach, and I saw one artillery round come down, and I don't know, maybe it's my imagination, but I swear I saw a couple of people flying through the air.

Bill Bader, US Navy veteran who served in Cuba in 1961

Probably the worst debacle in the history of the US Central Intelligence Agency (CIA), the Bay of Pigs invasion plan was ill-conceived, poorly executed, and doomed before it even began. Seeking to stage an invasion, trigger a general uprising, and overthrow the Cuban Communist regime of Fidel Castro, the force of anti-Castro Cuban exiles known as Brigade 2506 simply succeeded in being killed or taken prisoner.

After the Cuban revolution the Americans became increasingly concerned that Castro was falling into the Soviet orbit and introducing the poison of Communism into Latin America, traditionally considered by the US to be its own special sphere of influence. In March 1960 President Dwight D. Eisenhower had endorsed a CIA plan called the "Program of Covert Action against the Castro Regime," based on a successful CIA action in Guatemala in 1954. In that case CIA-sponsored radio stations had broadcast propaganda to stir up the population against the left-wing premier, preparing the ground for action by a CIA-trained militia that garnered enough popular sentiment to stage a successful coup. The Cuban "Program of Covert Action" underwent multiple revisions as Eisenhower was succeeded by the new president, John F. Kennedy, but in essence it called for anti-Castro Cuban exiles to be trained by the CIA in Guatemala, and then stage an invasion of Cuba with US naval and air support. It was believed that once Castro had lost one battle, the population would rise up against him.

THE CUBAN PROBLEM

Original versions of the "Program" called for a large-scale invasion near Trinidad, Cuba, but Kennedy had the CIA water down the operation to a smaller-scale landing at two beaches on the Bahía de Cochinos. This is usually translated as the "Bay of Pigs," but in fact the "Cochinos" in question are probably fish. Cubans know the invasion as the Playa Girón incident, after the name of one of the target beaches. Air cover was essential to the success of the operation, and initially Kennedy agreed that American bombers would take out Castro's air force on the ground, while cover would be provided over the beaches as the landing went ahead.

In Guatemala, 1,400 Cuban exiles trained under CIA guidance. Each was given a number, but to make the force seem larger than it really was, the first number used was 2500. The brigade took its name from the designation of the first casualty in training, and became Brigade 2506. On April 13th, 1961, the man in charge of the task force that would ferry the men to Cuba and assist in the landings, Jake Esterline, cabled the Brigade's handlers to request an evaluation. Colonel Jack Hawkins cabled back his assessment: "These officers are young, vigorous, intelligent, and motivated . . . Without exception, they have utmost confidence in their ability to win. They say they know their own people and believe after they have inflicted one serious defeat upon opposing forces, the latter will melt away from Castro . . . I share their confidence."

CHICO IS IN THE HOUSE

CIA confidence was misplaced in almost every aspect of the operation. For instance, the "covert" part of the Program seems to have been forgotten. According to a secret memorandum of 1963, in conversations between Fidel Castro and attorney James B. Donovan, declassified by the CIA in 2001, Castro "said that his advance information of the invasion was obtained in detail from the American press. Through the press he was aware of the formation and training of the invasion force." Forewarned, Castro took steps to protect his vulnerable air force by hiding his aircraft; he also doubled the training of artillery personnel and prepared roads to allow rapid deployment of troops to the probable landing site, which he claimed to have guessed.

ORIGINAL ENDORSER
The Bay of Pigs invasion scheme was originated under President Eisenhower.

© Public domain

On April 15th, B-26 bombers attacked Castro's airfields but failed to knock out his air power. The international backlash against these strikes only served to convince Kennedy to scale back direct US involvement further, and he canceled the planned air cover for the landings. When he eventually relented to allow two warplanes to be in attendance, a mix-up over the difference in time zones between Cuba and Nicaragua, from where they launched, meant that they would arrive an hour late.

On April 16th, Radio Swan, the radio station set up just off the Cuban shore to broadcast agitprop, repeatedly broadcast a message cooked up by CIA operatives, intended to spook the Castro regime into believing it was a coded transmission for underground resistance groups:

"Alert! Alert! Look well at the rainbow. The fish will rise very soon. Chico is in the house. Visit him.

The sky is blue. Place notice in the tree. The tree is green and brown. The letters arrived well. The letters are white. The fish will not take much time to rise. The fish is red."

In the early hours of April 17th, despite warnings that Castro still had operational aircraft but that no US air cover would be forthcoming, the task force began landing supplies, Brigade troops, and their CIA handlers. The landing site at Playa Girón was poorly chosen, offering access to little more than a swamp, with no hope of reaching the safety of the mountains to the south. Local militia penned in the landing force until large numbers of regime troops began to descend on them. Castro's air force showed up and began to inflict serious damage on the ships of the task force, damaging one ship which ran aground with hundreds of brigade troops still aboard. At 9:30 a colossal explosion caused CIA operative Rip Robertson, ashore at the landing zone, to radio his colleague Grayston Lynch in alarm: "God Almighty, what was that? Fidel got the A-bomb?" "Naw," replied Lynch, "that was the damned *Rio Escondido* that blew." The freighter *Rio Escondido*, loaded with ammunition and gasoline, had been sunk with a direct rocket hit.

PRE-REVOLUTIONARY
Fidel Castro in America shortly before the Cuban Revolution.

© Public domain | Library of Congress

The task force was ordered to pull back from the coast, abandoning the invasion force. With no supplies or air cover, the Brigade was doomed, but it fought bravely. Attending the annual Congressional Reception on April 17th, the president's brother, Robert Kennedy, took aside Senator Smathers of Florida and told him, "The shit has hit the fan. The thing has turned sour in a way you wouldn't believe." By 2 p.m. on the 18th the landing force had surrendered, and shortly afterward the Brigade's commander, Román José "Pepe" San Ramon, transmitted his last signal:

"Tanks closing in on Blue Beach from north and east. They are firing directly at our headquarters. Fighting on beach. Send all available aircraft now! . . . . I have nothing left to fight with. Am taking to the woods. I can't wait for you."

Over the next few days 1,190 members of the Brigade were taken prisoner; 114 had been killed. Castro claimed that around 150 regime troops had

NOTHING LEFT TO FIGHT WITH

been killed, although American sources put the number far higher. The Brigade prisoners were eventually released in December 1962, in exchange for $35 million of medicine and other supplies.

The affair was a humiliating disaster for both the CIA and Kennedy, who appear to have had their wires crossed all along. The CIA had been working under the assumption that when push came to shove, Kennedy would back up the invasion with American military intervention, so that it didn't really matter how likely it was to succeed on its own merits. Meanwhile, Kennedy had relied on the rather flimsy assumption that, even if the invasion failed, the brigadiers could melt into the hills to start a guerrilla campaign. In a secret meeting with a Kennedy aide, Che Guevara described the botched invasion as "a great political victory for [the Cuban revolution]." The impact of the raid was to drive Castro into the arms of the Soviets, leading in turn to the Cuban Missile Crisis. Kennedy, meanwhile, authorized the CIA to continue planning covert operations against Castro for years to come.

BATTLE

High casualty rate

Catastrophic defeat

Pyrrhic victory

Tactical blunder

Appalling conditions

TERROR AT TET: HUE

1968

Antagonists: People's Army of Vietnam (PAVN: N. Vietnamese army, aka NVA) and Viet Cong (S. Vietnamese Communists) under General Vo Nguyen Giap vs. US Military Assistance Command Vietnam (MACV) and Army of the Republic of Vietnam (ARVN: S. Vietnamese army) under General William Westmoreland

Casualties: Americans (victors): 119 killed; ARVN: 363 killed; PAVN/VC: ca. 7,500 killed

Fighting house-to-house is the dirtiest of all fighting . . . Just as a rat must be drawn from his burrow to be eradicated, an enemy soldier, burrowed in a building, must also be pulled from his hiding place to be eliminated. Normally, he will not come out without a fight. The attacker must go in and dig him out.

Major Ron Christmas, Company Commander in Hue

© Public domain

In November 1967 the Vietnam War appeared to be going well enough for the commander of US forces in Vietnam, General William Westmoreland, to tell the National Press Club in Washington, DC, "With 1968, a new phase is starting. We have reached an important point when the end begins to come into view . . ." Events would prove him right, although in the opposite manner to which he intended. In January 1968, during the Vietnamese New Year holiday of Tet (a traditional ceasefire period), the North Vietnamese launched a colossal operation involving a series of strikes across the whole of South Vietnam, including the capital Saigon. Over 170 sites were hit, and although the majority of the attacks were beaten off within days, some turned into drawn-out battles. The worst of these was Hue.

IMPERIAL CITY

Hue is the old imperial capital of Vietnam. Though not far from the border with North Vietnam, it had been quiet for most of the war as the Viet Cong insurgents and NVA seemed to steer clear of it out of respect.

In the buildup to the Tet offensive American intelligence had clearly indicated something was imminent, but it was a struggle to get the ARVN to cancel holiday leave and put their troops on readiness. Accordingly, the city was poorly defended when the attack was launched in the early hours of January 31st, as insurgents who had infiltrated the city in disguise linked up with ten NVA/VC battalions; soldiers flooded into the capital, mixed with New Year's revelers. Their main target was the Citadel, a thick-walled ancient imperial palace, and soon the Viet Cong flag was flying from the top of the palace. The rest of the city fell equally quickly, with two exceptions—an ARVN command post in the northeastern corner of the Citadel, and a compound housing a garrison of MAVC US advisers.

BOOSTER
William Westmoreland, commander of MACV, was known for his positive assessments of the war.

Here there was fierce fighting as Marines and army troops fought off NVA/VC assaults. The compound was renamed the Frank Doezema Compound in honor of an US army specialist: when the attack broke out Doezema raced to his assigned post, a guard tower, and insisted on manning the heavy machine gun despite incoming fire. As rockets and other ordnance pounded the tower, wounding all the soldiers within,

Doezema stayed at his gun spraying bullets at NVA/VC in an overrun police station, and according to some accounts cutting down a number of attackers loaded with explosives before they could blast open the compound. He continued firing until hit by a rocket that inflicted terrible wounds, and with helicopter evacuation impossible because of the firefight, he bled to death. He was posthumously awarded the Distinguished Service Cross for valor and several veterans of the compound credit him with checking the initial onslaught and saving all their lives.

With the city mostly under control, the NVA/VC started to round up so-called "enemies of the people," such as government sympathizers and Catholics, and up to 6,000 civilians are believed to have been murdered in the course of the battle at Hue. But the fight back began almost immediately, as Marines and other units were brought in to relieve the besieged MAVC and ARVN compounds. One of the first units to enter the city, "Golf" Company, 2nd Battalion, 5th Marines, advancing past a movie theater, were startled to come face to face with a life-size poster of a cowboy with drawn six-shooters. It was advertising *Massacre Valley* starring Franco Nero.

In the close-packed, narrow streets of the old city, the fighting to take back Hue from approximately 10,000 NVA/VC negated much of the usual US advantages of superior air and artillery power. The Americans and their ARVN allies found themselves in a Stalingrad-style battle, retaking the city house-by-house. Enemy snipers and booby traps turned the streets into killing zones, so the Americans quickly learned to develop new tactics. They acquired tear-gas launchers to flush defenders out of buildings, and concluded that if they could not get down the streets safely, they would have to go through the walls. Lieutenant Colonel Marcus Gravel, commander of a Marines battalion, explained the procedure: "One Marine would place a plastic C-4 charge against the wall, stand back, and then a fire team would rush through the gaping hole."

After two days US Marines and ARVN had secured the bank of the Perfume River, opposite the Citadel, but with the bridge blown the Marines had to stage an amphibious assault. Not until February 23rd were the last

© Public domain

ABANDON HUE
Civilians crossing the Perfume River to flee the fighting in Hue.

IN ORDER TO SAVE THE CITY

NVA/VC dislodged from the Citadel, and pockets of resistance continued elsewhere until the 25th. Half of the city had been leveled in the intense fighting, leaving 116,000 of the 140,000 residents homeless.

Although the Tet offensive had been beaten back with heavy losses to the North and insurgent forces, and the battle at Hue was a hard-won victory for the Americans and their South Vietnamese allies, the torrid scenes of combat relayed to Americans on their televisions won Giap a strategic victory. The American public and the opinion formers around President Lyndon Johnson had only recently been assured that intervention had practically won the war. Now it was conclusively demonstrated that the conflict was far from over. After Tet the Americans began planning for a withdrawal that would ultimately see the triumph of the Communists and the conquest of South Vietnam.

TRIED AND FAILED: BASRA

1982

BATTLE

High casualty rate

Catastrophic defeat

Pyrrhic victory

Tactical blunder

Appalling conditions

Antagonists: Iranian Army, Revolutionary Guards, and Basij militia under Ayatollah Khomeini vs. Iraqi army under Saddam Hussein

Casualties: Unknown (inconclusive result)

I saw tens of thousands of young boys, roped together in groups of about twenty to prevent the faint-hearted from deserting, make an attack [on the minefield].

East European journalist covering the Iran–Iraq War, 1984

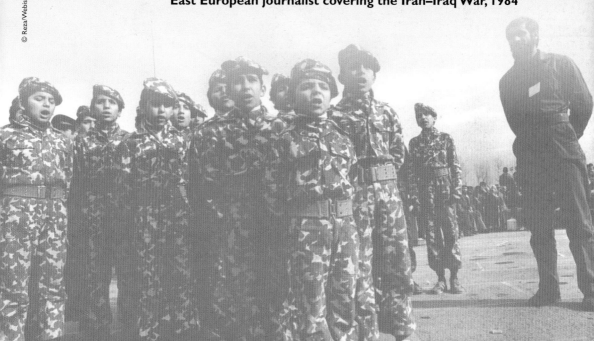

© Reza/Webistan | Getty Images

The Iran–Iraq War was one of the longest and bloodiest conflicts in history, yet also one of the least known in the West. Triggered by the September 1980 invasion of Iran by Iraqi troops under Saddam Hussein, it soon degenerated into a bloody stalemate between enemies characterized by complementary failings. The Iraqis, funded and supplied at various points by the Soviets, Gulf Arab states, and America, boasted great advantages in technology, armor, and supplies, but were unable to make these count owing to poor training, unit-level leadership with little initiative, low morale, and overbearing centralized command. The Iranians had huge manpower and great religious and patriotic zeal, but were let down by poor coordination between regular military and paramilitaries, outdated and insufficient technology and armor, and ill-judged interventions by unqualified commanders-in-chief. The two sides combined to produce a perfect storm of inconclusive but horrifically bloody battles that cost vast numbers of casualties to very little effect.

OPERATION RAMADAN

The invasion of Iran was successful at first, but poor planning meant that the initial advances ran out of steam without achieving decisive strategic blows. In addition, Iraqi attempts to knock out Iranian air power on the ground largely failed. In strongholds beyond the limit of the Iraqi advance, the Iranians regrouped and turned the tide, driving the invaders back across their own borders by May 1982, regaining the strategic initiative.

Saddam Hussein now began to seek a way out of the conflict, offering to negotiate a settlement in June. But by now control of the war on the Iranian side had passed into the hands of the clerics, and Ayatollah Khomeini, influenced by hard-line colleagues, overruled his military advisers and insisted on an aggressive persecution of the war. In July the Iranians prepared for what would become one of the largest land battles since World War II, Operation Ramadan, an assault on the southern city of Basra. Basra had a strong Shi'ite majority, which would tend to make it more sympathetic to the Shi'ite regime of the Iranians, and was strategically vital, controlling Iraqi access to the Gulf, oil shipping lanes, and vast offshore oil fields.

At 10:15 p.m. on July 13th, Operation Ramadan commenced with three army divisions and 30,000 Revolutionary Guards and Basij advancing 6 miles (10 kilometers) into Iraqi territory, only to be pushed back 3 miles (5 kilometers) the next morning by Iraqi counterattacks aided by helicopter air support. The primary tactic employed by the Guards and the Basij militia was the "human wave" frontal assault, where religious zeal was supposed to compensate for technological and tactical inferiority. Inevitably, this led to horrific casualties.

The worst aspect of the human wave tactic was the use of barely trained militia, ranging in age from as young as 9 to over 50, to clear paths across minefields by running into them. According to popular legend, the recruits for these militia were either brainwashed or press-ganged into compliance, and equipped with pathetic tokens of impending martyrdom such as plastic or wooden "keys to paradise," religious slogans on their uniforms and burial shrouds in place of guns, which were in short supply. Whether these claims are true or merely constitute Western anti-Iranian propaganda is not clear, but in a later operation in 1984, an Eastern European reporter claimed to have seen gangs of boys, chained together to prevent any from fleeing, herded onto minefields.

Over the next two weeks the Iranians repeatedly threw reinforcements onto the battlefield to meet the same fate, prompting the description of Iranian tactics as "tried and failed." Up to 70,000 Guards and Basij may have been sent into battle with little chance of survival, as the Iraqis proved themselves competent at engineering strong lines of defense with obstacles, minefields, flooded areas, barbed wire, ditches, and trenches.

AYATOLLAH
Khomeini, the Iranian supreme leader, personally directed military strategy in the Iran–Iraq War.

The Iranian assault ended inconclusively, with massive casualties incurred for the gain of a strip of land just a few miles deep, only to be repeated in August. Similar operations farther north produced no better results and the war settled into a stalemate. Later Iranian advances simply prompted external powers to start boosting the supply of money and arms to Iraq to counterbalance any shift in the regional balance of power, and the war ground to a halt in 1988 when the two sides finally agreed a ceasefire. The war as a whole is thought to have cost over a million lives on both sides, with Iranian casualties far outstripping Iraqi ones owing to their "human wave" tactics.

FURTHER READING

Thermopylae

Bradford, Ernle. *Thermopylae: The Battle for the West*. Boston, MA: Da Capo Press Inc, 2004.

Matthew, Christopher, and Matthew Trundel. *Beyond the Gates of Fire: New Perspectives on the Battle of Thermopylae*. Barnsley, UK: Pen & Sword Military, 2013.

Internet History Sourcebooks Project: www.fordham.edu/Halsall/index.asp

Gaugamela

Lane Fox, Robin. *Alexander the Great*. London, UK: Penguin, 2004.

Ledering, Jona. "What Happened at Gaugamela?" www.livius.org/aj-al/alexander/alexander_z7.html

Asculum

Fields, Nic. *Roman Republican Legionary 298–105 BC*. Oxford, UK: Osprey Publishing, 2012.

United Nations of Roma Victrix: www.unrv.com

Cannae

Goldsworthy, Adrian. *Cannae: Hannibal's Greatest Victory*. London, UK: Phoenix, 2007.

O'Connell, Robert L. *The Ghosts of Cannae: Hannibal and the Darkest Hour of the Roman Republic*. London, UK: Random House, 2011.

Teutoburg Forest

Clunn, Tony. *The Quest For The Lost Roman Legions*. El Dorado Hills, CA: Savas Beatie, 2009.

Wells, Peter S. *The Battle That Stopped Rome: Emperor Augustus, Arminius, and the Slaughter of the Legions in the Teutoburg Forest*. New York, NY: W. W. Norton, 2005.

Watling Street

Kaye, Steve. "Can Computerised Terrain Analysis Find Boudica's Last Battlefield?." British Archaeology: www.archaeologyuk.org/ba/ba114/feat3.shtml

Trow, M. J. *Boudicca: The Warrior Queen*. Stroud, UK: The History Press, 2005.

Webster, Graham. *Boudicca: The British Revolt Against Rome AD 60*. London, UK: Routledge, 1999.

Edessa

Dignas, Beate, and Engelbert Winter. *Rome and Persia in Late Antiquity: Neighbours and Rivals*. Cambridge, UK: Cambridge University Press, 2007.

Farrokh, Kaveh. *Shadows in the Desert: Ancient Persia at War*. Oxford, UK: Osprey Publishing, 2007.

De Imperatoribus Romanis: www.roman-emperors.org

Adrianople

Goldsworthy, Adrian. *The Fall of the West: The Death of The Roman Superpower*. London, UK: Phoenix, 2010.

MacDowall, Simon. *Adrianople AD 378: The Goths Crush Rome's Legions*. Oxford, UK: Osprey Publishing, 2001.

De Re Militari: Society for the Study of Medieval Military History: deremilitari.org

Yarmouk

Kaegi, Walter E. *Byzantium and the Early Islamic Conquests*. Cambridge, UK: Cambridge University Press, 1995.

Nicolle, David. *Yarmuk AD 636: The Muslim Conquest of Syria*. Oxford, UK: Osprey Publishing, 1994.

Horns of Hattin

Bartlett, W. B. *Downfall of the Crusader Kingdom: The Battle of Hattin and the Loss of Jerusalem*. Stroud, UK: The History Press, 2010.

Keda, B. Z., and Yad Izhak Ben-Zvi, eds. *The Horns of Hattin: Proceedings of the Second Conference of the Society of the Crusades and the Latin East*. Jerusalem & Aldershot, 1992.

Liegniz

Jackson, Peter. *The Mongols and the West*. London, UK: Longman, 2005.

Saunders, J. J. *The History of the Mongol Conquests*. Philadelphia, PA: University of Pennsylvania Press, 2001.

Agincourt

Curry, Anne. *Agincourt: A New History*. Stroud, UK: Tempus Publishing, 2006.

Keegan, John. *The Face of Battle: A Study of Agincourt, Waterloo and the Somme*. London, UK: Pimlico, 2004.

Agincourt Project: www.agincourt.soton.ac.uk

Towton

Goodwin, George. *Fatal Colours: Towton, 1461 – England's Most Brutal Battle*. London, UK: Phoenix, 2012.

Sadler, John. *Towton: The Battle of Palm Sunday Field*. Barnsley, UK: Pen & Sword Military, 2011.

Towton Battlefield Society: www.towton.org.uk

Tenochtitlán

Levy, Joel. *Lost Cities*. London, UK: New Holland, 2011.

Conquistadors: www.pbs.org/conquistadors/index.html

Pavia

Giono, Jean. *Battle of Pavia*. London, UK: Peter Owen, 1965.

Konstam, Angus. *Pavia 1525: The Climax of the Italian Wars*. Oxford, UK: Osprey Publishing, 1996.

Mallett, M. and Christine Shaw. *The Italian Wars 1494–1559: War, State and Society in Early Modern Europe*. London, UK: Pearson, 2012.

Cajamarca

Diamond, Jared. *Guns, Germs and Steel*. New York, NY: W. W. Norton & Co, 1997.

Conquistadors: www.pbs.org/conquistadors/index.html

Ostend

Duffy, Christopher. *Siege Warfare: The Fortress in the Early Modern World 1494–1660*. London, UK: Routledge, 1996.

Simoni, Anna E. C. *The Ostend Story: Early Tales of the Great Siege and the Mediating Role of Henrick van Haestens*. Houten, The Netherlands: HES & De Graaf, 2003.

Marston Moor

British Civil Wars: www.british-civil-wars.co.uk

English Heritage Battlefield Report: Marston Moor: www.english-heritage.org.uk/content/imported-docs/k-o/marston.pdf

Vienna

Stoye, John. *The Siege of Vienna: The Last Great Trial Between Cross & Crescent*. New York, NY: Pegasus, 2007.

Wheatcroft, Andrew. *The Enemy at the Gate: Habsburgs, Ottomans and the Battle for Europe*. London, UK: Pimlico, 2009.

Malplaquet

Holmes, Richard. *Marlborough: Britain's Greatest General: England's Fragile Genius*. London, UK: Harper Perennial, 2009.

Battlefield Anomalies: www.battlefieldanomalies.com

Torgau

Showalter, Dennis. *Frederick the Great: A Military History*. Barnsley, UK: Frontline Books, 2012.

Szabo, Franz A. J. *The Seven Years War in Europe: 1756–1763*. London, UK: Longman, 2007.

Bunker Hill

O'Shaughnessy, Andrew. *The Men Who Lost America: British Command During the Revolutionary War and the Preservation of the Empire*. London, UK: Oneworld Publications, 2013.

Philbrick, Nathaniel. *Bunker Hill: A City, a Siege, a Revolution*. London, UK: Doubleday, 2013.

Stephenson, Michael. *Patriot Battles: How the War of Independence Was Fought*. London, UK: Harper Perennial, 2008.

Pollilur

Holmes, Richard. *Sahib: The British Soldier in India 1750–1914*. London, UK: Harper Perennial, 2006.

"The Tiger and the Thistle: Tipu Sultan and the Scots in India": www.tigerandthistle.net

Eylau

Petre, F. Lorraine. *Napoleon's Campaign in Poland, 1806–07*. Barnsley, UK: Greenhill Books, 2001.

The Napoleon Series: www.napoleon-series.org

Albuera

Esdaile, Charles. *The Peninsular War: A New History*. London, UK Penguin, 2003.

British Battles: www.britishbattles.com

The Peninsular War: www.peninsularwar.org

Borodino

Lieven, Dominic. *Russia Against Napoleon: The Battle for Europe, 1807 to 1814*. London, UK: Penguin, 2010.

Zamoyski, Adam. *1812: Napoleon's Fatal March on Moscow*. London, UK: Harper Perennial, 2005.

The Napoleon Series: www.napoleon-series.org

Leipzig

Harvey, Robert. *The War of Wars: The Great European Conflict, 1793–1815*. London, UK: Robinson, 2007.

Hofschroer, Peter. *Leipzig, 1813: The Battle of the Nations*. Oxford, UK: Osprey Publishing, 1993.

Alamo

Davis, William C. *Three Roads to the Alamo*. London, UK: HarperCollins, 2000.

Tucker, Philip Thomas. *Exodus From The Alamo: The Anatomy of the Last Stand Myth*. Oxford, UK: Casemate, 2011.

The Alamo: www.thealamo.org

Texas State Historical Association: www.tshaonline.org

Gandamak

Dalrymple, William. *Return of a King: The Battle for Afghanistan*. London, UK: Bloomsbury, 2013.

Kekewich, Margaret. *Retreat and Retribution in Afghanistan, 1842: Two Journals of the First Afghan War*. Barnsely, UK: Pen & Sword Military, 2011.

Trousdale, William. "Dr. Brydon's Report of the Kabul Disaster and Documentation of History": www.khyber.org/history/a/dr._brydons_report_of_the_kabu.shtml

Balaclava

Brighton, Terry. *Hell Riders: The Truth About the Charge of the Light Brigade*. London, UK: Penguin, 2005.

Royle, Trevor. *Crimea: The Great Crimean War 1854–1856*. London, UK: Abacus, 2000.

Woodham-Smith, Cecil. *The Reason Why*. London, UK: Penguin, 1971.

Solferino

Brooks, Richard. *Solferino 1859*. Oxford, UK: Osprey Publishing, 2009.

Carmichael Wylly, Harold. *The Campaign of Magenta and Solferino 1859: The Decisive Conflict for the Unification of Italy*. York, UK: Leonaur, 2009.

Battlefield Anomalies: www.battlefieldanomalies.com

Antietam

Sears, Stephen W. *Landscape Turned Red: The Battle of Antietam*. Boston, MA: Houghton Mifflin, 2003.

Murfin, James V. *The Gleam of Bayonets: The Battle of Antietam and Robert E. Lee's Maryland Campaign, September 1862*. Baton Rouge, LA: Louisiana State University Press, 2004.

American Civil War: www.civilwarhome.com

Civil War Trust: www.civilwar.org

Gettysburg

Adkin, Mark. *The Gettysburg Companion: A Complete Guide to the Decisive Battle of the American Civil War*. CITY, STATE: Aurum Press, 2008.

Sears, Stephen W. *Gettysburg*. Boston, MA: Mariner Books, 2008.

News in History: www.newsinhistory.com

Sedan

Fermer, Douglas. *Sedan 1870: The Eclipse of France*. Barnsely, UK: Pen & Sword, 2008.

Howard, Michael. *The Franco-Prussian War: The German Invasion of France 1870–1871*. London, UK: Routledge, 2001.

Wawro, Geoffrey. *The Franco-Prussian War: The German Conquest of France in 1870–1871*. Cambridge, UK: Cambridge University Press, 2005.

Little Bighorn

Perrett, Bryan. *Last Stand! Famous Battles Against the Odds*. London, UK: Cassell, 1998.

Philbrick, Nathaniel. *The Last Stand: Custer, Sitting Bull and the Battle of the Little Big Horn*. London, UK: Vintage, 2011.

Little Bighorn Battlefield: www.nps.gov/libi/historyculture/index.htm

Khartoum

Asher, Michael. *Khartoum: The Ultimate Imperial Adventure*. London, UK: Penguin, 2006.

Nicoll, Fergus. *The Mahdi of Sudan and the Death of General Gordon*. Stroud, UK: The History Press, 2005.

Thompson, Brian. *Imperial Vanities: The Adventures of the Baker Brothers and Gordon of Khartoum*. London, UK: HarperCollins, 2010.

Tannenberg

Showalter, Dennis E. *Tannenberg: Clash of Empires, 1914*. Dulles, VA: Brassey's Inc, 2004.

Sondahl, Birrion. "The Battle of Tannenberg, 1914." www.militaryhistoryonline.com/wwi/articles/tannenberg.aspx

Wertheim Tuchman, Barbara. *The Guns of August*. New York, NY: Presidio Press, 2004.

Gallipoli

Hart, Peter. *Gallipoli*. London, UK: Profile, 2013.

UK National Archives: www.nationalarchives.gov.uk

Gallipoli Association: www.gallipoli-association.org

Verdun

Horne, Alistair. *The Price of Glory: Verdun 1916*. London, UK: Penguin, 1993.

First World War: A Multimedia History of World War One: www.firstworldwar.com

The Somme

Keegan, John. *The Face of Battle: A Study of Agincourt, Waterloo and the Somme*. London, UK: Pimlico, 2004.

MacDonald, Lyn. *Somme*. London, UK: Penguin, 1993.

Source Documents on the Battle of the Somme: www.johndclare.net/wwi_somme_docs.htm

Caporetto

Farina, John. "Caporetto: A Fresh Look": www.1ha.org/caporetto.htm

MacDonald, John, and Zeljko Cimpric. *Caporetto and the Isonzo Campaign: The Italian Front 1915–1918*. Barnsely, UK: Pen & Sword Military, 2011.

Thompson, Mark. *The White War: Life and Death on the Italian Front, 1915–1919*. London, UK: Faber and Faber, 2009.

Singapore

Barber, Noel. *Sinister Twilight: The Fall of Singapore*. London, UK: Phoenix, 2002.

Smith, Colin. *Singapore Burning: Heroism and Surrender in World War II*. London, UK: Penguin, 2006.

Thompson, Peter. *The Battle for Singapore: The True Story of Britain's Greatest Military Disaster*. London, UK: Piatkus, 2006.

Stalingrad

Bastable, Jonathan. *Voices from Stalingrad: Unique First-Hand Accounts from World War II's Cruellest Battle*. Newton Abbot, UK: David & Charles, 2007.

Beevor, Antony. *Stalingrad*. London, UK: Penguin, 2007.

Cassino

Holmes, Richard. "The Battle of Monte Cassino." www.bbc.co.uk/history/worldwars/wwtwo/battle_cassino_01.shtml

Parker, Matthew. *Monte Cassino: The Story of the Hardest-Fought Battle of World War Two*. London, UK: Headline, 2004.

Hürtgen Forest

Astor, Gerald. *The Bloody Forest: Battle for the Huertgen*. New York, NY: Presidio, 2000.

The Battle of Hürtgen Forest: http://hurtgen1944.homestead.com

The Battle of Hürtgen Forest: http://home.scarlet.be/~sh446368/home.htm

Iwo Jima

Newcomb, Richard F. *Iwo Jima*. Boston, MA: Holt McDougal, 2002.

Naval History and Heritage Command: www.history.navy.mil

Iwo Jima Memoirs: http://iwo-jima-memoirs.tripod.com

Dien Bien Phu

Windrow, Martin. *The Last Valley: Dien Bien Phu and the French Defeat in Vietnam*. London, UK: Cassell, 2005.

Fall, Bernard B. *Hell in a Very Small Place: The Siege of Dien Bien Phu*. Boston, MA: Da Capo Press, 2002.

Bay of Pigs

Rasenberger, Jim. *The Brilliant Disaster: JFK, Castro and America's Doomed Invasion of Cuba's Bay of Pigs*. London, UK: Robert Hale, 2011.

"Bay of Pigs: 40 Years After." The National Security Archive: www.gwu.edu/~nsarchiv/bayofpigs/index.html

Hue

Hammel, Eric. *Fire in the Streets: The Battle for Hue, Tet 1968*. Pacifica, California: Pacifica Military History, 2006.

Marine Corps Association: www.mca-marines.org

Vets With A Mission: Vietnam History and Educational Site: www.vwam.com/

Basra

Johnson, Rob. *The Iran–Iraq War*. London, UK: Palgrave Macmillan, 2010.

Hiro, Dilip. *The Longest War: Iran–Iraq Military Conflict*. London, UK: Grafton, 1989.

"Tactics and Strategy of the Iran–Iraq War." Small Wars Journal: http://smallwarsjournal.com/jrnl/art/ghazalah%E2%80%99s-phased-analysis-of-combat-operations-part-two-of-three